Empowering Housewives in Southeast Turkey

Empowering Housewives in Southeast Turkey

Gender, State and Development

Kübra Zeynep Sarıaslan

I.B. TAURIS
LONDON • NEW YORK • OXFORD • NEW DELHI • SYDNEY

I.B. TAURIS
Bloomsbury Publishing Plc
50 Bedford Square, London, WC1B 3DP, UK
1385 Broadway, New York, NY 10018, USA
29 Earlsfort Terrace, Dublin 2, Ireland

BLOOMSBURY, I.B. TAURIS and the I.B. Tauris logo are trademarks of
Bloomsbury Publishing Plc

First published in Great Britain 2023
This paperback edition published in 2025

For legal purposes the Acknowledgements on pp. xi–xii constitute an
extension of this copyright page.

Series design by Adriana Brioso
Cover image: Dancers, by Kübra Zeynep Sariaslan, 2013.

A catalogue record for this book is available from the British Library.

A catalog record for this book is available from the Library of Congress.

ISBN: HB: 978-0-7556-4648-7
PB: 978-0-7556-4652-4
ePDF: 978-0-7556-4649-4
eBook: 978-0-7556-4650-0

Typeset by Newgen KnowledgeWorks Pvt. Ltd., Chennai, India

To find out more about our authors and books visit www.bloomsbury.com
and sign up for our newsletters.

To those who do the invisible housework in academia.

Contents

Acronyms and Abbreviations

ADEM   family support centres (*Aile Destek Merkezleri*)

AKP   Justice and Development Party (*Adalet ve Kalkınma Partisi*)

ASAP   Ministry of Family and Social Policy (*Aile ve Sosyal Politikalar Bakanlığı*)

BDP   Peace and Democracy Party (*Barış ve Demokrasi Partisi*)

ÇATOM   multipurpose community centres (*Çok Amaçlı Toplum Merkezleri*)

CEDAW   Convention for Elimination of All Forms of Discrimination Against Women

CHP   Republican People's Party (*Cumhuriyet Halk Partisi*)

GAP   Southeast Anatolia Project (*Güneydoğu Anadolu Projesi*)

GAP RDA   GAP Regional Development Administration (*GAP Bölge Kalkınma İdaresi Başkanlığı*)

HDP   People's Democratic Party (*Halkların Demokratik Partisi*)

KADEM   Women's and Democracy Association (*Kadın ve Demokrasi Derneği*)

KADER   Association for the Support of Women Candidates (*Kadın Adayları Destekleme Derneği*)

KSGM   Directorate General of Women's Status (*Kadının Statüsü Genel Müdürlüğü*)

NACIDER   Association for Prevention of Honour Crimes (*Namus Cinayetlerini Önleme Derneği*)

PKK   Kurdistan Worker's Party (*Partiya Karkerên Kurdistanê*)

SIDA   Swedish Development Agency

SODES   Social Support Program (*Sosyal Destek Programı*)

SYDV   Social Assistance and Solidarity Foundation (*Sosyal Yardımlaşma ve Dayanışma Vakfı*)

TIGIKAM   Centre for Entrepreneurial Women in Tigris (*Tigris Kadın Girişimciler Derneği*)
UNDP   United Nations Development Programme
UNICEF   United Nations Children's Fund

Acknowledgements

This book was made possible thanks to the invaluable contributions of several people I met over the past ten years. I especially owe gratitude to those who accepted me into their lives and opened previously closed doors for me. I've tried my hardest to be worthy of their trust.

This book has born from my research for my dissertation, which was funded by the Swiss National Science Foundation. I would like to express my deepest gratitude to my exceptional academic supervisors for their guidance. If I am a social anthropologist today, it is because of Peter Finke's persistent encouragement since the beginning of my studies. I profited a lot from the knowledge and wisdom and also inspirational stories that Heinz Käufeler generously shared with me. Most importantly, I would like to thank Sabine Strasser whose contribution to the growth of this project and to me is beyond words. Her warmth and academic commitment are heartening and delightful to behold. I am happy to have the pleasure of working with her for my postdoctoral research as well.

My sincere appreciations are extended to all my distinguished colleagues Emilia Róża Sułek, Olivia Killias, Dilyara Müller-Süleymanova, Stefan Leins, Dominique Müller, Wolfgang Wohlwend, Mustafa Akçınar, Jovana Dikovic and Annuska Derks from the University of Zurich, and Veronika Siegl, Gerhild Perl, Julia Rehsmann, Luisa Piart, Annika Lems, Danaé Athalie Leitenberg and Julia Eckert from the University of Bern, who gave strength to me in various ways throughout the six years of my doctoral studies. I should also mention that I gained a lot of knowledge from the students who came to the seminars I led.

Many lengthy discussions and thought-provoking exchanges that happened at various times and places allowed me to put my ideas into these pages. I am grateful to Nermin Pınar Erdoğan for chasing ladybugs with me – sometimes at the top of the Mount Nemrut and other times at the bottom of the world. I am lucky to have the kind and sensitive words of my teammate Annelies

Kuijpers in my ears whenever needed. I was very fortunate to have met Erol Sağlam, who inspired me with his elegant ideas while writing the proposal of this book. I am truly indebted to Anna Wyss for being a rock-solid support in my challenge to remain in academia (and life?). I am grateful to my pen friend Yakup Deniz Kahraman for putting me first and reading earlier drafts of this book with a discerning eye. I chose my words in this book as if my cousin Hazal Mine was going to read them, and I owe her a debt of gratitude for her place in my mind. Also, I am thankful to the anonymous reviewers whose constructive criticism greatly improved the manuscript, as well as Sophie Rudland and Nayiri Kendir at I. B. Tauris for their excellent editorial support.

I am indebted to my dearest friends – near and far – for taking good care of me while I was writing this book. 'Dear nice people', a.k.a. Vera Ryser, Emre Sarıgöl, Eva Käser, Sally Schonfeldt, Güneş Direk, Ufuk Olgaç, Leonie Grüter, Deniz Subaşı, Shpresa Jashari, Lea Zwimpfer and Adnan Öztürel enabled me to live an emotionally prosperous life in Zurich, something that not everyone could have the chance to. They all have a hand in this too.

Lastly, I am grateful to the members of my loving and happily extended family – my parents Zehra and Nadir, my brother Özgür, my sister *outsider* Sezin and my dearest niece Naz – to whom I will always be indebted for everything that I am and have come to be.

Preface

As a product of Turkey's national modernization project, during most of my childhood I had no curiosity about the eastern part of my country. Although I had travelled to various parts of Turkey as a tourist, I had never seen what was going on in southeast Turkey. If I thought about it at all, it was as 'a country within a country',[1] far away from the capital city Ankara, my hometown. From schoolbooks I had learned that people in the region mostly lived in a traditional way in villages. In geography lessons, we had been told about the different dams on Turkish rivers. It was particularly important to memorize the names of some of these dams because, according to the textbook, the Turkish state was engaged in one of the biggest and most successful projects in the world named the 'Southeast Anatolia Project' (or simply GAP, the Turkish acronym for *Güneydoğu Anadolu Projesi*). The GAP was based on irrigation channels and large dams on the Tigris and Euphrates rivers, and it was a topic that was covered in geography lessons, again and again, every year. It never was completed – and it is still not complete today. I knew the GAP so well that it took me some time to forget it.

My curiosity about southeast Turkey started after I came across *Women Die in Batman*, a journalistic study carried out by Müjgan Halis (2001) about the massive scale of suicides by women in this region. Halis's book focused on one province, Batman, where suicide numbers were particularly high. She argued that female suicides were associated not only with poverty, political underrepresentation and prolonged neglect of the people of the region by the central government in Ankara, but also with the Turkish state's military intervention against the Kurdish nationalist movement and its human rights violations under the state of emergency. Reading about the first-hand experiences of fellow citizens – things I learned to ignore and only watched on TV – was like opening a Pandora's box for me as an undergraduate sociology student in the early 2000s. Looking retrospectively at historical developments in Turkey in the 2000s, I see various groups and actors making constant efforts of 'gendered racism' (Alkan 2018), that is coupling northern Kurdistan as a geographical area and Kurdish people, as the dominant group in this area, with 'culture' and 'traditions' of extreme physical violence against women.

The part of the fertile land between the Euphrates and Tigris rivers that is called Mesopotamia within Turkish Republican territory is described as 'the Southeastern Anatolia Region' in official Turkish schoolbooks. It was one of seven territorial units of Turkey named after geographical locations and the statistical differences among the regions. Newspapers and tourism brochures refer to it simply as 'the east' or *Doğu* in Turkish. Kurds, on the other hand, call the area 'northern Kurdistan' or *Bakur*, meaning 'the north' in Kurdish, underlining the transnational character of the ethnic group that is spread across Iran, Iraq, Syria and Turkey. And yet others consider it a part of 'western Armenia' or Արեւմտեան Հայաստան or Arevmdian Hayasdan, pointing to the fact that the area was once inhabited by a thriving constellation of Armenian communities until their violent destruction and expulsion in 1915 (Leupold 2020). In other words, this is a politically contested area and the way it is named has a meaning in terms of the political positioning of the self. Throughout the book I will use the different names of this locality interchangeably, depending on the content, but I will mostly use 'southeast Turkey', following its geographical denomination and stripping it of any ideological positionings.

Despite the fact that the region has the most fertile land for agricultural production historically, it has been listed since 1968 as a priority area for state development policies and one of the least developed parts of Turkey (Gezici and Hewings 2004). Bordering Iran, Iraq and Syria, it is the only part of Turkey that is predominantly populated by ethnically Kurdish citizens, alongside Turks and other minorities, such as Arabic, Assyrian and Armenian groups. The conflict between the Kurdistan Worker's Party (*Partiya Karkerên Kurdistanê*, PKK), the armed organization of the Kurdish national movement, and the Turkish Army had been waged for thirty years since 1984 – the year I was born. As a result of this war almost all provinces of the region have been under a state of emergency on and off for fifteen years since 1987 (Güneş and Zeydanlıoğlu 2013), and it had been under martial law and emergency regulations almost continuously since 1927 (Jongerden 2007). It was only in 2002, when Recep Tayyip Erdoğan's Justice and Development Party (*Adalet ve Kalkınma Partisi*, AKP) came to power, that the state of emergency was lifted.[2]

However, its wider implications remain intact. Sociologist Handan Çağlayan (2019) described women's suicides in the region as 'state of emergency suicides', underlining the way that political oppression went hand in hand with patriarchal constraints.

While the national press represented women's suicides in lurid and sensationalist ways and reproduced the centre–periphery divide between eastern and western cities in Turkey (Yılmaz 2004), artists responded to these tragic cases in various ways. One representation of these suicides was the novel *Snow* (2005), in which the Nobel Laureate writer Orhan Pamuk narrates the political atmosphere of Turkey in the 1990s and deals with the 'epidemic' of women's suicides. Pamuk's novel sets the story in Kars, a city in north-east Turkey, not in the southeast. In response, the inhabitants of Kars fiercely criticized Pamuk for 'insulting' them. For Kemalist Karsians, the suicides as honour killings, which was an extension of a traditional way of life, had no place in their city. In contrast, many Karsians emphasized that they supported the 'progressive' (*ilerici*) establishment ideals of the Turkish Republic, such as secularism and scientific enlightenment, and its founder Mustafa Kemal Atatürk (Sarıaslan 2021).

Turkey has played an active part in establishing and expanding international norms of gender equality and women's human rights in the name of Western modernization – especially since the 1980s. In return, the international conventions on human rights have put pressure on the Turkish government to develop corresponding regulations and to allow civil society organizations to engage in effective lobbying and campaigns. Turkey has been a party to the Convention for the Elimination of All Forms of Discrimination against Women (CEDAW) since 1985.[3] As an international bill of rights for women, CEDAW 'targets culture and tradition as influential forces shaping gender roles and family relations' (UN Women 2000). Also, after becoming a candidate for full membership in the EU in 1999, Turkey was asked to take the necessary steps to prevent 'honour crimes' in the annual progress reports of the EU (European Commission 2004). Feminist activists, bureaucrats and scholars from Turkey were actively engaged with these processes both as individual actors and in organized collectives (Tekeli 2017). In 2004, Turkey sponsored the United Nations Resolution on the Elimination of Crimes against Women and Girls Committed in the Name of Honour. Leyla Pervizat, a political scientist and feminist activist from Istanbul, was the initiator of this resolution. In an interview, she condescendingly explained the actual impact of the resolution as follows:

> In one of the smaller cities of the [south-east Turkey], women were conducting a women's human rights awareness workshop. When an illiterate participant, who was not a fluent Turkish speaker [compared with her native Kurmancî] asked about the resolution, it was explained to her that this is a resolution from the United Nations. Of course, she also did not know what the United Nations was; so this was also explained to her. Then, after hearing that the resolution is about the crimes of honour and at some far distant place called New York, some people took the effort working on this issue [...], she said, 'Oh, you mean that honour killing is not my destiny?' (Pervizat 2007)

In response to the growing public attention to the suicides in southeast Turkey, the then UN Special Rapporteur on Violence against Women, Yakın Ertürk, visited Batman and other cities in the region. As a feminist scholar involved in post-1980 women's movement in Turkey, Ertürk actively worked for the institutionalization and legalization of women's human rights in Turkey. She was struck by the contradiction between the increase in the number of suicide cases and the recent efforts made by the state in the region in terms of gender equality. She suggested that the suicides were intimately linked to honour crimes as well as to political and ethnic tensions and underdevelopment in the southeast (Ertürk 2007). Meanwhile, US Department of State prepared a report on human rights in Turkey, which also happened to cover cases of honour killings. Relying on studies of women's advocacy groups in the region, such as the Kamer Foundation, the report pointed to 'conservative Kurdish families in the southeast or among migrants from the southeast living in large cities' as the ultimate cause of violence against women (US Department of State 2006).

In this context, a large group of deputies representing different political parties in the Turkish Parliament worked to establish a parliamentary investigation commission on custom and honour killings and violence against women and children. Based on this commission's report, the Prime Minister's Office released a circular named 'Measures to Prevent Custom and Honour Killings and Violence against Children and Women'. The circular was binding for all local governors of all provinces in Turkey. It contained an action plan that would later become the basis of gender-mainstreaming projects, which aimed to make policies and public institutions sensitive to the gendered needs of women. Signed by then prime minister Erdoğan, the circular stated that education and development are fundamental issues in the fight against gendered violence. Although the circular did not indicate a specific region, it emphasized the term 'culture' (Resmi Gazete [Official Gazette] – 26218 2006), a term that is essentially racialized (Abu-Lughod 2008) and could be interpreted as an allusion to Kurdish communities.

Both the policy recommendation of the UN Special Rapporteur and the ultimate state policy name problems of education and economic development in the southeast Turkey as the underlying reasons for these acts of violence and women's suffering in the region. Interestingly, however, none of these accounts refers to the impacts of the massive scale regional development project, the GAP. Neither did they to its women's empowerment programmes.

Although the GAP dates to the first years of the republic, it was first institutionalized in 1989 as a result of cooperation between the Turkish Government and the United Nations Development Programme (UNDP). The director of GAP at the time celebrated the master plan because it 'would serve not only as a tool for meeting physical progress and achievements but also as an instrument for social engineering' (Ünver 2001: 7). In line with global trends in development since the 1990s, the GAP project is based on an idea that development goes beyond infrastructure and includes 'social goals'. Since then, it measures success with indicators, such as people's quality of life and the reduction of what is referred to as the 'gender-based and regional welfare gap' (GAP 2014b).[4] To achieve these goals, the GAP works in coordination with the UN, the EU and non-governmental organizations (NGOs) to run an extensive network of social projects to strengthen rural education, participatory urban rehabilitation, urban–rural integration and community development, and to promote women's empowerment.

Over time, third-party gender projects have been concentrated in southeast Turkey more than in any other part of the country. In these projects, women are marked as a disadvantaged group and hence have become the target of social projects that aim to empower them via education and employment, which are intended eventually to increase women's participation in public life and decision-making processes. These projects continue and have always been well received by most of the *housewives* living in the urban settlements of the region. And yet, despite these decades-long engagements by the Turkish state and intergovernmental organizations in women's empowerment through project-based initiatives to provide alternative opportunities for women, women's suffering in the region has not really withered away and may indeed have even been further aggravated – as may be illustrated by the wave of suicides in Batman.

Puzzled by the perseverance of patriarchal oppression despite political and social activities to mitigate it, I here explore the workings of these women's empowerment projects and ask: Why did these initiatives fail to deliver their promises? How were they operationalized in everyday life? How did the women involved perceive these initiatives? How is traditional practice used to explain underdevelopment and gendered violence in this context? How does empowerment operate within this sociopolitical setting?

In *Empowering Housewives*, I explore how women negotiate with state policies, development programmes and funding agendas, all of which are working together to empower them. I approach women's empowerment programmes in southeast Turkey with ethnographic curiosity and treat them as a category of practice by underlying diverse modalities of relations, changing alliances, accommodation, tolerance and conflicts. I look at a constellation of discourses, such as development and women's human rights, as well as orientalist or culturalist arguments based on gendered racism as strands of discourses and practices that are built on the foundation of Turkish nationalism and fashion gendered subjectivities. I focus on how women use the tangible and intangible extensions of these assumptions in their everyday life struggles and come to forge themselves as agents at the intersections of these discourses and practices. In this book, my aim is to provide a self-reflexive and vivid ethnographic representation of women in southeast Turkey who want to be strong as housewives, professionals, single women, girlfriends, wives, mothers, daughters and daughters-in-law, and who want to be involved in decision-making processes in their families, in their neighbourhood, in their city and in their country as right-bearer citizens, struggling against their relatives, neighbours, children, men and women who limit their autonomy, and aim to be loved, listened to and respected.

Introduction

This study is primarily dominated by the word 'development' because it examines projects that are aimed at women's empowerment and are funded by institutions, such as the Swedish *Development* Agency and the EU to eliminate regional discrepancies. The analysis aims at describing the everyday lives of women who spend most of their time in centres that have been opened within the scope of a state-sponsored regional *development* project in cooperation with the UN *Development* Fund. The arguments presented throughout this book draw on the ethnographic research I conducted in a province I name Tigris between 2013 and 2014, a period when the political field was dominated by the Justice and *Development* Party under the leadership of Erdoğan. This list could be expanded, but the point I am trying to make is that development denotes different meanings for these diverse actors and institutions involved. This multiplicity does not only make it impossible to limit the study to one angle, such as Europeanization or Turkey–EU relations. It also calls for unwinding these tangled threads and exposing how the concept of empowerment interlace through them, while examining the politics of gender and women's human rights in relation to development discourses in Turkey.

An anthropology of development is a useful way of capturing the multiplicity of meanings as it offers tools to understand the connection between development and various forms of governance, from colonial rule to the nation-state and transnational governance. Notions of development and enlightenment were central in colonial discourses, where the 'natives' were constructed as backward or childlike, and the colonizers as logical agents of progress (Gardner and Lewis 2015). Aiming primarily at capitalist growth, development later became a tool of modernization, promoting new norms and values such as individual initiative, risk taking, innovation and independence from familial limitations and customary duties; relying on technical interventions of knowledge and expertise; and requiring large-scale, expensive infrastructure to support heavy industries as well as a centralized state to make massive investments (Crewe and Axelby 2012: 6–7). This modernist conception of development undermines contextual specificities as it works through 'travelling rationalities' from the developed to the undeveloped (Mosse 2011: 3). Development is, then, an alternative form of colonialism, where powerful international players were able to force their interests, values and beliefs on the populations of the developing lands.

As the 'evil twin of anthropology', development once permitted the colonial rules to establish their power through technical interventions based on the empirical knowledge gained from the discipline. By focusing on the impacts of modernization in agriculture and on processes of capitalist transformation and urbanization, most early anthropological studies were sympathetic to development projects (Ferguson 1997). Critical anthropology of development scholarship, led by Marxist and feminist researchers and inspired by Michael Foucault's work on governmentality, made significant contributions and changed the field's complexion. Their critiques, however, did not slow or stop development, but were subsumed by newer development policies. Recognizing and reflecting on the critique of development's discursive power, my approach in this book is similar to that of anthropologists who value 'ethnographic treatment of development as a category of practise', or the study of how development emerges and produces historical and cultural contexts, and how it shapes and is shaped by distinct subjectivities (Mosse 2013: 229). Therefore, I look at both what development does with women and what women do with development through a genealogy of empowerment revealing 'power struggles and battles over domination, use, and meaning' (Garland 2014: 373).

Genealogy of a rhetoric: Empowerment

When development emerged as a vision to fight against poverty, disease and oppression in post-war era, gendered dimension was completely missing. The productive role played by women in households in addition to their reproductive roles as mothers, and their importance within the economy, were recognized by policymakers only after Ester Boserup's (1970) work showed that development was a gendered process, and therefore, has different outcomes for women and men. In light of Boserup's findings, the women's committee of Washington DC offered American policymakers a strategy called 'women in development' to integrate women's productive role into development projects (Rathgeber 1990). Historically speaking, this was the moment in which liberal feminists adopted 'the equity approach', which called for the equal treatment of women and men, and therefore, the provision of equal opportunities for both sexes (Parpart, Connelly and Barriteau 2000). However, this 'add-women-and-stir' method ignored global differences in gender relations and institutional settings (Razavi and Miller 1995). As a result, during the UN World Conference on Women in Beijing in 1995, a new approach was developed to address the demand for the acknowledgement of differences, together with equality. This strategy is known as 'gender and development'.

Meanwhile, the UN Conference on Environment and Development that took place in Rio de Janeiro in 1992 had significant implications for women's role in development. The conference created a paradigm shift in development approaches by calling for global awareness on the 'relationship between human rights, population, social development, women and human settlements – and the need for environmentally sustainable development' (UN 1997b). Accordingly, an action plan named Agenda 21 was prepared at the UN level and major groups were identified. As primary targets of the new sustainable human development paradigm, women constituted one of these groups (UN 1997a).[1]

Within the scope of the gender and development approach, 'gender mainstreaming' was introduced as a new policy tool to harmonize plans, policies and institutions with a top-down focus on gender and paying particular attention to women's needs (Rai 2003). By ensuring women's participation in decision-making processes, this approach promised that 'women not only [will] become a part of the mainstream, they [will] also reorient the nature of the mainstream' (Jahan 1995: 19). Simultaneously, 'empowerment', which later became a widely used concept in the development vocabulary, appeared in the declaration of the World Summit of Social Development in Copenhagen in 1995 (Mohanty 1995). The term was adopted from grassroots political activist groups from the economic South that aimed to shift 'political, social, and economic power between and across *both* individuals *and* social groups' (Batliwala 2010: 13; emphasis in the original).

At the interplay between the state's desire for governance through development and grassroots communities' desire for equality and freedom, the history of development progressed in parallel to the history of women's rights. A focus on human rights also suggests enlargement of the object of governance from national citizen to transnational humanity (Feldman and Ticktin 2010). That is to say, a global gender (equality) regime had been established to regulate the well-being of gendered bodies by international conventions, institutions and people that operate at local, national and transnational levels (Walby 2004). The Council of Europe Convention on Preventing and Combating Violence against Women and Domestic Violence – known as the Istanbul Convention – as one of the most recent international documents produced for policymaking demonstrates increased determination to set a global gender regime (Peroni 2016). However, what is less transparent is how these regimes work, and how they interact with cultural and religious norms, and travel on the ground to different localities (Kandiyoti 2010; Kardam 2011; Walby 2004).

Unlike the growing body of literature on assessing women's empowerment in the context of Turkey focusing on EU-funded projects (Titrek, Bayrakçı and Güneş 2014), cooperatives (Çınar et al. 2021), entrepreneurship (Akyüz et al. 2019; Altan-Olcay 2014, 2016) and migrant experiences (Rivetti 2013), I expose different meanings and manifestations of women's empowerment programmes. Aiming to contribute to the literature on vernacularizing transnational gender norms (Alnıaçık et al. 2017; Gündüz-Hoşgör and Smits 2007), in this book I look at the encounters between different discourses of feminisms, the NGO-ization of women's movements and the translation of these processes into bureaucratic structures in the name of empowerment.

Depoliticization back and forth

What does empowerment mean, then? Can we measure its successful implementation? Or is it a process that needs to be contextualized? Is it a goal to achieve and if so, by whom? Is it a tool that serves political purposes? What is its function and what kind of politics does it support?

In her book *Logics of Empowerment* (2008), Aradhana Sharma uses governmentality to emphasize the close connections between empowerment and neoliberalism and its self-regulatory aspect. Based on her ethnographic study on northern India, she focuses on the agency and diversity of women in utilizing empowerment practices and also negotiating their identities during the encounters created by state-funded projects run by NGOs. Building on Victor Turner's ideas of performance and Judith Butler's ideas on performativity, Sharma argues that development is 'staged' and 'performative':

> Development encounters operate as social dramas in which development identities, hierarchies, and norms are shaped and challenged, actors are fashioned, and different visions of development and modernity are articulated. (Sharma 2008: 93)

Similarly, based on her ethnography on training civil servants about human rights in line with the EU harmonization process in Turkey, Elif Babül (2017) focuses on the performance of government workers in front of a transnational – mostly Western – audience. While boundaries are negotiated during these encounters, the performances of both government workers from Turkey, including judges, imams (Muslim religious leaders) and the police, and foreign representatives of the harmonization industry reveal the 'ambiguity inherent to organizational practices and bureaucratic structures' (Babül 2017: 172). I understand empowerment as a rhetoric that informs performances.

In her article on reflections of the measurement of empowerment, economist Neila Kabeer defines it as 'the expansion in people's ability to make strategic life choices in a context where this ability was previously denied to them' (1999: 437). In this sense, empowerment is a process of change rather than a fixed state, and the social actors of this process are the disempowered themselves. This means nobody can be empowered externally (Kabeer 1999). Kabeer (2021) also points out the conditions of choice as well as consequences of choice. Similarly, Jo Rowlands (1997) conceptualizes empowerment by analysing personal experience to understand how power operates in everyday lives and developing the self-confidence to act for change towards a better state as the 'power within'. She argues that empowerment relies on the 'power within' together with the 'power to', or collective action to challenge structural bases of inequalities. However, the version of empowerment that dominates discourses and practices fails to accommodate this relationality (Cornwall and Edwards 2015). When this link is absent, a paradox emerges between powerless groups who do not have the means even to want change and demand rights (Berry 2015). In this book, I show how this paradox is negotiated in women's praxis.

In the aftermath of neo-Marxist theory and informed by Paolo Freire's (2000) ideas on functional education and political consciousness, the search of women in the Global South to empower themselves, rather than merely being the beneficiaries of the Northern altruism, dominated debates on gender and development in the 1980s (Sen and Grown 1987). Given the professionalization and institutionalization of development, however, individual actors do not have the knowledge that experts possess to change social reality (Escobar 1988). Developmentalism entails 'a set of discourses, practices and institutions that accompany "development" as a technical, political, ethical and intellectual project' (Madhok 2013: 2). Building on these ideas, one of the strongest critiques of development comes from the discipline of anthropology. James Ferguson argues in *The Anti-politics Machine* (1990) that development schemes expand state bureaucracy and power by defining poverty as a technical problem that can be solved by expertise and scientific interventions rather than political ones (Ferguson 1990).

Replacing the concept of poverty in development discourse with that of gender inequality and violence against women in empowerment, it is possible to argue that the latter is also an anti-politics machine. Empowerment depoliticizes arguments made by leftist and feminist groups by turning them into technocratic buzzwords, such as 'community participation', 'ownership', 'gender-based development', and 'beneficiaries' (Cornwall and Brock 2005; Merry 2011). All these technical interventions displace the feminist political project for equality and justice with economic goals of capitalist growth (Cornwall, Harrison and Whitehead 2007). Depoliticization, however, is not a unidirectional process. People make use of the discourses and practices of the empowerment industry as ordinary actors involved in the processes of depoliticization in their everyday life choices. As Lamia Karim (2008) illuminates with her work on micro-credit in rural Bangladesh, women make use of the opportunities provided to them in ways that end up disempowering others, or what she calls 'empowerment through debt'. While the empowerment industry depoliticizes women's problems, local elites can find ways to benefit from it in various ways. Therefore, as I aim to show in this book, empowerment has complex and unexpected consequences that can produce new relations and identification processes.

For more than a decade now scholars have called for the empowerment concept to be rescued or detached as a feminist product from the way that it is promoted and practised worldwide by the development industry (Batliwala 2014; Cronin-Furman, Gowrinathan and Zakaria 2017). For instance, Cecilia Sardenberg (2016) differentiates between 'liberal' and 'liberating' empowerment. Whereas the former departs from the liberal idea of individual growth and regards empowerment as an instrument for economic development, the latter lies in the efforts by organized groups against patriarchy. Liberal empowerment also contributes to creating careers in the development industry for women who are already well off and educated. Going beyond this liberal and liberated dichotomy, my research shows how different understandings of empowerment merge and operate together in southeast Turkey.

Women's praxis: An assemblage

'Rather than emerging fully formed from a single source, many improvement schemes are formed through an assemblage of objectives, knowledges, techniques, and practices in diverse provenance' (Li 2005: 386). Consequently, women's agency and diversity, and the ambiguities that emerge in multiple layers in empowerment practices, including their everyday life experiences, the political positionings of NGOs and the bureaucratic structure of the state, present a rich field of study. Where the state, NGOs, international funding institutions and businesses come together and form an assemblage, the practices of women's empowerment produce unexpected consequences, which include making political activism and transformation possible. How this assemblage comes into being, or what gives power and legitimization to this assemblage to act in different localities, is the main question that I deal with while examining the interplay between the participants of this research and the assumptions and expectations that are imposed upon them.

By practical extensions of the empowerment rhetoric, I mean the multi-layered field of mostly project-based practices of empowerment that entail various social actors. To define this field of practice, I use the term 'women's praxis', which is my conceptualization of the emic term *kadın çalışması* (women's work for women) used by the participants of this research, especially by practitioners, that is, those who build their self and career through paid or voluntary positions created by empowerment processes. I use *praxis*, in the sense of 'theoretically informed and self-reflexive human action devoted to the emancipation' (Nonini 2016: 242). Women's praxis, therefore, is used to refer to all activities, such as advocacy, trainings and workshops, addressing women's gendered needs and carried out by state-sponsored organizations or NGOs that are organized by or for women with varying agendas and political interests. In principle, the field of women's praxis as women's work for women includes all kinds of relations between the institutions and actors involved, in the form of alliances, negotiations and conflicts. This term contains the subject position of women as both actors and targets of empowerment processes.

In the field of women's praxis in southeast Turkey, empowerment practices constitute three strands of activities. Education is the first of these strands. It includes efforts to ensure that girls go to school as well as to multiply adult education practices to build new skills for women. Employment is the second strand of praxis. However, this term does not necessarily refer to creating permanent jobs for women. The last strand of women's empowerment practices clusters around their participation in public life, or an acknowledgement of the idea that women also have a voice, and therefore, they should also have a say in decisions and plans that would have an impact on their lives. These three strings of practices are integrated into women's empowerment to create the ground for further activities, such as the development of policies and further strategies, the establishment of institutions and the creation of careers. For instance, gender mainstreaming as a globally embraced strategy to realize gender equality creates its own gadgetry expanding through the bureaucratic structure and existing machinery of states from the centre to the remote localities. Meanwhile, awareness workshops, which aim to cultivate 'power within', enable women to reflect on their personal experiences through the filters of empowerment rhetoric and take up positions on their involvement with education, employment and participation activities (Sarıaslan 2019).

Culturalist foundations of 'progress'

All these efforts to 'empower women' are paradoxical. They are far from being a part of the broad and ambitious feminist project of empowerment that has been defined in relation to gender and development. Instead, they are remnants of the enduring promises of modernization theory and its local interpretation in Turkish history. Women's empowerment rhetoric in south-east Turkey is assembled on the everlasting narrative of *progress*, which is central to a narrative of the impartial modernization project of the Turkish Republic. While it was the case in Kemalist modernization, it is also dominant in the neoconservative ideology of the AKP and its development policies. In this context, feminist ideas have had only a selective influence on efforts to empower women. Therefore, the gender regime is elasticated through ongoing processes of negotiation. I argue that the main outcome of understanding empowerment as anything other than a process whereby women acquire power is the expectation that women must ceaselessly 'progress' towards a constantly redefined ideal, a 'new woman'.

As a centrally planned social engineering enterprise, the GAP is primarily an extension of Turkey's modernization project (Bilgen 2019; Çarkoğlu and Eder 2005). This project defines an evolutionary progress as a break with the Ottoman past and on binaries, such as Islamic–secular, traditional–modern and backwardness–development. In the early 2000s, the secularist narrative of progress in the public imaginary of the state in Turkey was dominant. According to this narrative, 'liberating women' meant de-culturation and embracing a modern way of life (Navaro-Yashin 2002). But ironically, this profoundly gendered ambition expected "the new woman" of the new republic to conform to tradition while representing modernity (Kandiyoti 1987; Saktanber 2001).

When the Turkish Republic was established in 1923 after the collapse of the Ottoman Empire, the state implemented policies that aimed at guaranteeing equal access to education for women and encouraged elite women in particular to join the formal workforce. This selective encouragement not only maintained the class position of the elite but also set clear boundaries between classes by preventing rural men and women from achieving upward mobility (Saktanber 2002). Despite its professed egalitarianism, the new republic has overall recoiled from radically overhauling the societal dynamics underpinning patriarchy and continued to maintain unequal power relations, leaving 'the double standard of sexuality and a primarily domestic definition of the female role, virtually untouched' (Kandiyoti 1987).

Cultivating innocence

The Kemalist republic expected citizens to commit themselves to modernization for the progress of the nation, 'just like the officially wedded spouses in a love marriage' (Özyürek 2006: 80). At the same time, however, it does not fully include non-Sunni and non-Turkish groups – such as Armenians, Alevis and Kurds – as full citizens (Maksudyan 2005; Ünlü 2016; Yeğen 2009). Moreover, over history the Turkish nation-state has systematically located 'tradition' in southeast Turkey, and in this way, fixed Kurdish identity with 'tradition', as Dicle Koğacıoğlu (2004) shows in her seminal article on the 'tradition effect'. Her analysis underlines that framing honour killings as a problem relating specifically to culturally distinct minorities or regions suffering from social and economic disadvantages reduces the state's responsibility to prevent gender-based violence and conveys the message that violent acts may be acceptable under certain conditions (Koğacıoğlu 2004).

It was in this setting that Kurdish women who sought freedom and autonomy and felt identified with the opposition of the PKK to traditional gender roles, gradually joined the armed struggle against the Turkish state (Çağlayan 2019). Yet, in the report of a workshop about women's problems in the region organized in 2012 by the AKP's Women's Branch with representatives of the media, civil society organizations and public institutions such as the GAP Regional Development Administration (GAP RDA), the term 'women' is equated with 'Kurdish women' and is also referred as a singular entity. Omitting most of the section that explained why Kurdish women joined the PKK, the report concludes:

> The woman of the region [*bölge kadını*] is both a victim and a great power for the solution of problems they experience. Women are in idle and passive positions in the eastern and south-eastern Anatolian regions [and] all kinds of projects should be implemented to activate them, to take them out of the hierarchical order, to increase their status in the society, and to give them a position in the region. (Ak Parti 2012b)

As anthropological scholarship shows, the gendered experiences of women are more complex and diverse than such singular and one-dimensional framings as ethnicity, or a rigid understanding of 'culture', can offer. Lila Abu-Lughod (2013) criticizes the erasure of political agency in highly political contexts, together with the idea of 'saving [other] women' from the dangers of their culture, which has to be improved and modernized in line with Western liberal ideas of women's human rights. For her, this kind of understanding is dangerous in itself, because it has already been utilized to create grounds for military interventions in Afghanistan and Iraq. The logic of saving other women legitimizes military interventions in Turkey's Kurdistan as well. Also, feminist scholars agree that patriarchal militarist systems and the gendered citizenships of nation-states leave little room for women's political agency (Altınay 2004; Butler, Gambetti and Sabsay 2016; Çağlayan 2019; Düzel 2018; Yuval-Davis 1997). In this context, by openly showing their political agency and joining the Kurdish national movement, Kurdish women fighters not only challenge gender norms but also break free from the subject position defined by Turkish nationalism (Düzel 2018; Käser 2021; Schäfers 2018) and offer a new feminine political subjectivity (Aretxaga 1997).

In the context of southeast Turkey, then, women's empowerment is a useful rhetoric for the construction of the docile subject. In contrast to Kurdish female fighters, housewives, 'free' from the messiness of the market and politics, but also 'victims' of the violent culture that they were born into, constitute the perfect candidates for the powerful to direct their will to empower. Moreover, housewives are attracted by empowerment workshops based on making traditional handicrafts or refining 'feminine skills', which promise to build upon their domestic caring duties (Harris and Atalan 2000). Offering the potential to become 'new woman', which also fits into the modernization narrative, housewives in southeast Turkey provide to the state the subjects which it needs to govern.

Based on her ethnographic scholarship on transnational humanitarianism, Miriam Ticktin argues that innocence became a central ethico-moral concept for the contemporary political imagination, even in places 'where principles of democracy, individual freedom, universal equality, and religious toleration may no longer hold a central place' (2017: 578). She explicitly includes Turkey, referring to 'moral and epistemic purity', as well as innocent figures, such as women, who are assumed to be far from politics (Ticktin 2017). This image of innocent recipients in need of help justifies the outpouring of aid to such areas. Thus, the institutional practices of the state and other organizations that target women, and particularly housewives, in the southeast fall within this framework of political morality. I argue that in stark contrast to those who manifest their political agency and are repressed by military power, the production of modern housewives legitimizes governance in the southeast as focusing on docile, innocent, victimized subjects that need to be saved and empowered.

Making use of feminisms

Not only do modernist progress meta-narratives but also feminist political projects serve for constructing a certain national identity – as current discussions on femonationalism articulate how xenophobic and racist politics couple with Islamophobic feminist discourses in transnational contexts (Farris 2017). From a reverse perspective, however, various feminist ideas and their practical outcomes can be useful for women to fashion their subjectivity and to form their agency. Throughout the book, I use feminisms in plural to underline a variety of possible interpretations of feminist ideas by various actors and in different forms. I will particularly tackle with two kinds, which are namely state feminism and project feminism.

Educating women is a part of many state formation practices (Najmabadi 1998; Shakry 1998). In its expectation that female citizens must be modern housewives first and foremost, the 'state-led promotion of women's equality in the public sphere' is referred to as state feminism (Navaro-Yaşın 2000; White 2003). In the setting of these ideas, the global discourse of development – implying progress towards modernism from tradition (Kandiyoti 2010) – has been powerful with a promise of increasing the social status of women in the Third World. In the southeast of Turkey, utilizing opportunities provided by the sustainable human development framework of the GAP and its empowerment rhetoric, national women's organizations claim to work *for* and *with* women. By running projects on education, employment and gender equality as well as on the elimination of gender-based violence, development discourse has gone beyond its original scope and brought women to the fore. In this process, women's NGOs became prominent in their interventions in local advocacy and policy processes. Initially criticized for having no political claims by various political activist groups, these activities by women's organizations and the constant competition among one another to receive funds from the state or other parties have been labelled 'project feminism' (Bora 2006; Lang 1997).

Yasemin İpek (2006) documents how state feminism and project feminism can be connected in her ethnographic analysis of discourses of civil society organizations. She shows that the Kemalist citizenship project placed strong emphasis on individualism in the shape of self-improvement and self-confidence, which were available only to those who had an education. She also points out the indebtedness of urban middle-class women, who had legally unhindered access to education and employment thanks to the work of the Kemalist regime in the twentieth century, unlike those living at the periphery of modernization, and therefore, defined by their lack of consciousness and education. She argues that premises of state feminism continue to inform women's civil society practices today (İpek 2006). More recent examples of women NGOs in Turkey under the AKP governments in the forms of GONGOs, or government-organized NGOs (Çelebi 2022), however, provide a new state feminism repertoire that supports extension of state power within women's organizations and to the civil society in general through their practices (Kütük-Kuriş 2022). In this sense, state feminism evolves and manifests itself in new forms.

The women's movement was also effective in supporting state-led Westernization. Although support for gender equality has never been a political priority, Turkey was active in institutionalizing international norms of women's human rights owing to its strong women's movement. In fact, transferring international women's human rights discourses and practices to Turkey was the main goal of the post-1980 women's movement in Turkey – a group of women activists who remained united regardless of their ideological differences, whether they were secular, Islamists or Kurdish (Tekeli 2010). In this way, the women's organizations emerged as new political actors engaged in wide political contestations, including anti-war efforts and peace-building (Arat and Altınay 2015; Yıldırım 2019).

In this book, I seek to understand women's engagements with activities and services offered to them as packaged in the meta-narratives of progress. Acknowledging the variety of feminisms and feminist ideas, what state feminism evolves into and how it informs project feminism in respect to the idea of modernist progress is yet another question I address. In other words, I wonder what new ideal woman the state aims to create today and what feminist ideas it mobilizes for this aim. Considering the women's praxis that I investigated, the ideological positionings of organizations were shaped not only by alliances with the representatives of Republican Kemalism but also by their connections with the new neo-Islamist conservative elites of the AKP.

Housewives 'in progress'

Most of the women I met during the fieldwork defined themselves primarily as *ev hanımı* (housewives). I use 'housewives' as a category produced by the discourses and practices of empowerment problematized by the literature I introduce and discuss further on. Also, I do not replace it with 'homemaker' to keep the term's reference to marriage, which, is highly relevant to my discussion.

Deniz Kandiyoti (1988) addresses the paradoxical role that women play in the reproduction of their own domestication as housewives and offers the term 'patriarchal bargain' to explain these women's rational choices as well as the unconscious deal that they make with men to ensure their own security and protection in exchange for their autonomy. According to her, development projects challenge this bargain within the household and put it into crisis. In such moments, 'women often resist the process of transition because they see the old normative order slipping away from them without any empowering alternatives' (Kandiyoti 1988: 282). A decade after her work on bargaining with patriarchy, she revisited her conceptual framework, which was based on 'simplifying assumptions' about the institution of the household and overlooked women's agency (Kandiyoti 1998: 148). I intend to answer her call for careful contextualization that adopts a perspective where women are the subjects of change.

While the professionals and volunteers saw themselves as 'helping other women' in my study, the participants were hoping to improve themselves. In this exchange, the housewives who were participating in empowerment activities aimed to involve in self-making, that is to build up their womanhood. During encounters between women with different backgrounds, class-based differences are translated into a constructed dichotomy between Eastern/ traditional and Western/modern in Turkey, and resulted in a process of mutual othering. Gül Özyeğin (2001) defines a similar mutual othering in the encounters between middle-class women and families of doorkeepers living in the same apartments in Ankara in the 1990s. She says:

> Articulations of class inequality through the criticism of gender enable the domestic workers to define their own identities against urban middle-class femininity and, in the process, to reaffirm the value of traditional femininity and their own moral superiority as women and mothers. (Özyeğin 2001: 149)

There is also an effort to close the gap between the two classes. In her research on domestic work and speaking to Özyeğin's analysis, Aksu Bora (2005) argues that the class difference between employees and employers result in different perceptions of womanhood, which are conflictual but interrelated. Therefore, Bora challenges the assumption of 'sisterhood' that gathers all women onto the common ground of womanhood. In this way, she takes Özyeğin's arguments further and claims that it is possible to have 'class mobility' within womanhood, where middle-class housewifery is perceived as the ideal (Bora 2005). This ideal womanhood includes body image as well. Based on her ethnographic studies on women-only sport centres in Istanbul, Sertaç Sehlikoğlu (2021) shows that women selectively reject and appropriate the ideas of the various patriarchal systems that defend the superiority of a specific body image (or set of images). These systems are either rooted in different ideologies in the political scene of Turkey, such as secular modernism and Islamic doctrines, or in global capitalism (Sehlikoğlu 2021).

Offering the subject position of housewives to be saved or empowered via empowerment rhetoric and its practical extensions, state-sponsored development, including all the organizations and actors involved, creates opportunities from which women in southeast Turkey can benefit. While making use of the services and opportunities offered to them, women do not necessarily follow the designed empowerment paths and processes. Unexpected consequences of planned schemes emerge from the ways in which the housewives fashion their own subjectivities and negotiate norms of womanhood with their agency – whether it be of resistance or submission, as we learn from Saba Mahmood (2004). Precisely because of this uncertainty, development remains as a need to be met in the region and sustains itself as 'a design of absence', and the region remains as 'the representation of lack', may it be skills, infrastructures or a prospect of future (Akıncı et al. 2020). In this context, I argue that the construction of innocent housewives legitimizes discourses and practices of state-led developmentalism, and this process repeats itself in a loop, which keeps housewives 'in progress'.

Empowering families

How useful is the modernist idea of progress for today's institutions and actors? The women who utilize the opportunities provided to empower themselves face structural limitations that are defined by the continuity of the gendered regime of Turkey. Berna Yazıcı (2012) illustrates the lack of alternatives in the process of women's empowerment in contemporary Turkey. In her ethnographic research on the contrast between the actual lives of urban women with socioeconomic vulnerabilities and the political rhetoric of the government, Yazıcı shows that celebration of a strong family is a discursive tool of the AKP to excuse the state from its social care responsibilities:

> Younger generations will be encouraged to take care [of] and live together with elderly parents, and for children in need of protection, return[ing them] to the family and foster family services will be prioritized. (Ak Parti 2012b, quoted in Yazıcı 2012)

Political discourse on the family is not new. It has been the core unit of modern Republican society 'to create harmony between the paternalist order of families and the paternalist order of the state' (Yilmaz 2015: 374). However, what is new under the AKP, in contrast to the modern nuclear family model, is that now there is an emphasis on a three-generational extended family, which is the classic patriarchal family to which Kandiyoti's 'patriarchal bargain' had been built upon in the 1970s.

Ethnography from Turkey shows that women and children are defined as victims instead of bearers of rights and they are expected to be grateful and obedient in return for the protection provided by the 'masculinist state' (Babül 2015). Adopting a neoconservative framework, the masculinist state defines the structural limitations for women who empower themselves at the same time as it refrains from its responsibilities for protecting those who do not fit into the ideal definition of family and who require shelter, money or protection for themselves and their children. 'Mothers' and 'wives' are the 'permissible roles' for women in this perspective (Çavdar and Yaşar 2019: 60).

Through ethnographic examples of how women make use of the narratives that work upon them and configure their subjectivities, I show how they define their own paths and the directions in which they want to progress and enhance their agency. While doing so, I also pay attention to the role of the state as the key mediator or the filter between transnational ideas and practices, as well as their local footprint in women's praxis. Whether they are national, international or supranational, all organizations and bodies must act in terms of the state's laws, regulations, institutions and officers under the conditions of late capitalism. This means that none of the projects that I introduce in the following chapters can be set in place without the legal permission of the state – and to a great degree, without the political consent of the AKP. Therefore, an analysis of empowerment requires to pay close attention to the intersection of the state, international NGOs and business (Elyachar 2005), as the concept of transnational governmentality provides a comprehensive tool to grasp power relations in a world where 'boundaries are blurred' (Ferguson and Gupta 2005). Consequently, since the 1990s no ethnographies of Turkey have been able to shift the focus away from the state (Kaplan 2003; Navaro-Yashin 2002; Özyürek 2006). What is new in the state, however, is the experience of a single-party government. The AKP has been in power for two decades, and this is experienced for the first time in the history of Turkey since the 1950s.

Context of the research: Times of hope

The empowerment rhetoric holds onto the culturalist understanding of progress and adapts to the political needs of the day defined by those in power. I focus on the political changes in Turkey, which have been brought about by the governments of Recep Tayyip Erdoğan's AKP, affecting everyday life in Turkey over its two decades of rule.

The AKP came to power in 2002 as a defender of 'conservative democracy,' which is based on a view of modernity that does not exclude tradition (Akdoğan 2004). While embracing Republican values, such as laicism, the

AKP also conformed to its legacy of liberal economic transformation of the 1980s and 1990s (Öniş 2004). Sceptics were anxious about what they perceived as the Islamist and clientelistic tendencies in the AKP, even though it appeared to consist of a model of religious democracy that was convincing both to certain Euro-American powers and to some other Muslim societies (Tuğal 2016). Owing to its rapid privatization of government business enterprises and of natural resources like forests and rivers (Evren 2022), Turkey's economy was growing after the crisis of 2001 (Erensü 2018). Thus, despite the inequality of income and high unemployment, among other vulnerabilities of its financial system (Herr and Sonat 2014), Turkey was identified in the UNDP's 'Human Development Report' in 2013 as an influential actor in the global political arena (Malik 2013).

In the early 2000s, the AKP adopted a language celebrating participation, multiculturalism and negotiation; terms that became popular after the 1960s and were widely used in the development industry as well. These concepts were formally filled in the series of reforms and regulations in legislative and bureaucratic structures after negotiations for Turkey's full membership to the EU started in 2005. Celebrating Ottoman cosmopolitanism, Turkey became a brand as a model of democracy for other Muslim societies in the Middle East (Iğsız 2014). However, this model reduced participation into elections, equated freedom only with religious freedom of Sunni Muslims and perceived civil society organizations as a third sector to bear the burden of public services on behalf of government instead of being a political field for citizens to act within (Doğanay 2007). This ensured that the short period from the mid-2000s to the late-2000s in Turkey which had raised the hope for more democracy and freedom remained an illusion.

This is particularly clear in the AKP governments' gender policy and perspective on the Kurdish question.[2] Gender equality has never been the priority of politicians, whose political perspectives tend not to be very stable, and support for gender equality has always depended on the sociopolitical context in Turkey (Kardam and Acuner 2002: 103). In the early 2000s, however, to bring its legal system in line with the EU, the government promised to enact a set of reforms, ranging from the expansion of rights and freedoms to the elimination of regional disparities (Tek Turan 2016). Building their arguments upon the promises of the harmonization process of EU membership, the women's movement cooperated closely with the state in various campaigns.

The reforms recognizing sexual and bodily autonomy and the rights of citizens – especially women – in the Turkish Penal Code of 2005, in particular, is renowned for showing a determination to end violence against women. However, after the constitutional referendum in 2010, the authoritarian turn in the AKP, primarily in its political discourse, dominated the country (Esen and Gümüşçü 2017; Yabancı 2019). In this process, women's bodies and sexualities were increasingly utilized by the AKP 'as discursive opportunity structures that ensure the maintenance of the patriarchal gender regime' (Cindoğlu and Ünal 2017: 41). For example, after Erdoğan said, 'I consider abortion as murder', other state representatives followed his lead and targeted women as well as doctors performing abortions (Özgüler and Yarar 2017; Ünal 2019). As a result, abortion as a legally acknowledged right for all women became inaccessible for many women due to this de facto ban (Karakaş 2019; Tekerek 2015). Furthermore, especially during the summer of 2013, when a wave of public demonstrations and civil unrest followed protests against the urban development plan for Istanbul's Taksim Gezi Park, women became more politically visible than ever. Erdoğan subsequently increased his verbal attacks on feminists and politically active women in general, and the debate became heated (Tekay and Üstün 2013). In the wake of AKP rule and its political agenda for a neo-Islamic conservatism, 'a rights-based account of gender equality as a political concern (whether understood as an egalitarian or a transformative project) has lost significant ground' (Acar and Altunok 2013: 20).

The AKP has partially acknowledged that the Kurdish language and symbolism may be used in public – mostly due to grassroots movements making use of the climate of the EU accession process for Turkey (Ayata 2011). The AKP lifted the state of emergency rule in southeast Turkey. Kurdish culture and politics, as well as civil society organizations and activities in the region, became more visible as an extension of the so-called 'peace process' when I was conducting my fieldwork. In 2013, the peace process and negotiations to solve the Kurdish question continued. Under the scope of the EU negotiations, the AKP government tolerated the use of the Kurdish language in public. Thus, speaking Kurdish and listening to Kurdish music publicly or having meetings in Kurdish were possible during the time of my fieldwork, although they all became difficult again afterwards.[3] In fact, no peaceful and sustainable solution could be achieved on the Kurdish question.

Legal reforms were far from answering the demands coming from the target population (Biner 2007; Tambar 2016) and 'remained under the shadow of neo-Ottoman performances of multiculturalism that challenged the Republican imaginations of a homogenous national body only in rhetoric' (Dağtaş 2018: 363). Therefore, despite the change in the political regime in Turkey, the central powers continue to use the broad contours of the existing repertoire, especially in the fields of gender policy and the Kurdish question – with interpretations and modifications defined by the needs of the day.

In sum, I scrutinize transnational discourses on women's human rights and women's empowerment that are entangled with development discourses and practices are present in southeast Turkey. However, they are necessarily filtered through the national politics and needs of the day, namely the populist and capitalist ideology of the AKP. These discourses are negotiated and turned into practices on national and local levels by several organizations and actors, who are not necessarily supporters of the dominant ideology and sometimes have multiple belongings. On the one hand, these practices inform local discourses of gender relations and create awareness about gender inequality. On the other hand, social projects targeting women do not directly challenge the patriarchal social structure. Therefore, these projects create limited spaces of manoeuvre for women but do not necessarily contribute to the improvement in their social status. Moreover, the discrepancy between the established ideas of the republic, which have supposedly been abandoned to a great extent, and the populist government in power offer an extra dimension to the overall frame. However, demands and policies for more development and more education were pouring into southeast Turkey via various channels in the 2010s. Against this setting, I was curious about how women in southeast Turkey understood, contributed to and made use of the discourses and practices targeting them in the political atmosphere of the early 2010s, the climax of the time for hope.

An ethnography of women's praxis

In the 2000s, a generation of social scientists in Turkey was outspoken about and critical of certain state practices, including discrimination and violence against some ethnic, political and religious groups. Accordingly, topics and people that had previously fell in the blind spot of academic curiosity[4] started to attract scholars as understudied subjects of investigation. Bearing in mind Kirin Narayan's (1993) critique of the dichotomy between the native and the foreign anthropologist, I stress that these studies were written from insiders' perspectives – meaning they were conducted by researchers who are members of the researched groups. I belong to this generation of researchers, although I do not have an ethnic identity other than Turkish, and culturally, I ought to position myself among the Sunni Muslims of Turkey – but not the Alevis or Christians, for instance – and therefore, cannot offer a specific insider's perspective for any minority groups. Also, in terms of discriminatory state practices against minoritized groups of the nation, my Turkishness has granted me privileges. Although I problematized these privileges to the extent that I could see, hear, feel and acknowledge them, I still possessed them, in contrast to most of the people I encountered in Tigris. My intention while writing this book has never been to claim the field within Kurdish Studies, and therefore, I refrained from any attempt of giving voice to Kurds. Having said that, I also considered my own vulnerability as an observer as well as possible stigmatization and marginalization because of the topic I study (Behar 1997; Berry et al. 2017).

Right after I completed my fieldwork, Turkey underwent a series of critical events. First, the local elections took place in March 2014 and the pro-Kurdish political party, People's Democratic Party (*Halkların Demokratik Partisi*, HDP), emphasizing pluralism and human rights, not only in party constitution but also in practice, won many municipalities in southeast Turkey. In August the same year, Erdoğan was elected as the president of the republic in the first presidential vote. Then, in the parliamentary elections of June 2015, the AKP's votes decreased dramatically for the first time. On the other hand, the HDP got 99 per cent of the votes in southeast Turkey, crossed the 10 per cent election threshold[5] and entered the parliament as the third party after the main opposition party, which is the Kemalist secular's Republican People's Party (*Cumhuriyet Halk Partisi*, CHP). This was a strong manifestation of Kurdish citizens' will for self-representation within parliament. However, the president Erdoğan rejected a coalition option when the new composition in the parliament did not permit a single-party government and the elections were held again. This also reflected nationalist anxiety about the autonomy of Rojava region as an outcome of the Syrian civil war, which, together with the peace process, was celebrated by Turkey's Kurds. Between the two elections deadly suicide bomb attacks took place in the town of Suruç, Urfa (or Şanlıurfa) province (with thirty-four people killed and more than hundred injured) and in Ankara (107 killed and more than five hundred injured).[6] While the state halted the peace process and renewed military operations in towns in southeast Turkey, the Kurdish youth declared self-governance in these same towns. In this context and after the bomb attack in Ankara on 10 October, the AKP's votes increased and thus the fourth single-party government was established in November 2015 (*Hürriyet Daily News* 2015). After the coup d'état attempt in July 2016, a state of emergency in the whole country was declared. According to the Human Rights Foundation Turkey, between 16 August 2015 and 1 June 2017, there have been at least 218 officially confirmed curfews in ten provinces of the southeast and the eastern Anatolia regions. The foundation estimates that almost 2 million people have been affected by these curfews in terms of their right to life, their right to health and other fundamental human rights. Meanwhile, those criticizing the military operations of the government, including lawyers, journalists, academics and artists, were oppressed and even risked being detained, prosecuted and killed, as in the example of the assassination of Kurdish human rights defender Tahir Elçi. The novelist Aslı Erdoğan, who was imprisoned for her reports for the pro-Kurdish newspaper *Özgur Gündem*, summarizes what I kept in my mind throughout the fieldwork:

> I'm not Kurdish, nor am I politically active. But I have written about Kurdish issues. According to a UN report, 2,000 civilians died in the south-east. If you start asking why they died, you pay a high price. It's an attempt at intimidating us, so-called 'white Turks': Don't get involved, let us deal with the Kurds as we wish, or we will punish you more severely than the PKK. (Erdoğan 2017)

While writing under the shadow of these events, however, I searched ways to arm myself against *white tears* and followed those who break with 'white fragility', or react in defensive, sad, angry or disrespectful ways to evidence of racism as a member of the majority in the society (DiAngelo 2018). Having said that, I do not deny that I became emotionally and morally charged from the time I was first curious about the research site, ever since I was a sociology student and since the time I first learned about the suicide cases in Batman. Just as anthropology's persistent search for the exotic other (Käufeler 2019) directed me to look for the 'country within', working on 'the East' was almost an instinctual choice. My engagements with feminist ideas were also influential but also Chandra Mohanty's criticism (1988) of what we call today 'white feminism' – ignoring differences among women – created a tension in me, that I had to face throughout the whole research process, during and after the fieldwork, and while working on my records, photos and field notes. They are still with me as I write this book.

It's critical to consider the book's cover at this point as well. Like many researchers writing ethnographic monographs, I was unsure if one particular image would adequately illustrate the nuanced nature of the stories I narrate in my book. It was also crucial to utilize a shot I took rather than one that is generic and with which I personally have no connection. One of my very first photos I ever took in Tigris is the one on the cover. It captures a folkloric dance group of young girls dressed in glittery stage costumes with bright purple bandages wrapped around their foreheads. Some colleagues I asked for input said that 'it did not reflect the theme of my book'. I am aware that no better cliché than folkloric dance can function to reduce women in southeast Turkey into exotic objects, as some of the discourses I discuss in this book do. But if some would argue that this image is 'orientalizing' women, as it was the first thing that comes to the mind of an ethnographer friend dealing with gender and sexualities, I could defend my choice by saying that 'people orientalize themselves anyways', as another expert of this specific topic immediately replied. Despite the controversies this image would provoke, however, I stayed behind my choice primarily because of the *movement* it captures, as a director of photography working in documentary films made me realize when I asked her professional opinion. She also decoded the camera's angle which invites not only to look *at* but also to look *with* – and even dance with – the dancers, which suits well to a self-reflexive ethnography. With these interpretations in mind, I resized and re-coloured it to conceal some information and highlight others. Still, similar to ethnographic films, in this image as well 'there is always much more detail [than] is governed by the interpretation, and viewers may derive knowledge from this material independently' (MacDougall 2019: 138). In the end, despite the ambiguity of this image, I am confident that it both tells something about positionality of the author of this book and is not totally irrelevant to my fieldwork. It was taken during the Women's Day celebration on 8 March 2013 organized for the participants of the multipurpose community centres, about which I will talk extensively in the following pages.

During the fieldwork, many people misinterpreted my place of origin due to my physical features and thought that I was from the region. In most of the cases, speaking of Ankara damaged the initial warmth of any encounter because the capital city, where I am from, is symbolically central to the Turkish nationalist modernization project (Tuncer 2018). This positioned me as an outsider. American anthropologist Marjorie Shostak (2000), reflecting on her research in the Kalahari Desert, once asked: 'What was it like being a woman in a culture so outwardly different from my own? What are the universals, if any, and how much would I be able to identify with?' (Shostak 2000: 5). I had more or less similar questions while conducting this research. On the one hand it sounds absurd to draw an analogy between the two cases, as women in southeast Turkey are not to me as women in Kalahari Desert were to Shostak. However, the ignorance I share with a large majority of Turkish citizens and the distance I felt were not very different from hers, as I aimed to show at the very beginning of the book. On the other hand, I was born and raised into similar gender norms that the participants of this research were shaped by and shaped into. Moreover, we were gendered citizens of the same state and bound to each other by experiences of womanhood. Therefore, they were not 'outwardly different from my own' and I was not a total outsider. In general, I developed a curiosity about the women in southeast Turkey while bearing in mind the critique of feminist ethnography about the assumptions that women all over the world had similar gendered experiences. I took the insider/outsider dilemma in feminist research as a constructive force by looking at how the women who shared their lives with me perceived me. I acknowledged fluidity and complexity in perceptions of my persona through the moments of interaction and shared emotions and anxieties.

Although we had lived different lives, we had similar demands in terms of our rights over our bodies. On one occasion, I felt how unexpectedly close and empathetic we could be. It was when I was invited for the first time to a picnic with a group of women of my age who were married and having children. I attended the picnic immediately after a tiring night journey back from a one-day trip to Istanbul, where I went to witness, albeit rather briefly, the occupation of Gezi Park. Early in the morning, without having changed my clothes, I was enjoying the food that my interlocutors had prepared for the picnic. While we were chatting about our lives, one of them asked me whether men in Ankara cared about marrying a woman who was not a virgin. Still under the influence of the angry, libertarian spirit of the Gezi uprising, I replied furiously and said 'I would never allow a man who cared about something like virginity to be part of my life'. However, shortly after I realized the heaviness of my words for my audience, whose lives were populated by exactly the kind of men I had criticized. Fortunately, they were not upset or offended but rather genuinely agreed with my view.

Anonymizing the research setting

Despite all the fair and impartial intentions of feminist ethnography, it makes research participants vulnerable to exploitations of their intimacy. This is because the things people tell researchers cannot always be told to others, especially in texts like academic writings that are intended to be open and engaged to the public. Therefore, the dilemma that feminist ethnographers face while *writing women's stories* is central to my research. Although I present data mostly about mundane facts of everyday life, which were not always intimate, the very existence of 'the women's voice' alone has the potential to cause harm. What I mean here is that activism gives a voice to women, varying in form from advocacy, legal or psychological support and awareness creation to friendship and tacit gestures of critique. As I will describe in detail in the chapters of this book, local interpretations of feminist ideas vary from establishing collectivities, such as women's organizations, to individual attempts to make shadowy protests. I show how women claim spaces for themselves to alter power relations by negotiating the boundaries defined by norms, institutions, discourses and their own communities. This will add important knowledge to the reductive and dominant view that is taken about women in the south-eastern part of Turkey – the source of dangerous traditional practices and violence against women. Without neglecting gendered power relations, this book will focus on women's struggles for a better life – individually and collectively.

My interactions were mostly in public settings, such as women's centres, NGO offices, formal gatherings, streets and cafes. Moreover, I was interested in a wide range of topics comprising political participation, women's status in the society, their access to education and their employment opportunities. However, my questions provoked women to tell me personal stories and also to give me emotionally loaded answers, simply because larger meanings and well-remembered snapshots from their biographies were attached to these topics. For example, education was a painful experience for women and thus difficult to talk about, because it was related to their early memories as daughters who were craving for the love and attention of their parents, which was instead directed to their brothers. Furthermore, I also asked some intimate questions and experienced moments of self-disclosure. I listened to women telling me stories of the different forms of oppression that they experienced in their everyday lives. During the in-depth interviews they also shared their experiences of sexual violence and abuse, which were sometimes hard to hear.

While analysing the data, I spent a considerable amount of time deciding what exactly I wanted to tell. Only after developing my initial ideas and the language to express them could I focus on the question of what I *could* tell. My apprehension about the problem of preserving anonymity, which is an essential principle of ethnographic writing, put me in a difficult situation. Realizing that the use of pseudonyms would not eliminate the probable harm, I concluded that there were not many options other than writing about the research setting incognito to ensure the safety and well-being of my interlocutors. The choice of an anonymous setting is inspired by feminist anthropologists who invited to blur the boundary between the fact and the fiction in ethnographic writing. By no means my work is a creative fiction, but it acknowledges the construction of the 'truth' in any nonfiction genre (Visweswaran 1997).

In the following pages of this book, I have concealed all the information that would allow an interested reader to identify the urban setting in which I worked. That is why I have changed some geographical, historical, political and biographical details and call the city Tigris after the river that defines the eastern border of the geographical region known as Mesopotamia. I used the English name of the river to avoid disambiguation with Dicle, the name of another city in the region. Moreover, as it is also the Armenian name of the river, the name 'Tigris' preserves the Armenian touch that is still visible in the public façade of Tigris.

Tigris is one of the cities representing an urban settlement in the south-east Anatolia region, which is composed of nine provinces. It is not a green city, although a small river goes through it, creating a narrow valley of green gardens and separating the old city centre of Tigris from the new one. Residents of Tigris are interested in neither the old town nor the green valley. They prefer the new town, which was built in the 2000s and offers large apartments with good infrastructure and modern buildings. Accordingly, most of the public services are located in the new town. On the other hand, the old town attracts tourists who want to see historical monuments, and the poor newcomers to Tigris, who can only afford the cheap accommodation available among the ruins of the past. The residents of Tigris, who also spent their childhood in the town, are nostalgic about the old times, an attitude that is common in other parts of the region and that erases the conflicts and crimes of the past (Biner 2020; Öktem 2005; Wohlwend 2015). Here, I refer not only to the Armenian Genocide but also to other crimes against Assyrian, Jewish and Alawi communities in the region. During the short-lived pluralism and multiculturalism of the AKP, bilingual settlements like Tigris were promoted for representing the country's heterogeneous composition that has been a legacy of Ottoman cosmopolitanism.

Similar to other cities in the region, Tigris had received massive internal migration from Kurdish villages during the 1990s as a result of the state policy of village evacuations (Jongerden 2010). This migration triggered tensions between the Arabic-speaking and Kurdish-speaking inhabitants of Tigris. Moreover, because it is close to the border with Syria, peripheral neighbourhoods populated by Kurdish people a decade ago were slowly becoming places in which predominantly Syrian refugees could afford to live during the time of my fieldwork. In general, new building constructions were defining the feeling of the urban space in Tigris, which was a common trend in the whole country.

While the old town had been swamped under the dust of renovation and rehabilitation projects since the mid-2000s, new residential buildings, a university campus with tennis courts as well as a shopping mall (where the only movie theatre of Tigris exist) were being erected in the new town. The relation between the politically motivated interests of local elites with different ethnic backgrounds and the construction industry–based economic agenda of the government was mostly controversial but together they were changing the silhouette of the urban landscape and defining daily public conversations in Tigris.

Points of entry

Amongst all the other cities in the region that the GAP covers, I decided to conduct my research in Tigris because it was not directly influenced by the infrastructural efforts of state-sponsored development. However, the number of social projects targeting women and youth was higher in Tigris than in other places. International interest from the UN and the EU were concentrated in Tigris because it was relatively safe from military conflict, compared with other cities in the region due to its multi-ethnic composition. I talked to women who were targeted by the development business of the nation-state of Turkey and also by globally framed women's human rights concerns. I included actors and institutions with transnational, national and local connections. For this reason, my field is multi-levelled, and my analysis is multi-focal.

Apart from my connections through university circles, I used three main points of entry. Firstly, relying on the general framework of the research project that I was part of, I took the GAP, and multipurpose community centres (*Çok Amaçlı Toplum Merkezleri* or ÇATOMs) as its women's centres as my primary targets. During my preliminary research in the summer of 2012, I conducted informal interviews with experts, or public officers with social science backgrounds, working to coordinate GAP's sub-projects targeting women and youth. I visited the GAP RDA in Urfa, which is the public institution that is responsible for the coordination of projects that are run under the scope of the GAP, and I discussed my research questions with the coordinator of the UNDP project, Gönül Sulargil. The UNDP has mounted various projects in the region since 1995 in cooperation with the GAP. Sulargil took me to one of the oldest women's centres and introduced me to the supervisors (*saha çalışanı*) and participants (*kursiyer*), whose amicability shaped my expectations. As I explain in detail in Chapter 1, ÇATOMs were established by GAP and the UNDP in the 1990s as sex-segregated public places for women with the idea that the social and economic position of women is directly reflected in household welfare [as] reformative projects of women's status are a necessity in terms of human rights and important to increase social welfare. (GAP ÇATOM 2017)

The GAP RDA was established under the Prime Minister's Office but was switched to the Ministry of Development in 2011 and to the Ministry of Industry and Technology in 2018. This project-based, and therefore, temporary institution's term of duty has been prolonged many times since it was established in 1989. The GAP RDA is the first regional development agency in Turkey. However, currently, alongside it in the GAP region, there are three regional development agencies, which were established after the new classification of economic regions in line with EU harmonization processes. Therefore, in Tigris, besides the GAP regional development agency, there was also what I call the Mesopotamia development agency involved in the coordination of regional development. These two agencies had no connection. In fact, there were times when their plans were in conflict. While the Mesopotamia development agency had an office in Tigris, the GAP RDA had no local administrative unit. However, individual public officers working for local directorates of the Ministry of Agriculture were assigned as the GAP representatives in each province. I met the GAP representative of Tigris, but soon afterwards I realized that this official was rather deeply involved in rural development and infrastructural investment activities. Therefore, I kept the ÇATOMs as one of the reference points for my study in Tigris and paid regular visits to Al ÇATOM and Mor ÇATOM. As I note in the following chapters, these ÇATOMs are named after the neighbourhoods where they were established. As I did for all individuals' names, I used pseudonyms for neighbourhoods, and therefore, for the ÇATOM names.

The ÇATOM supervisors allowed me to conduct my research in their facilities and I also informed the tutors (*kurs eğitmeni*) of the different handicraft ateliers about my research. Focused on different handmade production techniques, these ateliers function both as classrooms where participants learn and artisan workshops where standardized designs are produced. I attended the handicrafts atelier in Mor ÇATOM and the ceramic atelier in Al ÇATOM as a participant, even though tutors did not treat me very seriously as a trainee. In the times that I spent in ÇATOMs, I had conversations with tutors and met regular and irregular participants of the ateliers. Some tutors avoided talking to me about delicate matters like marketing or the pricing of goods produced in ÇATOMs, but they did not refuse to let me into their atelier.

Both ÇATOMs had their own daily routines. Also, their ateliers differed in terms of group dynamics and rhythms of work. I tried to keep a balance in the density of my participation in these two different centres accordingly. Although I could establish relations with the women in the ÇATOMs that were not necessarily close but were quite stable, for example, with a tutor I call İlknur from Mor ÇATOM and a supervisor I call Emel from Al ÇATOM, I met them in non-professional settings only occasionally.

The second door I approached without hesitation was a branch of the Kamer Foundation in Tigris. Kamer is a well-established civil society organization, focusing specifically on gendered violence in the region since 1994 in cooperation with national and international organizations and funding institutions. The headquarters of the Kamer Foundation is in Diyarbakır, or Amed in Kurdish, but it has branches in all eastern and south-eastern provinces in Turkey, including Tigris. The connections that I had established in Kars, where I had previous research and professional work experience, facilitated my access to Kamer. Before my actual research, I visited the office in Diyarbakır to inform the administration of the foundation about my project and also to get updates about the most recent activities of the foundation.

A small group of women working in Kamer's Tigris office offered me their friendship, besides the warmth and the comfort of their office, whenever I needed them during my research. They allowed me to participate in their awareness workshops that I describe in Chapter 5 and other activities involving women from various backgrounds. The reader will learn more about Nalan, the representative of Kamer's Tigris Office, whom I accompanied regularly and with whom I conducted a biographical and expert interview. I also include the life history of Hazal, a volunteer of Kamer. People involved with Kamer were central actors of both women's work for women in Tigris and my field experience.

The third place where I always felt welcomed in Tigris was the office of the gender mainstreaming project that was run by UN agencies, namely the UN Population Fund and the UN Development Fund. Having worked in the same project as the local coordinator of Kars before this research, I was familiar with its structure and activities. Moreover, the local coordinator of Tigris was a young woman from Izmir named Oya. She allowed me to participate in and observe the activities that she was carrying out. She also kindly hosted me at her house for a couple of months and supported me with her friendship.

These three initial points of entry enabled me to cover a large field of women's praxis, including the activities of women's organizations and public institutions in Tigris. I learned about newly established family support centres (*Aile Destek Merkezleri*, ADEMs) that were replicas of ÇATOMs while Oya was telling me about her daily meeting schedule. In the following chapters, I refer to ÇATOMs and ADEMs together as women's centres. Although my observations in ÇATOMs are more numerous than those in ADEMs, I have enough data to show the differences in how they approach women in Tigris, as I show in Chapter 1, and their similarities in the services they provide, as I will focus on in Chapters 2 and 3. My connections with Kamer's Tigris office helped me to meet women from the Women's Desk Unit of the municipality and that is how I encountered Aliye, one of the key research participants. It is also how I was able to follow one gender awareness project from the beginning. However, sometimes I established relations by myself, as a total stranger without any references. For example, it would have been unlikely for me to meet and engage with Sibel, one of the key figures in the women's praxis of Tigris, as I explain in Chapter 3. If I had not seen the signboard of her NGO and decided to visit her office without any prior notice, I probably would have missed the chance to hear her story, which on its own shaped the whole structure of this book.

Organization of the book

Training programmes for capacity-building, promoting and providing financial support for formal education, and gender awareness workshops are the primary pathways used in women's praxis for empowerment. Speaking to the anthropological literature on gender and development, the following three chapters situate these technical interventions to promote education, employment and participation in a socio-historical context and analyse responses to them using women's life stories. In this way, I reveal the continuity in the gender policy of Turkey, which keeps women's demands for their share in the public realm in suspension. The last two chapters focus on the top-down and bottom-up approaches to empowerment, which are gender mainstreaming and awareness building. I trace these ideas via two case studies I followed. Throughout the book, I examine substantial claims of women's human rights discourse and modes, which are built on the foundation of development practices in southeast Turkey.

Chapter 1 introduces women's centres, referred to as 'second homes' by my research participants, and shows how they aim to achieve women's integration in the public sphere by offering them alternative education and employment opportunities. It does so by mapping out the ÇATOMs of the GAP RDA opened in 1995 and the family support centres opened by the Ministry of Family and Social Policy by the third AKP government in 2012. Exploring the idea of creating a strictly delineated space for women in the public realm, the chapter juxtaposes women's centres in contemporary Turkey with similar historical examples, namely girls' institutes, established in the late 1920s.

To illustrate how the participants in these educational activities make use of, negotiate, subvert or outright challenge the imperatives for women's education in northern Kurdistan, Chapter 2 introduces the life stories of women. The cases of Aylin and Halime demonstrate how women develop different and sometimes counter-intuitive strategies, ideals and pathways through their engagement with the programmes provided by women's centres. By following the fights of programme staff İlknur and Tuğba for an egalitarian dispensation of financial benefits to ensure that every participant earned approximately the same amount of money regardless of their skills, the chapter studies the involvements, prospects and discourses as well as the cultivation of an entrepreneurial ethos among the interlocutors. I also introduce Melek and Filiz and show how they failed in their endeavour to be entrepreneurs.

Chapter 3 focuses on the issue of political participation and demonstrates that women's praxis in NGOs can not only enhance their prospects to participate in political processes but also creates opportunities for the ruling party to expand its networks of power within civil society organizations. It begins with the story of Efsun, a woman who had been working as a supervisor in a state-sponsored women's centre and then attempted to run for the parliamentary elections. It also follows the career path of Sibel as a successful NGO president to illustrate the ways in which civil society organizations actively serve the state's interests. Highlighting the way that conservative outlooks towards women enable NGOs to benefit from funding opportunities, the chapter argues that gender equality and women's empowerment discourses, along with culturalist arguments, are used to maintain existing unequal power relations, especially in the extension of state power over civil society.

Chapter 4 brings the reader into the meeting room of the women's rights coordination committee, a local quasi-official gender-equality organization, to flesh out what happens behind closed doors. This extended case study of a meeting describes interactions between various actors as representatives of different institutions – and ideologies – and shows how they negotiate their claims based on assumptions of an imagined singular category of 'women'. The chapter asserts that project-based efforts for gender equality of a temporary nature provide a platform for exchanging ideas to design a woman-friendly future, yet they fail to inform policies unless they are supported by bureaucratic structure – even in informal ways.

In Chapter 5 I follow the self-making processes of two women who go in opposite career directions that are created by the women's praxis. This chapter addresses the limited autonomy and room for manoeuvre of non-governmental institutions and actors in women's praxis, even though they engage closely with decision-makers. The chapter brings all institutions and people introduced previously in the book together within the story of Aliye, a municipal employee who aimed to build a career for herself in the NGO sector created by women's praxis. Focusing on the ways she deals with the challenges she encounters in a locally funded gender project, I show how she mobilizes her kin relationships instead of bureaucratic power. Building on the settings of the awareness workshops that primarily target housewives and aim to create awareness of gendered roles as well as gender-based violence, this chapter also introduces the story of Hazal, who aims to have a career in women's praxis by volunteering for an NGO. Choosing an opposing path to one followed by Aliye, Hazal ends up as an employee of the municipality. The chapter shows how the gap between her existing self and the person she would like to be troubled her.

In the Conclusion of the book, I repeat that interventions for empowerment are legitimized in this locality through culturalist reasoning on gendered violence, by reflecting on the political developments after I had finished my fieldwork.

1

Second Home

In the first months of 2014, Turkey was heading towards local elections. There were flyers on the streets, billboards screaming slogans, and a fervent atmosphere in Tigris due to the tension between hoping for stability with an AKP mayor and hoping for change under the HDP. On one occasion, I was invited to a lunch party in a hotel by a woman whom I was planning to interview. I wanted to talk to her about the local NGO she works for over lunch but instead, I found myself in a crowded campaign event for the ruling party's mayoral candidate. The gathering was organized exclusively for women's organizations. During his speech, the mayoral candidate said:

> We plan to open cultural centres where civil society organizations can have their meetings, and where women get vocational education and literacy training, produce handicrafts and contribute to the household economy.

This comment surprised me: what did he mean when he said, 'contributing to the household economy', while women were already responsible for everything reproductive – caring for children, the elderly, the disabled and the sick, not to mention doing the housework and other domestic work. Also, I was curious as to whether he intended to compliment civil society organizations for covering state services by providing alternative education opportunities for women. Finally, I wondered why the mayoral candidate wanted to organize this event in a four-star hotel and promised to open new centres instead of paying a visit to one of the numerous ÇATOMs that had been opened in Tigris by the GAP two decades before? Several similar centres for women had also been opened by the Turkish government in 2012 in Tigris and in other cities in southeast Turkey. While this was the case, I wondered, what made women's centres, which were replicas of each other, still relevant and in demand?

Creating a public space exclusively for women is not a new idea. Moreover, while the idea behind the design and establishment of these centres is to encourage women to get out of their homes and to engage more in 'public life', what actually happens is they reproduce women's domestic roles as mothers, wives or housewives. This is why the AKP mayoral candidate came up with the good old idea of establishing women's centres. And this shows that the objective of creating the ideal woman persists. Regardless of their differences, women's centres serve this objective, even while they are presented as part of the state's social policy.

I examine what women do with this offer in more detail in the following chapters. The aim of this chapter is to situate two kinds of contemporary women's centres in southeast Turkey in a historical context. These centres are at the heart of women's praxis in Tigris and in the larger GAP region. They are firstly, the ÇATOMs of the GAP, which were opened in line with global development trends with a strong emphasis on human rights and sustainability, and secondly, the ADEMs of the AKP government.[1] On the one hand, these two centres share the same heritage of past ideas, which is to form ideal gendered citizens by defining a location for them. The idea of second home was institutionalized in 1930s and accommodated by the ÇATOMs in the 1990s and by the ADEMs in the 2000s. On the other hand, contemporary women's centres in southeast Turkey are different from each other because they originate from different political projects. Their agendas and approaches are informed by political projects, which are discrete and seemingly in direct opposition to each other: namely Kemalist secularism and neoconservative Islamism. These differences also give rise to hints about the projections of 'the national home' imagined by different power holders of the time.

Kemalist vision of emancipation: Girls' institutes

A graduate of a girls' institute has the power to earn her own money depending on her own initiative. She can move to professional life by opening her own atelier. Or she can pursue the goal of raising the next generation in a good and healthy way by turning housewifery into a craft, a profession. (Özkonuk 1947: 13)

In 1947 Rezan Özkonuk, a reporter on *Home*Work: Household, Handicrafts, and Women's Journal (Ev*İş: Ev, Elişleri ve Kadın Gazetesi)* wrote this extract in a series of articles on girls' institutes. Public schooling for girls was established in the Ottoman Empire for the first time during the Tanzimat period in the late nineteenth century with the aim of making the children of the nation progress and preparing them for industry. These schools were turned into girls' industrial schools and used educational models found in harems that include classes in embroidery, music and religion with modifications according to the needs of industrial production (Akşit 2011: 303–4). After the disintegration of the Ottoman Empire, the newly established Turkish Republic took over this legacy of girls' education. The difference between the two forms of girls' institutes (*kız olgunlaşma enstitüleri*) was that while the previous institutes were for orphans, the new ones offered a harem curriculum for the daughters of local elites, who preferred education to be segregated by gender (Toktaş and Cindoğlu 2006: 739). The school buildings were the material manifestations of the modernization process, and therefore, gave the impression that modern Kemalist women had a public presence (Bozdoğan 2001). Consequently, all these articles by Özkonuk start with a description of the institutes' modern buildings. This spatial aspect continues to be symbolically charged and politically relevant to contemporary women's centres in southeast Turkey as well.

State feminism in Turkey, or Kemalist women's rights discourse, as Ayşe Saktanber (2001) puts it, refers to the revolutionary break from the Ottoman past and 'the fundamental element in the character of the Republic' (323). Equal citizen status for women was ensured by legal regulations for them to have opportunities for education, employment and political participation, and in this way, as Deniz Kandiyoti (1987) asserts, Turkey was distancing itself from the *Kinder-Küche-Kirche* ideology of fascist dictatorships of the time. However, as both authors argue, the new regime paradoxically expected the new woman of the republic to fall in line with tradition at the same time as representing modernity. With an emphasis on home, as women's place in the society, 'the domestication of the feminine figure constituted the principle basis for Republican reforms regarding the new Turkish woman and public space' (Tuncer 2018: 36).

In a similar fashion, girls' institutes were not necessarily intended to produce a labour force for the labour market. Instead, they aimed to create modern housewives who would be the carriers of the Republican world view. Girls' institutes were intended to 'ensure that the new modern state had the proper type of woman, a kind of role model consistent with the state's Westernized, secular image' (Gök 2007: 96). The need for girls' institutes also shows that making women into modern citizens was different from the roles envisaged for men (Kandiyoti 1997). A modern female citizen was a good mother and housewife, and who was responsible for the reproduction of the next generation. In this way, a 'Western type of secular patriarchy'[2] replaced the 'Islamic patriarchy of the Ottoman times' (Zehra Arat 2010: 58). Accordingly, women were trained to be good housewives and learnt about scientific methods of housekeeping (Akcan 2009; Navaro-Yaşın 2000).

The literature on the ideal woman was limited to the experiences of upper-class urbanite Turkish women until studies of the experiences of other ethnic identities started to get underway. This is described in a pioneering unpublished study by Sevim Yeşil (2003) on the boarding school of Elazığ Girls' Institute, which was established after the Dersim Rebellion in 1937.[3] Yeşil collected the biographical narratives of women who had graduated from this school and showed that being educated was a tool for upward class mobility, as they could get out of the village and marry an educated man. More importantly, however, the Elazığ Girls' Institute shaped their self-perceptions and ethnic affiliation. Yeşil says:

> These women have internalized the themes of civilization and progress, the basic emphases of the Kemalist ideologies, and they accept the backwardness of their own ethnic identities and traditional lives, perceive themselves improved and civilized, and believe that they recorded significant progress when compared to their preschool conditions. (2003: 154)

The memoirs of Sıdıka Avar, the supervisor of Elazığ Girls' Institute between the years 1939 and 1959, were published in 2004. In her review of the book, Delal Aydın argues that the examples in the book on the interaction between Avar and the local people summarizes the 'pronatalist, sexist, paternalistic and imposing aspects of the assimilationist social engineering project' of the Republican era (Aydın 2009: 260). Focusing on Avar's memoirs, historian Zeynep Türkyılmaz (2016) challenges the constructed image of the Republican woman as a peaceful and passive housewife and shows that women were actively involved in nation-building practices in the east. Borrowing the concept 'maternal colonialism' from critical scholarship on indigenous populations, Türkyılmaz argues that Avar 'co-opted the premeditated, genocidal, disciplinary education policies and single-handedly transformed them into an 'affectionately' carried out, gendered, and only 'symbolically' violent project of assimilation and maternal colonialism' (2016: 169).

Such historical studies of women's education and roles, as defined by Kemalist ideology in the early Republican regime, are not only relevant because they give information about the sociopolitical specifics of southeast Turkey. They also contributed to the ongoing self-criticism of the feminist movement in Turkey together with making an impact on the close interaction between Turkish and Kurdish feminists in the late 1990s.[4] As a result, some feminists, such as those following the feminist magazines *Pazartesi* in the 1990s and *Amargi* in the 2000s, distanced themselves from Kemalism and took a critical stance towards the state's oppressive policies in Kurdish cities in southeast Turkey (Diner and Toktaş 2010: 50). For example, *Pazartesi* published an article written by Ayşe Düzkan, who travelled to southeast Turkey and observed what was happening in the ÇATOMs. Based on the interviews that she conducted with women from Kurdish activist circles, Düzkan criticized the GAP for its 'hidden agendas', such as the assimilation of Kurdish women and the exploitation of cheap labour for the emerging industries in the region via the ÇATOM project (Düzkan 1998). While other feminists positioned themselves close to the state and against the Kurdish movement (Diner and Toktaş 2010: 50), Düzkan's critique did not come from that perspective. Consequently, in the next issue of *Pazartesi*, anthropologist Ayşe Gül Karayazgan criticized Düzkan for speaking on behalf of women who actually participated in ÇATOM activities, rather than talking to them, listening to their demands and showing respect for their decisions (Karayazgan 1998). Karayazgan critiqued Düzkan's othering tone instead of emphasizing sisterhood and creating a sense of 'we-ness'. Although Karayazgan's critique undermined power relations between men and women as well as between the state and its (in this case Kurdish) citizens, which should be taken into consideration while hearing and representing women's voices (Sözer 2004: 2–6), it was a warning to some feminists, who 'defined themselves in reaction to the state and then defied the state feminism of the Kemalist founding fathers' (Arat 2000: 121–2).

Contemporary women's centres also define and train women as primarily 'modern housewives of the nation' attached to the ideal of 'progress' as the previous institutions did. Moreover, critique of the centres in southeast Turkey echoes similar debates on assimilation and nationalism that are solidified in the example of Elazığ. I give more insights on these criticisms in the following chapters. However, first, I continue with the story of how ÇATOMs and ADEMs were created, to illustrate the involvement of local, foreign, national and transnational institutions in 'progressing women' in southeast Turkey in different directions.

Developmentalist vision of empowerment: Multipurpose community centres

Officials from the GAP RDA told me the history of ÇATOM in reference to a series of studies conducted between the years 1992 and 1994 (Akşit 1993, 1994; Gökçe 1994; Saltık 1994; Sencer 1993). These policy-oriented studies that provide the legal basis for the ÇATOM aimed to support development plans that were in accordance with the everyday life of the local populations. 'GAP Region Population Movements Research' was one of them. Carried out by (all-male and non-Kurdish speakers) scholars from the Middle East Technical University Sociology Department, the research showed that rural to urban migration did not necessarily alter rural social structures, but instead, people preserved their lifestyles, languages and family structure – with minor modifications only if necessary. According to this research, the rate of speaking Turkish among women – especially older women – was not as high as it was among men. Therefore, the 'integration' of rural migrants in city centres was an important issue to address.

Another complementary study was undertaken adding women's perspectives, which had been neglected in previous ones. The Development Foundation of Turkey, an Ankara-based NGO, conducted the survey. The report, entitled *Status of Women in the GAP Region and Their Integration into the Process of Development* (1994) showed that women wanted to increase their income and become more knowledgeable and educated. Also, 67 per cent of women responded to the question whether they wanted to be 'the way they are' saying 'no' (Türkiye Kalkınma Vakfı 1994). The report recommended the development of alternative ways of employing and educating women and young girls in poor neighbourhoods, especially those in the poor areas of urban centres that received migrants from rural settlements (Ünver and Gupta 2003). Accordingly, several programmes were designed for different target groups living in urban areas. For example, one category of women was imagined as becoming the local development experts of the future. Selected among women who were 'eager to work with local people, interested in development issues, preferably educated, familiar with local culture, willing to take initiative, and young', this group was planned to be trained to become 'women leaders' coordinating the social projects of the GAP directly in the field (ibid.). These women later became field supervisors of the ÇATOMs, which were established in line with the GAP social action plan.

The GAP social action plan was prepared in a seminar organized by the GAP RDA and the UNDP in 1994 with the participation of experts and professionals from academia, civil society organizations and the public sector. With this plan, the GAP was officially registered as a 'sustainable human development' approach. In 1995, the Turkish government and UNDP agreed on the programme entitled 'Strengthening Integrated Regional Development and Reduction of Socioeconomic Differences in the GAP Region' or the 'GAP Sustainable Development Programme' (Resmi Gazete [Official Gazette] – 22937 1997). The original contract was signed in 1996, and activities began in August 1997. Composed of dozens of small projects, the umbrella programme was funded by the Turkish government ($1,500,000), the UNDP ($700,000) and third-party sources (Türkiye Kalkınma Vakfı 1994). The project was elaborated into further sub-projects with the support of the government of Switzerland in 2000. It was run by the GAP RDA – which was then under the Prime Minister's Office (Ibid.).[5] These projects were designed to strengthen rural education, participatory urban rehabilitation, municipal wastewater disposal in small and medium-size communities, urban–rural integration and community development programmes. Ambiguity and diversity in the norms and concepts, 'poverty' in particular, in the UNDP's vision of GAP have been criticized for reducing the political and social complexities of the regional context into problems that can be solved via technical interventions (Özgen 2005).

One of the sub-projects was the 'Pilot Project for the Improvement of Rural Women's Status and Enhanced Participation in Local Development Processes'. It was based on the findings of the survey prepared by the Turkey Development Foundation. This pilot project aiming at 'training of poor women to equip them with skills that may enable them to participate in income-generating activities and motivate them to participate in community-based organizations' (Resmi Gazete [Official Gazette] – 22937 1997). To meet this aim, facilities entitled multipurpose community centres (*Çok Amaçlı Toplum Merkezleri*, or ÇATOMs) were envisaged to offer training and consultation activities for women.

The first ÇATOM was established in 1995 in cooperation between the provincial government of Şanlıurfa and the GAP RDA, and with the support of the United Nations Children's Fund (UNICEF).[6] First established in Şanlıurfa and Mardin, in a short time ÇATOMs expanded to the other provinces in the region. Since 2008, ÇATOMs have been supported financially by the Swedish Development Agency. However, many philanthropic organizations, NGOs and companies have contributed in the past or are still contributing to the pool of financial resources of the ÇATOM project.[7] The General Directorate of Social and Human Development of the GAP RDA is responsible for the coordination of ÇATOMs. The Development Foundation of Turkey provides technical assistance, including the employment of workers and monitoring and evaluation of sub-programmes. I call ÇATOMs state-sponsored women centres because they are public institutions even though they do not have a permanent legal basis. In 2013, there were forty-two ÇATOMs in nine provinces in southeast Anatolia.[8]

The ÇATOMs were expected to transform into autonomous women's NGOs but they are still part of the regional development plans just as they were originally designed more than three decades ago. From 1995 to date, despite all efforts, women still face problems accessing state services. However, for officials, ÇATOMs have been successful in attaining the goal, changing the traditional position of women as 'passive receivers' and transforming them into committed and socially responsible citizens contributing to the well-being of their communities (Fazlıoğlu n.d.: 8). The *Turkey Country Report*, prepared in 2000 by the Ministry of Foreign Affairs for the World Water Forum, also applauded the ÇATOM project as 'a catalyst for change' (Ministry of Foreign

Affairs Department of Regional and Transboundary Waters et al. 2003). ÇATOMs are referred to in various policy documents including national plans today as well. For instance, national action plans for gender equality (2008–13, 2012–15 and 2018–23) recommend increasing the number of ÇATOMs to support women's access to health and education services. Also, the UNDP Turkey Gender Equality Strategy 2017–20 prescribes stronger collaboration with the ÇATOMs.

The ÇATOM model was successful in terms of serving to the nationalist and secularist project of the state in southeast Turkey. First, they provided Turkish literacy courses to women in northern Kurdistan, whose native language is mostly Kurdish, Arabic or neo-Aramaic rather than Turkish. In her critical accounts on the Turkish state's practices in the southeast, Nilay Özok-Gündoğan (2005) argues that 'social development' policies, including scholarships and supports for girls' schooling and Turkish literacy courses for adults, are nothing other than governmental strategies in addition to military interventions aiming to put an end to political resistance in the region.

Secondly, ÇATOMs bridge the gap between contradictory state practices, which promote girls' education on the one hand and ban the headscarf in public, including schools, on the other. Women's centres provide an alternative education for girls who are prevented from schooling due to several reasons, one of which being their parents' concerns about mixed education at schools where the headscarf is not allowed. Thus, while the headscarf ban was disempowering, alternatives to public schools were empowering. Leila Harris and Nurcan Atalan (2000) state that sex-segregation in education could be considered a short-term solution to increase girls' access to education in southeast Turkey. However, Harris reports that public officials working for the GAP RDA found the authors' proposal in contradiction with Kemalist gender equality goals (Ibid.). Harris (2008) proposes to understand such contradictions caused by practices of the Turkish state aiming to regulate gender with the help of post-colonial theorist Homi Bhaba's concept 'ambivalences', which explains how maintaining boundaries of national development inevitably creates opportunities for those very processes to be disrupted (1705). Citing the headscarf example, Leila Harris says, these practices are referred to by the European Union and other observers as instances of the Turkish state's 'undemocratic', 'amodern', and 'un-European' nature, rather than serving as evidence that Turkey is 'western', 'secular', and 'modern' (1706). My ethnography aims to bring out further examples of these contradictions and present them embedded in the history of the present.

Erdoğan's vision of rehabilitation: Family support centres

During my visit to the deputy governor of Tigris, he openly discouraged me from studying ÇATOMs. He said ÇATOMs were no longer of interest because the Ministry of Family and Social Policies had created new centres for 'our ladies' (*hanımlarımız*). In accordance with the ministry's name, they were called family support centres (*Aile Destek Merkezleri*, or ADEMs). These centres, opened under the scope of the Law No. 3294 on Encouraging Social Assistance and Solidarity of 29/5/1986 of the Ministry of Family and Social Policies, come under the civilian authority in every province and district as project-based entities. They provide various forms of training and handicraft courses directed to women. Their aim is not clear, but they are framed as social policy, as they were established in line with the demands of social assistance and solidarity foundations.[9] The first ADEM was opened in Tigris at the beginning of 2013.

It did not take me long to understand that ADEMs were replicas of the ÇATOMs because they offered exactly what ÇATOMs offer, plus Quran courses. I understand ADEMs as Erdoğan's vision of creating a public space for women that was in continuity with the earlier visions but had a new aim: neither to emancipate nor empower women but to rehabilitate them – and I will expand this rehabilitation logic in the following pages. At first glance, it seems that this development lies on a distinction between the Kemalist ideals of modernization built on the foundation of developmental efforts of the GAP on the one hand and AKP policies on the other. However, the political baggage accompanying the idea of defining a place for women in society by creating a space that feels like a 'second home', as in the example of these centres, is more complex than a simple dichotomy. What is evident, however, and has been noted by others, is that although the AKP's 'new mode of patriarchy' has unique characteristics of its own, 'it is familiar', because it identifies the family as the natural place of women (Coşar and Yeğenoğlu 2011: 567).

Creating publics

Although in feminist literature the act of exiting the home and participating in public life is often emphasised, and is always linked to women's empowerment and emancipation, there is very little grounded research analysing under what conditions women leave the home and enter public space. (Tuncer 2018: 4)

The analysis of the visions behind women's centres helps to understand the imagined public life for women, as I offered earlier. Further on, I will provide a careful observation of the ways that these centres operate with the aim to present information to understand how women imagine their life in public. Women's responses to the centres also reveal their agency and their take from prescribed roles and performances.

The annual ÇATOM report states that women cannot be equal participants in social life and cannot benefit from employment opportunities in southeast Turkey due to the high birth rates and household sizes as well as the low level of literacy and education in general in this region. Moreover, rural to urban migration creates extra burdens for women:

These problems have even worse consequences for women who are disconnected from social life and economic production because they confine themselves within four walls (*dört duvar arasına kapanarak*). If we define development as an increase of welfare, research shows that investing in women rather than men has a better influence on the welfare of children and the household. Accordingly, educating women, enlarging their horizons, bringing them together, providing them with income opportunities and making them active participants of social processes will increase the impact of development efforts and accelerate this process. Again, experience shows that when women's education level and their participation in employment increase, early marriages decrease, productivity increases, and therefore, the population growth rate decreases, children's education and success rate increase and the welfare of the household in general increases. ÇATOMs, with their community-based, holistic, flexible and participatory approach, are an important step towards the elimination of the negative conditions that women are in, and they present an innovative model and attractive centres for the target group. (GAP ÇATOM 2015)

Thus, in this quotation, the ÇATOM aim fits Naila Kabeer's definition of empowerment (1999). Also, it is framed as a social transformation project aiming to change traditionally defined gender roles in the southeast Anatolia region. These traditions force women to be 'confined in four walls', a common expression I heard many times, meaning they make a conscious decision to stay at home instead of going out and being under the surveillance of relatives and neighbours.

To reach these objectives, ÇATOMs primarily provide attractions that may take women out of their homes and make them visible. Apart from training and income generation, both ADEM and ÇATOM organize social events including seminars, exhibitions, excursions, picnics, visits to museums and the cinema as well as special celebrations, such as World Women's Day and Mother's Day. They are institutions for socializing women outside their homes. The centres work closely with public institutions and women to facilitate women's access to state's services. Both centres mediate social aid and ÇATOMs provide scholarships to young girls for their education. There are also reading rooms for school-age children in the ÇATOMs. Both ADEM and ÇATOM have day-care centres attached to them so that participants can bring their children with them. However, none of these care facilities are available to working women outside the ADEM and the ÇATOM.

According to the book entitled *Women, the Light of the Southeast: Existence of the Southeast Anatolian Woman with Her Stories and Photographs* (Fazlıoğlu et al. 2010), ÇATOMs were successful in keeping its promise to take women out of their houses. Under the title of 'some basic achievements', the project claims that it has rendered the 'invisibility of women visible' in the region through 'positive discrimination' (15). The book states that the ÇATOM project cultivates 'a healthy environment for dialogue among segments of society, which needs to be strongly supported by the public institutions and the non-governmental organizations', stressing the need to develop a 'human-centred, peaceful, democratic society'. It contains thematic chapters: 'Education', 'Entrepreneur Women', 'Human Rights', 'Health', 'Violence' and 'Honour'. Each chapter contains direct quotations from the participants of a ÇATOM project without any comments. In other chapters, there are photographs of women as well as their poems and drawings about the centres. While some of the women say that the ÇATOM gave them a second chance in life ('*Benim için ÇATOM'la tanışmak tam anlamıyla ikinci bir hayat'* [Fazlıoğlu et al. 2010: 25]), others define ÇATOM as a second home:

I come ÇATOM everyday with great enthusiasm

Owing to ÇATOM I have peace at home

Colourful prayer rugs, decorative towels

This environment with love embraces us

Better I learn, my heart is filled with peace

It just makes me happy when there is peace

Now time is less, new things came to my life

Towels, napkins and brightest prayer beads I make

With plenty of handicrafts my dowry is full

ÇATOM became to me just like a second home

Our lovely tutors made me so encouraged

They made our ÇATOM even more coloured

I wish lasts long this beautiful dream

All women'd smile with the help of ÇATOM (Fazlıoğlu et al. 2010: 86)[10]

As the poem suggests, when women go out and reach their second home, they produce handicrafts and earn money in return. In this way, as it is stated in the book *Women, the Light of the Southeast,* 'the poor at the bottom of the social pyramid are reached' (Fazlıoğlu et al. 2010: 15).

During my visit to the Nar ADEM, I learned that they also attract women with the promise of being able to 'contribute to the household budget'. Aiming to find out the difference between ADEMs and ÇATOMs I asked the director. However, she did not know about ÇATOMs except from hearsay:

In ÇATOMs participants have paid employment, I mean, they earn according to what they produce. ... Also, we work directly with the Ministry [of Family and Social Policy], whereas ÇATOMs offer courses, only courses. Our institution is not a course centre [*kurs merkezi*]. We don't tell ladies [*bayanlar*], 'you'll come here and produce this amount of product until that time'. I mean, [we only say] 'come'. We only need them to enter this door. The deputy governor told me that this is a place where ladies can come to relax. He said, 'we want people to know that the state provides this kind of service to them'. Whereas both the ÇATOM and the public education centres are course centres.

In fact, ÇATOMs have more in common with ADEMs than the public education centres (*Halk Eğitim Merkezi*), which are adult learning centres solely focused on vocational education and training for the labour market under the Ministry of Education.[11] Graduates of public education centres get a certificate if they regularly attend and fulfil the requirements of the courses. If the participants of these courses are trained in handicrafts, for example, they can work as tutors in the centres. Whereas ÇATOMs and ADEMs are more flexible, and welcome housewives who might not attend courses regularly or complete tasks correctly due to their other obligations and priorities at home.

Centres provide training on various topics including Turkish literacy, civil law, home economics, hygiene, motherhood and childcare. For income generation, there are ateliers, which provide training focused on female skills, such as kilim weaving, textile painting, embroidering, tailoring and hairdressing. The goods produced in these ateliers are sold in fairs in big cities like Istanbul, Ankara and Izmir, owing to the cooperation between centres and municipalities in these western cities.

There is a close cooperation between the centres and the Ministry of National Education. The ministry has a pool of tutors, who are usually registered at people's education centres. Therefore, the centres borrow their tutors from the ministry. If a tutor already has an assignment or if there are no tutors for a specific course, then the centres hire external tutors. Sometimes women who were previously participants can become tutors, as I explain in Chapter 2. In this way, there is always a possibility of 'promotion'. Therefore, we can see that they create their own employment system or sector, with a capacity for upwards mobility, although this is very limited in terms of the number of job opportunities.

Participants in courses of both centres gave me almost identical reasons when I asked them about their motivation to come to centres. These answers are also very similar to those reported by previously conducted studies:

'I was bored at home, here I make friends'.

'It is cold outside, but I prefer to leave home where my in-laws' watch what I do constantly'.

'We produce, they sell. It is nice to earn your own money'.

'My son asks help from me for his homework because I can read and write now, I am more confident'.

'It is silent here, people focus on their work'.

'Doing handicrafts is like a therapy. Here I forget about myself and problems of everyday life'.

What I understand from the documents I found and the answers I got is that the ÇATOM's methods of addressing women's problems did not change over time and they were also adopted to the core by the ADEMs.[12]

According to the GAP website, every year more than 10,000 people participate in ÇATOM courses and events, about 200 women find a job and around 10 women start their own business (GAP RDA n.d.).[13] While the exact number of ADEM participants is not available, its ateliers have been full during my visits. This means that the centres manage to keep demand stable. Therefore, their difference is not in what they offer but in their ways of offering it.

Managers

Field supervisors (*saha çalışanı*) are responsible for the management of ÇATOMs. They are usually female[14] members of the local community. Accordingly, they are fluent in local languages, and they also have an insider's perspective. Every year ÇATOM supervisors come together to exchange their knowledge and experience in closed meetings. Moreover, supervisors also participate in workshops and training, which can be on several topics ranging from gender awareness to marketing and promotion, organized by the GAP RDA with the technical assistance of third parties. As a result, they are well-equipped professionals in gender work and have an in-depth knowledge of the context in which they work. In this way, field supervisors play the role of mediator between the local community and the central government.

In general, field supervisors hold their position for several years. Starting at a very early age and having worked for more than twenty years, some supervisors still hold their position. Emel was one of them. She was a high school graduate, daughter of a well-off Arab family. Since she was born and raised in Tigris, she knew what the everyday problems were, and accordingly, people took her seriously.

Emel felt uncertain only when dealing with state officials, who usually come from other parts of the Turkey and head to another destination after their compulsory term of office in the eastern provinces ends. These people were not locals, but they were very powerful in terms of decision-making processes, and it was useful and necessary to be close to them. It was my bad luck to meet her on the day when she could not arrange an appointment with the wife of the new deputy governor, so she was not in the best of moods.

When I entered her office, Emel was sitting on the other side of the table. There was a monitor showing the images captured by several security cameras in the Al ÇATOM building. She welcomed me and asked the purpose of my visit. I told her about my research and offered to give English-language courses voluntarily if anyone would be interested. After listening till the end, Emel said:

> People like you come here, and we welcome them. However, after they leave they write things that are not true about us and degrade our institution. Those people do not know anything about the reality of this region, and they think they are more intelligent than us. I do not like this attitude. I think it is disrespectful and mean.

Emel was suspicious about me because of what she said had happened before and because both the GAP and the ÇATOMs were still controversial issues in the region – and here I refer to the 'hidden-agenda' debate among feminist that I presented in the previous section of the chapter. Her performance – of an authority figure – was familiar to me from my encounters with other state officials. Then, a woman in her forties with short hair – I noticed because it was unusual – greeted us and served coffee. Having personnel to provide such a service, which I had not seen in other ÇATOMs, completed my impression that Al ÇATOM was a public institution with a hierarchical structure.

After some weeks, Emel got used to my presence and even invited me to several events. She also allowed me to interview the participants. This is how I learned about the story of the woman with short hair who served coffee to us. She had been subjected to systemic violence since childhood by her father and by her husband. She stayed in a women's shelter but left with her children because of her substance use disorder She was homeless for a while until the officials sent her to Al ÇATOM. Emel created a job for her, and she started to work as supplementary staff at the ÇATOM. With the help of Emel, who followed up her case with the police and the court, she found an apartment to live in with her children and benefited from the psychologists visiting Al

ÇATOM. She said, 'Emel Hanım is my friend, my mother, my father. She is everything to me. I love her very much'. I got the impression that if centres are a second home, the supervisors are 'everything' for women in need.

Similarly, ADEMs are also places where women can ask for help. However, Ebru, the director of Nar ADEM, frames these moments as personal problems rather than structurally shaped experiences that women undergo due to their gender. In Nar ADEM there is a special room where participants can share their personal problems with Ebru or a tutor, who can immediately get in touch with the relevant public institution, such as the hospital or the police, to help and find a solution.

Ebru and her husband are from the Black Sea region. He is a policeman and due to his compulsory term in the southeast, they moved to Tigris. Ebru was a teacher; however, she took a break from her career after having had her second child in Tigris. When the child was old enough to start kindergarten, Ebru was invited to be the director of the newly established Nar ADEM by the deputy governor of Tigris. She could not refuse this offer coming from a superior of her husband.

Although Ebru had command of neither of the local languages, she started to undertake household visits to attract women to Nar ADEM. While answering my questions about the ways in which she approached people she did not know, she spoke enthusiastically:

> First, I introduce myself and say, 'Look, I have a small child at home, and I left her home, at this late time of the day, only to talk to you. Don't you always say that the state doesn't do anything for you? On behalf of the state, here I am with the aim of taking care of you. I am not from Tigris, but I am here to do something for you and work for you'.

She says that in time men became supportive and allowed their wives and daughters to participate in the ADEM courses. However, there were times when the Nar ADEM had been attacked by a group of men, when Ebru had to close the doors and call the police.

As director of an ADEM, Ebru's role is more distant and formal than that of a field supervisor like Emel. The participants of the ADEM like and respect Ebru. However, in contrast to the ÇATOM field supervisors, she does not mediate between the state and women in Tigris. She is the director of the place, and she only represents the state. Both Emel and Ebru are at the top of the hierarchy of the individual centres that they manage. Although their titles differ due to the ideological positioning of the institution they represent, they are managers, and I use the term 'managers' in the rest of the text when referring to both 'supervisors' and 'directors'.

'Disadvantaged' neighbourhoods

When I asked more about the centre, Ebru explained that the ADEM project started in the eastern and south-eastern provinces because these are where the 'troubled' neighbourhoods are located. According to her, 'troubled neighbourhoods' are places where people 'live in tribes, so to speak' (*tabiri caizse, kabile halinde denen*) and 'estrange themselves from the rest of society'. There was also one ADEM in Mersin, 'because there are troubled neighbourhoods there too', Ebru says. Mersin is a coastal town near the Mediterranean Sea and receives migrants from predominantly Kurdish provinces. Therefore, although she did not once use the word 'Kurdish', I understood that she was referring to Kurds with her problematic definitions and particularly with the word 'troubled' while defining peculiar aspects of neighbourhoods.

In contrast to ethnic categorization by the ADEMs, the ÇATOMs define neighbourhoods with the help of the terms offered by the development jargon. Accordingly, ÇATOM targets 'disadvantaged neighbourhoods', which does not necessarily refer to the ethnic composition of the place but rather to the socioeconomic level of the inhabitants. Local administrators of the central government, namely governors (*vali*) and district governors (*kaymakam*),[15] decide which neighbourhood needs a ÇATOM and make their request to the GAP RDA accordingly.

In principle, ÇATOMs are mobile and temporary. They are named after the neighbourhoods in which they are opened and their names change when they move from one place to another. For this reason, it was difficult to keep a record of the number and locations of ÇATOMs since 1995. ÇATOMs can also be mobile in the same neighbourhood for several reasons. The ÇATOM in the Mor neighbourhood of my field site was one example. It was one of the first women's centres in Tigris and for a decade it operated in a large building set in a garden full of trees. In this building, which was rented by the GAP RDA, women had a good time. During my preliminary research visits, I had seen other ÇATOMs installed in renovated old buildings that provided a pleasant atmosphere. However, the Mor ÇATOM had to move to a rather more modest building and had to fit into the small rooms of two apartments in a residential building. This was due to budget cuts from the GAP RDA, according to the explanation of the supervisor. Conditions were so poor in the Mor ÇATOM that it did not seem like a state institution to me at first sight. The Turkey Development Foundation, which monitors the ÇATOM, also repeatedly reported the infrastructural problems of the premises that they used. Therefore, I wondered why anyone would voluntarily come to this kind of place every day.

It should be noted that the ADEM buildings are in better condition than the ÇATOMs as they get more support from the local funding provided by the provincial government. Moreover, ADEMs are better supported than other women's centres, as they are a service (*icraat*) of the ruling government, the AKP. For example, the prime minister of the time, Recep Tayyip Erdoğan, attended the opening ceremony of the Nar ADEM. I have also observed that the wife of the deputy governor spent much time in ADEMs but not in ÇATOMs.

ÇATOMs can also remain in the same place for a long time if they continue to be needed. For example, decades ago when the Al ÇATOM was established in the centre of the old town, the neighbourhood was not populated by poor people. However, over time, its demographic composition changed. Locals left the neighbourhood for better urban infrastructure elsewhere and rented their houses to migrants coming from rural areas. The Al ÇATOM became an important resource for Kurdish women to learn Turkish and to have access to healthcare as well as to the social support services of the state. After the outbreak of war in Syria, the residents of the neighbourhood this time changed to Syrian migrants. Since 2015, ÇATOMs have been involved in humanitarian projects for the Syrian women who have fled from the war (UNDP Turkey n.d.). Therefore, the constant movement of the population and poverty in the urban setting provides the raison d'être for keeping ÇATOMs going so they may mediate between the state and society in the Al neighbourhood.

In contrast to the Al, Mor and Nar neighbourhoods in the old town, those in the new town of Tigris did not need a women's centre. This does not mean that urban transformation was not taking place. However, the gentrification of the old town, urgently demanded by the tourism industry, had not yet reached aggressive proportions.

Politics in the centres

The ÇATOMs administration consists of the field supervisor and an administrative board composed of the field supervisor, one of the tutors and three participants (GAP ÇATOM 2004). According to the development expert at the GAP headquarter the board is evidence that GAP ensures 'participation' in development processes. This expert had been working with the ÇATOMs from their inception in the 1990s. Interested in the word 'participation', I asked him whether ÇATOMs also encourage its participants to go into politics, or, for example, to run during the local elections to become *muhtar*, that is, the elected representative of the state at the neighbourhood level. He liked my idea and found it innovative, but he said: 'This never occurred to us!' However, it was not *my* idea. Women's NGOs were already organizing training and encouraging women to take part in politics both in the region and elsewhere in Turkey. Later, another interviewee, who also had professional experience at the GAP RDA, reminded me of the larger problems of political representation in the region. In fact, she found my idea rather amusing: 'Even men can't run for elections in this region, let alone women!' Here she was mainly referring to the obstacles that pro-Kurdish parties face in parliamentary politics, such as the 10 per cent threshold. Moreover, entering politics requires both financial resources and the support of a large kinship network, 'and women have neither of these', she said.

'We absolutely do not get involved in politics', says ADEM's manager Ebru, when I ask similar questions to her.

> If you look at the handicrafts that they produce, you'll realize that it is all their colours [yellow, green and red, the colours of Kurdish flags]. I mean, they reflect [their ethnic identity] even in their work. Then I make a point of going up to them and appreciating their work. This time they smile back at me. ... Sometimes we go to the movies. For example, I don't understand Kurdish, but I watch Kurdish movies [refers to *Hükümet Kadın* series, only partially in Kurdish] with them. This makes them happy: 'You also watch together with us', they say.

Directors at the other ADEM in Tigris, which was in the Karakol neighbourhood, framed their involvement into national politics differently. Gülten, the manager of Karakol ADEM, shared responsibility of the centre with a co-manager named Nevriye. Both had graduated from university in other provinces and came back to Tigris, where they originate from. Gülten explains her role and the purpose of the ADEM project as follows:

> These centres were opened to create a home atmosphere [*ev ortamı*]. By this I mean to rehabilitate them [*onları rehabilite etmek*], teaching them things that they don't know, not only by offering courses but also by guiding them so that they can go out of their homes, break down their prejudices against the state and correct the wrong impressions that they have. ... She [Nevriye] is an Arab and I am a Kurd. I mean, there are a lot of wrongs, which they [people in the region] think are right. They have blind confidence [in the Kurdish movement] because they do not know the true reason for it, because they do not study it. We [want to] inform them about what they believe and what they serve so that they can still believe in whatever they want but at least do so consciously.

As these quotes illustrate, politics is defined strictly in relation to the Kurdish question and women's rehabilitation is a key word that is just as important as empowerment. I understand that rehabilitation has multiple meanings from the way that it was used in the context of ADEM's aim. First, as Gülten's quote indicates, ADEM aims to change Kurdish women's perception of the Turkish state and reshape their ideas about the Kurdish political movement and on identity politics in general. I explain the other meanings of rehabilitation in relation to empowerment further on.

ADEM aims to 'heal' and 'save' women by providing a second home to them, because the original/first home is the source of violence and problems intrinsically. The special room in Nar ADEM and Ebru's approach illustrate this second meaning of the term rehabilitation. The third meaning of rehabilitation refers to disciplining women, in accordance with the political project of the AKP as ideal Muslim mothers of the nation. Nevriye gave me an informative example of this last meaning of rehabilitation, which goes to the other pole of empowerment. She said:

> Once there was this pregnant woman, but she wasn't sure about having a baby. She came to ask me, '*Hocam*, here is the situation [...]' I told her that

she should never consider abortion because it is a great sin, it is equal to murder, may God forbid. Then months later she came back with a huge belly.

The pregnant woman addressed the ADEM manager as "hocam," just like many other participants did in other instances I observed. This is a word used differently in various contexts. It might mean (1) religious authority, (2) teacher, (3) mentor or guide. Because the managers of the centres are educated women, in this example it is used in the second and the third meanings. However, because ADEMs also provide Quran courses and because Gülten gives those courses herself, as a form of address *hocam* also refers to the directors' religious authority. This is not and can never be the case in the ÇATOMs. For instance, Tuğba a tutor working at ÇATOM would have a different answer in a similar situation: 'Once a woman asked me if using contraceptive pills is a sin. How would I know? I told her to go and ask to a *hoca*'. As a practicing Muslim who wears a headscarf, Tuğba had an abortion once because she thought that she was not ready for another child.

This example of differences in the guidance offered in ADEMs and ÇATOMs is telling. However, I put a caution to understand the difference between the two centres simply based on the secularist–Islamist divide. Following the warning of Sertaç Sehlikoğlu (2008) about scholarship of women in the Muslim societies, pious women do not always perform Islam in their ethical choices, as in the example of Nevriye's choice to advice pregnant woman not to have an abortion. I rather explain her act as a reiteration of conservative discourse of political power in her life (Kocamaner 2019). It is possible that tutors give advice, and perhaps this tutor also shared her opinion with the participant in this situation and did not want to share it with me. However, officially, Tuğba knows that although religious services are provided by the state in Turkey, this state institution (which is a ÇATOM) is not entitled to provide religious guidance. While in ADEM there is a clear prescription based on religious doctrines, in ÇATOM there is a negotiation process between the participants and the tutors and encouragement to seek more information, even though this information is again based on religious knowledge. In this way, the ÇATOMs stick to their basic principle, which is 'not to tell women what to do but to demonstrate what can be done under different circumstances' (GAP RDA n.d.). On their part, the ADEMs echo the popular political discourse adopted by AKP spokespersons when talking about the intimacy of women's bodies and sexualities with Islamic *spice*.

Conclusion

Establishing women's centres is a popular policy for addressing women's issues in both local and the central governments in Turkey, and this represents the continuity of a state tradition that goes back to late Ottoman times. The aim of these centres is framed in different ways, according to the needs of political projects of the time. However, defining a special *location* for women in public life and reproducing their home-based activities remain the means to help them 'progress' as even better housewives. Accordingly, the mayoral candidate of the ruling party, who is the carrier of this continuity, made use of existing repertoire in his election campaign that I mentioned at the beginning of this chapter. His vision was to establish centres where housewives produce handicrafts and contribute economically to their family, instead of acknowledging their contribution to household economy or opening a women's shelter, for example, in a city where gendered violence is high, and women's related needs are not met in the best way possible. While ÇATOMs detach self-consciousness from collective action and instead depoliticize feminist claims to empowerment, ADEMs do not problematize imbalanced power relations and use a vocabulary of rehabilitation.

In fact, although some NGOs involved in human rights advocacy in south-east Turkey have already drawn attention to the necessity of addressing psychological and physical rehabilitation (Yıldırım 2013), what the AKP government offers in their ADEMs is a different perspective. The frequent use of the term 'rehabilitation' in speeches of government spokespersons in last couple of years confirms that the AKP intends to extend the state into households in the region. As evidenced by the following press release from the Minister of Family and Social Policy, dated January 2016, rehabilitation took on a special meaning when military operations against Kurdish guerillas in northern Kurdistan were once more intensified:

> Our ministry and personnel cooperate with our armed forces closely [in the region]. We keep working on the ground for psychological rehabilitation and restoration. Both our social workers and our psychologist friends visit door-to-door and talk to children, the youth, the elderly, women, and the disabled one by one to find out their needs and provide financial aid. (Aile ve Sosyal Politikalar Bakanlığı 2016)

Whether it be for empowerment or rehabilitation, however, the differences between the women's centres' approaches do not make a sharp contrast in the services that they provide. Neither in the Kemalist republic nor in Erdoğan's response to it are women's needs fully met. Both women's centres discussed earlier are outcomes of projects which are planned to meet a particular goal for a limited period. In other words, they are not institutionalized and do not have a permanent legal basis in the bureaucratic structure. ÇATOMs were expected to become independent women's organizations over time; however, this did not happen. They were expected to become private artisan workshops, but this did not happen either, except in a limited number of cases. On the other hand, there is no such vision for ADEMs at all. By their very presence and stability over years, women's centers function to sustain women's position in the society and keep their 'alternative' options limited. Women still show an interest in them because their living conditions have not changed enough to decrease their demand for courses on housewifery skills. In the following chapters, I show how women negotiate with existing the conditions and opportunities provided, namely, education and employment.

2

Alternative opportunities

A local civil servant with an Arab ethnic background showed greater interest in my research than any other person during my fieldwork.[1] He once told me how difficult it was for him to get a higher education at a university even though he was very interested in the social sciences. He even invited me to have lunch with his childhood friends: a tailor, a businessman and a cook. We met in a quiet restaurant in the old town. I enjoyed the company of this group of middle-aged men and listening to their stories about Tigris. The most fascinating topics were the traditional handicrafts lost to time, and the good old days when women wove carpets at home during the cold winter nights. I asked them what they thought of the current state of women's employment. One of them said: 'For a woman, being a mother is the most important thing in the world.'[2] Other men agreed and noted that women cannot take on every type of job. Women could be teachers and gynaecologists or midwives, for instance. A female doctor was better suited for examining their wives. They then began a lengthy discussion about traditional healers, most of whom were women as well.

I felt a level of comfort and trust that enabled me to speak in more depth about sensitive topics because they were all kind and friendly. I asked whether men were primarily fathers if women were primarily mothers. They repelled my attack with humour but did not really answer my question. Next, I asked them directly whether women should work or not. The tailor answered my question seriously: 'There are some consequences of women working outside the home. We know how fashion models pay the price [bedel ödemek] for being famous'. By reducing the professional capacity of female fashion models to their sexuality, the implication was that successful career women must please powerful men sexually. It was common for my male research participants to use absurd and extreme examples with sexual connotations in conversation with me as a female researcher, but I was still offended at this. I said, 'I am a working woman too, and now I am eating and chatting with a group of men whom I barely know. What is the price I am paying now, you think?' After taking a moment to digest this, they loudly objected with one voice and told me mine was a different case. They said, 'You are an educated woman, you saved yourself. You are like a man'.

Anthropologist Julie Billaud opens her book *Kabul Carnival* (2015) with a story of a girl who decided to dress like a boy in order to bypass the rigid gender norms that became even more rigid during the decades of war in Afghanistan. I did not dress like a boy during my fieldwork. However, my parents made sure that I had received enough education to enable me to find a place for myself in a society which disadvantages women. The men in the restaurant were right, in this sense. My education negated my gender, or in other words, as soon as I became highly educated, my gender no longer mattered. Their remark was also pointing to the fact that the words 'women', 'education' and 'employment' come together in an uneasy way.

'It is not coincidental that most of the critical works [of feminist scholarship on Turkey] focus on girls' education' in the literature of Turkish citizenship (Türkyılmaz 2016: 169). As I have shown in Chapter 1, girls' education is an important aspect of Turkish modernization. At the intersection of various explanations about problems of schooling and political discourses framing the value and meaning of education differently, I wonder where women position themselves.

Women's praxis in Tigris is not limited to state-sponsored women's centres but also includes NGOs and other actors who work towards women's empowerment. For example, there were women cooperatives, which concentrate on producing high-quality products that have a constant demand in the market, and therefore, could be sold for good prices, instead of producing souvenirs for an oversaturated market. However, these cooperatives were not active during the time of my fieldwork. Moreover, state-sponsored centres dominate the field of income-generation activities because of their stability in terms of financial gain. This means that they open courses continuously in every semester and without interruption. For this reason, most of my data comes from ÇATOMs and ADEMs activities of which I could follow more closely.

In the centres, women were encouraging women to study further via long-distance education programmes or in formal education, in order to complete their high school education. However, the meaning and use of a diploma are very personal. While it may be a certificate that proves their qualifications for a future job opportunity for some women, for others it is a part of self-improvement and self-respect that makes them better mothers and wives. The value and meaning of a diploma, or education, differed according to a woman's family background, migration history, work experience and marriage status.

Alternative opportunities for education and employment are meaningful in women's lives in relation to other dynamics, which are namely stigmatization of Kurdishness and publicly visible Muslimhood in modernist narratives and the uncertainty of the path outside home – whether for education or work reasons – due to the gender policy of the state. Women reply to the stigmatization by developing a meaningful self without conforming to a victimhood position. They use it to benefit from opportunities to achieve their goals in life and to provide a better future for their children. The uncertainty, on the other hand, is useful for filling the positions of both housewife and working woman because it enables them to switch between these positions, depending on the conditions at the time.

Meanings of education

Most of the illiterate adults in the world are women. In Turkey, 2.8 million women are illiterate, and 3 million women do not have a primary school diploma (*Independent Türkçe* 2021). In the 2010s, southeast Turkey remained one of the regions with the highest percentage of women with no or little education although there has since been some improvement (Hacettepe University 2014). A survey shows that adult literacy is the lowest among 'housewives who live in the south-east Anatolia region' (Konda Araştırma 2016). In Tigris, Turkish literacy courses offered by the women's centres were in high demand in 2013. According to the annual report of ÇATOM for the year 2013, 758 women had attended Turkish literacy courses (GAP ÇATOM 2013).

Understanding the lack of education primarily as the outcome of the economic burdens of families and lack of state investment in the eastern provinces, private companies have launched corporate social responsibility projects starting in the early 2000s that essentially targeted girls' education. 'Dad, Send Me to School' (*Baba Beni Okula Gönder*) of Doğan Holding and 'Snowdrops' (*Kardelenler*) of Turkcell, a large mobile phone operator, are the most well-known examples of such projects that are run in rural parts of the country. Critical scholarship argues that companies locate 'gender issues' that are at a far distance from their own operations and in this way, neglect their own women workers' issues like sexual harassment, unequal payment and the glass ceiling (Türker and Yılmaz 2017: 170).

The campaign 'Off to School, Girls!' (*Haydi Kızlar Okula!*) launched by UNICEF and the Ministry of National Education in 2003 also explains the problem in girls accessing schooling not only by underdevelopment but also by 'traditional' gender roles in its brochure (UNDP 2020). This UNICEF project primarily focuses on the eastern provinces – starting in Van, near the Iranian border, which was one of the ten provinces of the country with the highest gender gap in education. Ethnography shows that the project had a positive impact and increased the willingness of families to send their daughters to school (Grabolle-Çeliker 2013).

Together with patriarchal norms (Kılınç, Neathery-Castro and Akyüz 2018), ethnic conflicts and nationalistic policies also prevent children in southeast Turkey from attending school. Since the first primary school curriculum was adopted in 1926, the centralized and nationalist character of school education intended to raise nationalist citizens remains unchanged (Altınay 2004; Kaplan 2006). Studies demonstrate that an aggressively ethnocentric form of Turkish nationalism is taught as a compulsory ideology to fight against threats to the very existence of a Turkish people both within and outside the country (Çayır 2014). Before 2012, when selective language courses in Kurmancî and Zazakî[3] were included in the curriculum, Kurdish was not taught in schools, although it is the native language of the majority of the population living in northern Kurdistan. However, even in the schoolbooks of these selected courses the word Kurd (*Kürt*) is used only once. In this context, the state's resistance to demands for education in the native language and the acknowledgment of Kurdish ethnic identity is yet another explanation for the low level of schooling in the GAP region. Sociologist Mesut Yeğen argues that due to this fact, Kurds hesitate to send their children to school (2009: 601). In an article that appeared in 2006, Yeğen also defines campaigns like 'Dad, Send Me to School' and 'Off to School, Girls!' as tools for the assimilative policies of the state in provinces where a Kurdish population dominates (Yeğen 2006). However, feminist scholar Handan Çağlayan (2013) says that the 'fear of assimilation' does not explains why only Kurdish girls – and not Kurdish boys – are prevented from schooling.

In their research conducted in Ankara on 'the life experiences of young girls who neither work nor go to school', Kezban Çelik and Demet Lüküslü (2010) quote young girls who regret dropping school and follow skill courses offered by the municipality. During my fieldwork, I have seen many young girls above fourteen years of age attending courses offered in women's centres. They told me that they did not like formal schooling. Neither the subjects taught nor the school environment appealed to them: 'School is boring'. In general, girls were reluctant to discuss their decision to drop out of school and some even reacted with fury to my questions. As one girl exclaimed: 'What is so great about school, Zeynep, for God's sake!' Thinking back, I came to realize that girls did not like to be questioned on the reasons why they stopped going to school, especially if their low level of education is associated with poverty and a stigmatized identity, such as Kurdishness and publicly visible Muslimhood. Moreover, it was even more unpleasant to have an educated woman from Ankara, where policies based on this kind of stigmatization are produced, asking such questions. After my unsuccessful attempts to talk to girls, tutors told me that it was because these girls had experiences 'that couldn't be told'. I understand that tutors meant that there were things that could not be told *to me*. Therefore, it is worth noting that the narratives of adult women that I present further on are products of a similar process of reflection.

Halime: 'not interested'

In an average afternoon at a women's centre in Tigris, from the open doors of the sewing atelier, you can hear the noise of sewing machines, the faint squeaks coming from the rusted legs of ironing boards and a quick clank of scissors. Imagine women sitting in tandem and working in the atelier. Most probably they had made it to the centre after having spent the morning at home dealing with housework. Possibly, you may hear them sharing stories with each other in low voices and receiving brief rejoinders from others. They do not speak much because everybody is concentrated on the work. Very often, a woman sits back and complains about the piles of textiles left undone. Rarely does someone take a smoking break. The sooner the piles are done the better, because routine household tasks await them, such as preparing dinner and picking children up from school.

While computer-learning students leave the centre after the day's session, the handicrafts ateliers upstairs have their day-long routine. Every couple of weeks, the tutor teaches her participants a new crocheting technique to decorate local textiles. She shows extra patience not only with the teenager participants of the atelier, who come every day in the hope of becoming a tutor in another souvenir atelier, but also with their favourite pop songs playing on loop as background music in the room. Meanwhile, in the next room of the souvenir atelier, the textile painting tutor shows students how to give a shadowy effect to the figures on the surfaces of items designed recently during a workshop organized by a 'philanthropic' organization from the country's commercial centre, Istanbul. The items will be sold online with labels including the full name of the woman who produced it, and they will be promoted as 'ethically and locally produced handmade goods to support women's empowerment'.

When I met Halime she was taking computer courses at one of the women's centres in Tigris, Al ÇATOM. When the centre was established in an old neighbourhood of Tigris, the neighbourhood was not yet dominated by poverty and populated by migrants fleeing from the war in Syria. I decided to approach Halime because she was not interested in ateliers where she could earn money, in contrast to other women. She was also wearing colourful headscarves and makeup, which was not a usual practice among regulars of ÇATOMs. Moreover, unlike the others she was not very talkative. However, when we found somewhere quiet to talk, it was she who initiated the conversation and told me out of the blue: 'I was dating someone, but it didn't work out'.

Intimate relations or stories from the past were not openly discussed with neighbours or relatives for fear of gossip. Therefore, having a private conversation with a stranger like me was an opportunity for her to 'remember beautiful memories'. On the one hand, dating was risky and not typical of girls of her generation. Therefore, her experience was something that separated her from her peers in the women's centre. On the other hand, like the others she had also been prevented from schooling. Her father had sent her to a Quran course after she completed primary school. He promised to send her to a girls' vocational high school where she could acquire a skill. However, when he died, her brothers told her that girls do not go to school because it is dangerous for them.

In her article on a spatial analysis of gender in Urfa, Bridget Purcell (2017) suggests that having a school education is a sign of wealth. In Halime's case, however, moving from a remote city in the east to the cosmopolis did not enlarge her opportunities. Urban life might have the potential to improve women's lives, but it depends on whether one focuses on the dangers or opportunities it offers (Tuncer 2018). In Halime's case, her brothers focused on the dangers of the city to a young women's dignity, such as sexual harassment. Moreover, the alternative path to education offered by the women's centre in Tigris was not accessible in Istanbul.

This is how Halime started to work in a textile workshop with her brothers at the age of fifteen. As a poorly educated and unskilled woman who has to contribute to the family budget, Halime was one of the unregistered women workers engaging in the hidden economic activities that constitute almost 50 per cent of all economic activity in Turkey (Kümbetoğlu, User and Akpınar 2010). She spent one year working there, and within this period, she developed friendships, earned enough money to buy a cell phone secretly and fell in love with another worker:

I met him in the textile [workshop]. But we were not going out or anything. We were just making eye contact and texting messages. He was from the west, born and raised in Istanbul. His family did not want [me]. I mean, one of their soldiers died a martyr here, I mean, because of the terror. They saw me as one [a terrorist].

Halime's family told her that she should stop hoping for a future with this young man from Istanbul because the families did not know each other. They preferred her to marry someone from their own extended family. Because of the family pressure, she says, she decided to marry the person of their choice:

> Then, [the man i am currently married with] came with his family to ask for my hand. I contacted the one in Istanbul. He said, 'No way, I'll elope with you!' I refused and said, 'I can't dishonour my family. My brothers and my grandfather's family would kill us. There's nothing we can do. Neither your family nor mine wants us to marry'. I got engaged, thinking that it would be easier than getting divorced.

Specifically, in Halime's case, marriage was a lifesaver. Although she was not happy with the poor conditions of her house in the old neighbourhood of Tigris, she was content with her marriage and two children. She described her husband as a forward-looking and indulgent person. She described her relationship with him as satisfactory and relaxed, compared with the strict control over her movements in Istanbul she experienced when she was a teenager:

> My brothers oppressed me. Going out was not allowed. One day, when I was thirteen or fourteen years old, I felt a tightness in my chest. When I opened my eyes, I saw the police while the doctor was giving me cardiac massage in the emergency room. The police led my family away and asked me what the problem was. I said, perhaps it was due to stress: 'You are an easterner [*doğulusun*], probably it is about family pressure' ... Thank God my husband is not like that.

The police officer realized that Halime's family's practices were violation of her rights while she was a child, and therefore, abusive. However, he did not report it. There are many dynamics at play here. First, varying images of Halime are related to the various representations of Kurdish women – even though the police officer silenced her ethnicity with a metonym, 'the eastern'. Secondly, Halime's gendered citizenship is at play in her encounter with the state representative. Thirdly, and finally, she holds a slippery position. Is she a terrorist or a victim of her culture? Images and perceptions of the victim to be saved and the national enemy/other overlap over the bodies of women living in southeast Turkey. Although Halime is aware of the imaginations her gendered body triggers as a Kurdish woman, she accommodates neither of the positions she openly talks about.

She wanted to work after getting married despite the furious objections of her in-laws. She found a job as a cleaning lady through her husband's connections in the AKP's local union and started to work at the women's shelter. However, she found the conditions of work burdensome and quit after a few months. Halime told me that she was interested in working as an assistant in a shop, pharmacy or beauty salon. However, all these jobs require a high school degree. Although Halime followed courses at the ÇATOM to earn an elementary school diploma, she was not prepared to continue her schooling via distance learning education or in other ways. While she was working at the cleaning job, her relatives and neighbours criticized her for leaving her children alone at home. She said, she felt very guilty as a mother, and therefore, she dropped her plans to work outside the house. However, she had an entrepreneurial spirit. A few years before, while taking courses in the women's centre, she had sold sandwiches to the participants. She had to stop this business because her equipment was stolen. After this incident, she stopped taking courses.

Halime started taking courses at the women's centre again with an urge to master communication technologies. 'Because something bad happened to me', she said, giggling. Then I listened to how she found pictures of her husband with other women on a USB stick. Her husband's infidelity made her upset, but she never considered divorcing him:

> What could I do, where could I go? [I knew that eventually] we'd make things up because we have children, so telling my mother would make things worse. Then, my brothers would get involved, and my relatives would turn against him. ... I know it is not his fault but his friends. Thank God that he hasn't done me wrong again since then. I stayed because of my children. Thank God that we are okay. And this is how I started back at the women's centre, with anger; and he could not prevent me from doing what I want after all that he has done to me.

After Turkey became a candidate for full membership in the EU in 1999, a civil society platform, mainly composed of the post-coup feminist groups and queer communities' organizations, was successful in putting pressure on the government. As a result, both the Civil Code (that importantly establishes the equal split of assets gained during marriage as the standard form of property ownership) and the Penal Code (that most importantly recognizes the sexual and bodily autonomy and rights of citizens, especially women) entered into force. In this way, the post-coup feminist movement in Turkey gained a significant victory and showed its power and determination to end violence against women (İlkkaracan 2007). However, Halime was doubtful that state institutions were willing to protect her. On the one hand, she had nowhere to go other than to her sister, who had convinced her to make up with her husband. On the other hand, marriage brings status, and a lack of this status can be mortal. Even if it might not be the case for Halime, gender-based violence and the killing of women are extremely common in Turkey, and divorced women are the primary targets of such crimes. Halime instead prefers to resist in intimate ways in the home, as Kandiyoti explains:

> The fact that resistance did not necessarily have to take overt and organized forms but could be expressed through covert and indirect forms of bargaining was particularly well suited to women's contestations of domestic power structures involving as they do face-to-face relations with intimates such as husbands, mothers-in-law, sons and daughters rather than encounters with the more impersonal workings of bureaucracies and state apparatuses. (Kandiyoti 1998: 144)

Halime's mother did not want her brothers to get involved in the Kurdish political movement and this is how they all ended up living close by their relatives in Istanbul. Owing to her migration experience, Halime had already learned as a child what it meant to be Kurdish. Later, being a Kurdish woman from the east created further problems when she made her initial choice of a spouse. After marrying the 'right' man, however, she returned to her hometown of Tigris and started to follow courses at ÇATOM as a bored housewife. However, although she was not sent to school, both because of their poverty and because of her brothers' perception of school as a place dangerous for girls and their honour, Halime did not register on distance education programmes like her friends. For Halime, the symbolic value of the diploma or the experience of formal schooling was irrelevant to her because her work experience at a young age had reduced the value of education by enabling her to earn money and meet new people. Despite her husband's betrayal, she decided to stay with him instead of going through the difficult path of divorce. Halime had to keep her marriage safe, and this was why she was determined to advance her skills in digital communication technologies to protect herself against her husband's possible future infidelity.

Aylin: 'I had bigger dreams'

Aylin was an eye catcher among others in the handicraft atelier with her smart comments and a good sense of humour. Later I learned that this forty-year-old woman with her modest look was very interested in the news. She was one of the very few people with whom I could talk about the political developments of the day, including the Uludere or Roboski massacre[4] that caused her face to drop; the Gezi uprising that she sympathized with because of her love of trees; the headscarf controversy, by defending her choice to cover her head; and the Kurdish question that she criticized with a nationalist instinct: 'I don't know what they want. Don't they have any rights? Everybody speaks Kurdish in hospital, for example. It is me who feels like a minority in Tigris'.

Aylin came to Tigris almost thirty years before when she got married. Previously, she lived in Van, a province in eastern Turkey, near the Iranian border. When the earthquake hit Van in 1976 her family moved to Istanbul. She was a senior high school student dreaming about going to university in Istanbul when her parents forced her to marry a cousin of hers, a primary school graduate living in Tigris:

> I was very sad, cried a lot, denied it. When my relatives were studying at the university, this [happened to me] ... I felt as if they had thrown me back into exile, to the East. I was very sorry, cried a lot, wanted to confront [them]. But I couldn't say anything to my parents. What could I say? If I said no, then [they would ask] whether [I was dating] someone else. It used to be very difficult to say no in those days, now girls can easily say whatever they think. I couldn't. This is how, [my parents] gave me away.

Her uncle, who was also her father-in-law, convinced her to marry by saying that she would get her high school qualification in Tigris. He said, she did not even have to attend classes because he knew people at the provincial directorate of education, who can help.[5] However, he did not keep his promise and Aylin did not get her diploma.

Aylin started to live with her uncle's extended family in a large mansion in the old town. Although everybody had their private apartments, they all ate together under the same roof. She spent her time doing housework with her co-sisters-in-law (*eltiler* and *yengeler*) who were married to her husband's brothers. These women who were living together under the same conditions possessed different levels of freedom, depending on their age, how many children and boys they had and the age of the brother with whom they were married. Their mother-in-law was responsible for organizing daily life at home.

When Aylin got pregnant at the age of seventeen, she was still dreaming about continuing her education. However, schooling was useless in the eyes of her new family, because it did not provide education that was useful for a woman's everyday life, such as how to feed a baby:

> I was in shock when I was told that I was pregnant at the health centre. I said 'No, I don't want it! ... I am still a child; how can I have a child?' We did not plan [it]. I was very sad. My husband was sad, too. He asked me why it had happened so early. It was my fate. I did not take good care of my baby; I couldn't breastfeed very successfully. My co-sisters-in-law got angry when they heard that I did not mix the infant formula with water. They said, 'What kind of a mother are you, and you call yourself educated?' But did I learn how to raise a child [at school]?

The other women in the house were the source of her troubles but also the source of information and solidarity for her. For example, Aylin started courses at the Mor ÇATOM with the help of one of them. This ÇATOM was providing a lot of training that was useful to housewives such as learning sewing, knitting, making point lace, childcare and sexual health. Also, the directors and trainers at women's centres encourage women to study and complete their education. As a director in an ADEM explains, their policy is to make sure that all participants complete their education even if they never take on waged work. A diploma is important for a woman to be a good mother and to allow her to help with her children's homework:

> Imagine: a woman sends her kids to school but cannot even help them with their homework. I mean, kids see their mother as their primary model in life, right? When the mother can't help her kids, they start to judge her differently. They think 'my mom doesn't know anything', even though she helped them until they started school. So [with a diploma] she manages to become a perfect mother in her children's eyes.

Aylin also registered to start high school again via long-distance education. Both Aylin and her daughters followed the long-distance education programmes, the alternative education solution offered by the state. Her daughters have wanted her to continue her studies to be able to take university exams. However, Aylin was not so sure. She says that being prevented from schooling hurt her very deeply and it is too late to repair the damage:

> I took the position of a housewife and remained there, I suppose. Yet my thoughts are broader than that. … Your capabilities are limited within the home when you are a housewife, I cannot improve myself, with the best will in the world. Now I say that I am free, but it would be much better if I could [have studied] before, when my kids were still young. Then I would be in a very different position than I am now.

For Aylin, the state, in the shape of the ÇATOM, gave what her family, her in-laws and her husband took from her: her right to education. Therefore, she was certain that the state could solve other problems including domestic violence and femicides, which were, in her opinion, the main problems in society. Although she did not find preventive measures and penalties satisfactory, the solution that she offered was in line with the existing policies of government, which was to focus on the family unit rather than the well-being of woman. For Aylin, it would be the best if psychologists or a counsellor would talk to people, visit households regularly to observe and correct wrong behaviour within the family.

The interruption to her educational life had a harmful impact on Aylin's self-perception and still upsets her many years later. During our interview, she often remarked on how happy she was to be able to attend the Mor ÇATOM: 'I have surpassed what I assumed was my own personal limits'. At first, she started to work at home by sharing her piecework workload with her co-sisters-in-law. They shared the profit from the sale of these handmade souvenirs with Aylin. When the field supervisor made a household visit, Aylin got a personal invitation to attend the courses at the centre because of her talent. Although her mother-in-law did not like the idea, Aylin got the permission of her husband. This is how she started to earn money and turned from being a housewife into being a working woman through the courses she attended.

Aylin needed the money because her husband has been unemployed, and the salaries of her working daughters were not always enough for household expenses. She used the money that she earned from the ÇATOM to cover her personal expenses, such as her travel costs when she had to go to the doctor, and so on. She was also providing her son, who was still of school age, with pocket money. She said, 'It frustrates me when I see that there is no money left in my purse, because I have got used to having my own money'. In fact, Aylin told me that she would like to have salaried employment. The only question that occupied her mind was whether the working environment would be safe for a woman:

> I mean, in the end you are a lady [*bayan*]. If the working environment is male [dominated], you can't be sure whether they will treat you respectfully. And what about your husband? He has to trust you ... I mean it is not only about whether you want to work or not.

The job market is not always safe for women, but ÇATOMs are safer. However, considering the time and labour invested and the established system of production in ÇATOMs, Aylin thinks that women should earn more money, at least an amount that enables them to stand on their own two feet:

> I wish the ÇATOM could be our bread and butter so that we wouldn't have to work somewhere else. We want [our ÇATOM] to work as a workshop that receives orders regularly. Many women come here in the hope of earning money and they become disenchanted when they realize that they can't really live on this money. Instead, they work as [domestic] helpers, to clean and cook until noon and earn 400 liras per month. It is not a waste of time. Who on earth would earn the same amount of money in a ÇATOM?

Conditions of employment

Because housewives are not included in the labour market, it is assumed that they do not participate in production processes and the economy. However, their unpaid care service, which is generally expected of women, ensures the reproduction of labour by protecting the health and well-being of family members (Oakley 1974). Housework entails not only the fulfilment of routine and labour-intensive activities, but it also places a mental load on women. Nevertheless, earlier feminisms tended to belittle housewives: women should have bigger dreams than having a good marriage and raising children and they should rather realize their potential by getting an education and making a career in a profession (Friedan 2013). However, being a housewife can be a status symbol and wage labour may not always mean empowerment for those who have to work hard outside the home (hooks 1981). Therefore, a wage-earning employment both empowers women and increases their own and their family's welfare but 'gender equality does not have to be achieved by participating in the waged labour force'.

In Turkey, when women find a job, it is usually home based or in the informal sector (Dedeoğlu and Elveren 2012), and they keep investing more time for unpaid work within the household than men (Öneş, Memiş and Kızılırmak 2013). In any case, women spend more time in care work, and for this very reason, Ferhunde Özbay (2019) suggests that women participating in the market economy as 'working women' can be seen instead as 'housewives participating in the market economy'. Therefore, methods of increasing women's participation in wage labour systems should also include dismantling the entire framework of gendered wage labour system that is based upon patriarchal norms.

Gülay Toksöz (2016) shows that although the numbers suggest that female unemployment slightly decreased in the period of AKP governments, a close look at the characteristics of employment reveal the fact that women remained outside the labour market and inside the informal sector. She shows that the officially recorded number of unemployed women is misleading because the number of women, who declared that they were ready and willing to work even though they were not actively seeking employment, should also be added in calculations (ibid.) as women's agency in work-related strategies are influenced by their class-specific differences (Beşpınar 2010).

Policies about childcare are illustrative in terms of women's care work. Working parents rely on their family networks for childcare because high-quality day-care centres are expensive and rare. The 'Grandmother Project' (*Büyükanne Projesi*) shows that the government supports this solution. According to this project adopted with modifications from an EU-funded project of the Ministry of Labour and Social Security, grandmothers who take care of their grandchildren get financial support, if the mother of the child is employed. Although the amount given was below the minimum wage, per month for a period of one year, the demand for this project was very high. Başak Can (2019) argues that the project manifests how solidarity between different generations of women is instrumentalized by pro-family social policies. In this context, day-care services provided by ÇATOMs and ADEMs do not accept children of wage labourer women.

Earning money creates moments when money breaks the husband's full power and control over women. As soon as housewives earn money, even if the amounts are small, they feel they are more independent and autonomous individuals. This is the progress referred to in the goals of the ÇATOM. The strict regulations in the ADEMs also hint to the potential of conflict between participating in the ateliers and importance of earning one's own money. Although women earn less than minimum wage from selling their products, the amount that they did earn was enough to give them independence in some life decisions. For example, one young woman was able to pay her exam fee, which costs 20 liras, and obtain a high school diploma. 'Now I work, maybe I can even go to the university, because I don't want to be like my mother and other women in this place, who gossip about each other and pity themselves all day long', she said.

A professional in 'feminine skills': Tuğba

Tuğba, the tutor of the textile-painting atelier, helped me to understand the symbolic value of money for women. She says earning even the smallest amount makes them happy, because it is not easy to ask for money from their husbands, especially when they want to give a present to a friend or buy something for themselves. Besides, the husbands themselves do not earn enough all the time. Therefore, it is very important for women to earn their own money:

> It is better than nothing. Women earn quite well even without going to fairs. Let's say we earn 350 Turkish liras in total and when I distribute this amount among eight to nine women, they are relieved. Aylin, for example, always works with me. Sometimes she earns more than I do. Not always, but she earns quite well.

According to Tuğba, Aylin was not only the most dedicated but also the most talented of a dozen participants in her textile-painting atelier. There were six women like Aylin who came every day, but they did not earn as much, because not all of them were equally skilled. For this reason, there were times that Tuğba designed a product for one person, who could stick with one simple thing. In this way, even women who are not exceptionally skilled can earn money. During the last fair (*kermes*) that they attended, participants of Tuğba's atelier earned approximately 900 TRY (100 USD) in total from selling a simple design. She said that women cried when she distributed everybody's share of the profit, because they could not believe that they could earn that amount of money.

Tuğba said that not many goods produced by her group of participants remained unsold. However, there were exceptions. In such cases women got jealous and gossiped. Tuğba had a clear explanation for it: 'How can I sell if you produce badly? People look at all of them and buy the best one. I can't tell people what to buy!' The myth that women have natural feminine skills in making handmade products was misleading, because not all women were equally good at it. Because production was based on skill, good design and quality control were difficult issues in women's centres, unless the women concentrated on producing very simple designs. This created discontent among participants and in the larger public. An NGO representative whom I talked to also highlighted this point: 'They produce unmarketable things there, things that have no economic value. In return, women expect to get some money, even at times when they do not produce something of good quality'.

Tuğba was a local urbanite woman in Tigris. She was the seventh and last child of a local middle-class family, born to an Arabic mother and Kurdish father. Her mother's family dealt in textile production and owned land. She grew up in a big house in the old town. During her visits to her sister living in Istanbul, Tuğba attended handicraft courses offered by the public education centre. She continued the same courses in Tigris and eventually became a tutor at the public education centres at the age of twenty. Meanwhile, both her parents had died, and she started to live with her brother's family. From an early age she had been receiving her parents' retirement payments, and thus she had been economically independent since her youth.

Working as a professional woman, Tuğba was not interested in marriage. However, a man in her neighbourhood showed an interest in her. She told me that at the beginning she refused to 'deal with him'. After some time, she decided to meet him and went to the market he owns. The man was openly thrilled. When Tuğba attempted to buy a hairpin, he attempted to offer it for free. She did not accept the gift and insisted on paying. Then he invited her to a patisserie, but she refused that, too. Instead, she gave him her phone number later via her sisters. With her brother's consent and her sisters' positive feedback based on their investigation of her suitor, Tuğba accepted the man's proposal. They got married when she was twenty-four. However, she did not want to have a child immediately: 'My husband used contraception, because I didn't know much about female contraception. I mean, he was twenty-nine years old'. Seven months after having her son, she was pregnant again. This time she decided to have an abortion. She told me that this had been a mistake because she could probably never get pregnant again after this operation. However, she did not believe that abortion should be banned: 'I mean, of course, pregnancies without marriage should be aborted.[6] You know, then people abandon babies if they are not allowed to have an abortion in these circumstances'.[7]

Tuğba stopped working at the public education centre after giving birth. However, she was still producing handicrafts for her relatives' dowry at home. The tradition of dowry creates a considerable market for women to sell their handicrafts. Participants on ÇATOM courses are respected when they sell their products to relatives for their dowry. For younger women, this means that they are good bridal candidates and are talented enough to generate additional income for their family to support their husband, when needed. After a break of ten years, Tuğba decided to go to work and applied to a ÇATOM. In this way, she positions herself as being a full breadwinner from the very beginning of her marriage and she finds herself powerful enough to offer help to her husband when needed: 'I don't want money from my husband. On the contrary, I have offered to help him many times, but he refuses'.

A breadwinner housewife: İlknur

Apart from their income-generation activities, centres also create employment for tutors and directors. Throughout the history of the ÇATOMs, upwards mobility has been possible within the hierarchical administrative structure, and Adalet Budak, the GAP development expert, is an example of this. Budak was part of the ÇATOM project from the very beginning. She was born and raised in Urfa. In the early 1990s she was a high school graduate participating in courses offered by the public education centre. She was also a student on an Anadolu University distance learning programme. She was offered the post of coordinator of the first ÇATOM established in Şanlıurfa and that is how her career started. Over the years, a charity organization established by a businesswoman from Istanbul sent Budak to New York for further education and training in the subject of development. She came back to Turkey and started to work as an expert at the headquarters of the GAP RDA in Urfa, coordinating social projects. At the time of the research, she was still responsible for coordinating the activities of ÇATOMs, including distributing scholarships distributed to girls who cannot go to school for financial reasons.

Like Adalet Budak, İlknur was also a product of a ÇATOM. As a young mother and housewife without a career plan, she attended ÇATOM courses. İlknur was known as a talented young woman in the village where she was born and grew up. She was the oldest daughter in a Kurdish family and was responsible for the household and for hosting guests. Men, including a neighbour of her relative, started to ask for her hand when she was fifteen years old. He was four years older than her, and she did not know him at all. 'It was a matter of destiny', she said. They entered into a religious wedding first and after three months, when they were sure that she was pregnant, they had an official wedding at the municipality. As she explained, 'A [religious] marriage is intended to prevent unmarried couples from sin'.

The newlywed couple decided to leave their hometown and moved to Tigris, where her husband would have better job opportunities. Although city life was difficult, the idea of moving appealed to İlknur from the beginning: 'We thought about it. In the village I was at home all the time. In Tigris I would be at home as well. It was fine with me'. However, it was not what she imagined because she was living far away from her relatives and very lonely with her newborn son. İlknur was 'stuck at home within four walls' and suffering from boredom before she enrolled into the Mor ÇATOM in her neighbourhood, with the support of her husband.

In the Mor ÇATOM she learned that she could earn money with her existing skill in difficult handicrafts, such as making *oya* lace. She followed courses regularly to develop her skills further. Over time, she mastered handmade souvenir production and after five years she became one of the official tutors of the Mor ÇATOM. As a working woman, İlknur was also proud of herself for earning money. However, during our interview she ridiculed the term 'working woman' because she was still a full-time housewife too. Her husband's reluctance to acknowledge her as a working woman frustrated İlknur: 'Husbands don't change. I tried hard to change him but failed. I work, he does too but he never shares the responsibility of housework with me'.

İlknur's husband was not pleased by the fact that she was fully committed to her career and spent a lot of time in the ÇATOM. When İknur demanded his help with the housework, he not only refused to share the responsibilities, but he also 'threatened' to take away her job. He reminded her that it was her decision to work and if it was difficult to fulfil her duties at home, she should consider leaving her job.

İlknur is proud of being good at cooking and cleaning, in contrast to her husband, who 'cannot even feed himself if he is alone at home'. While she highlights her skill in domestic work in contrast to her husband's neediness (*muhtaçlık*), she describes her place at home as essential for the survival of her husband and her family. This gives her the encouragement to negotiate her position in the household to be more equal. One of the topics to negotiate is how far away from home she can travel.

As the tutor of a handicraft atelier, İlknur has never gone to Istanbul herself to sell the goods, although she works hard in preparation for the fairs. When I asked her why, she smiled and whispered that her husband does not permit it. A few months before this conversation during an awareness workshop, which I will talk about in detail in Chapter 5, İlknur called upon the women to respect the decisions of their family and husbands, who, she said, were wiser than women. Remembering this previous exchange, I asked İlknur what she thought about husbands' control over women's mobility. She replied that ideally, women should not ask their husband's permission all the time and added that husbands do not have the right to control women. She prefers to 'inform' her husband, rather than 'ask' him. Even informing him is not necessary most of the time. Then she entertainingly told me how she has stopped informing her husband at times when she goes to the market for shopping. 'And he got used to it', she added.

İlknur's husband gets used to other things too. Her education is another example. Like many other women that I listened to, İlknur was not able to continue studying after primary school because there was no school in her hometown. However, after being a trainee of ÇATOM, she registered with distance education and was able to graduate from secondary school. At the time of the interview, she was about to graduate from high school and was making plans to register at the university. She said that having a diploma, even via the distance learning system, would make her feel stronger as an educated mother and wife in her family. However, her husband was very discouraging from the beginning. Although she learned appropriate techniques during her gender equality training in the ÇATOM, İlknur did not confront her husband with the argument that she had the right to continue her education. Rather, she persisted flirtatiously with her education plans. She paid exam fees with the money that she earned from the ÇATOM, and added bitterly: 'He felt offended when I took care of my own expenses without asking his help'. She giggled while telling me how his face turned black and blue when she told him that she passed her mathematics exams. I got the impression that she enjoyed this power game with her husband over money. In this way, she kept being an interesting and charming partner in her husband's eyes and convinced him to let her do what she wanted.

İlknur's next target was to get her bank card back from her husband. She had given him the card when she started to earn money. This submissive act was an indicator that although she was working outside the home throughout the whole day, it was all done to contribute to the household budget. She said she was perfectly fine with the idea that her husband controlled her income if he spent it on their common expenses. In the end, he was not spending her money for his own luxurious consumption, or abusing her labour. However, she said, 'Sometimes when we fight, I find myself thinking: What if I asked for that bank card back now?' For her, the bank card was a symbol of her valuable financial contribution to the family, and therefore, keeping it showed that her voice, her opinions and her decisions deserve to be considered as much as her husband's.

In short, İlknur's story illustrates progress. She pushes the boundaries defined by her husband in their relationship and she can do it due to her regular contribution to the household working as a full-time tutor at the Mor ÇATOM. Here she was orchestrating women's production well and was working hard to find ways to sell their goods. The participants and other tutors respected her in return. She was always the first to come in in the mornings and the last to leave in the evenings because, she said, she loves her job and does her best to do things better. She was also interested in being a field supervisor in the future. Meanwhile, some teenagers in the ÇATOMs also hoped to become tutors. In this way, İlknur was a role model. However, there are very limited numbers of tutoring positions available.

Dreams of entrepreneurship: Filiz and Melek

> I was confident of myself but could not prove it. I felt better after paying regular visits to the ÇATOM, attending courses and meeting new people. My family also recognized [the change in me] and started to support me differently. While I used to need permission even to go out for a walk, my family gives me full support when I say that I plan to open a shop.

These are the words of an ex-ÇATOM participant in a promotional video produced in 2011 (GAP 2014a). In average, one in 10,000 ÇATOM beneficiaries establishes a business every year (GAP ÇATOM 2015). Because ADEMs are very new and have not released a report, it is not possible to make a comparison between them. However, participants were eager to find a way to establish their own businesses. In fact, managers of the ADEM had already developed a project to buy sewing machines for women who are enthusiastic about earning money from home and producing simple goods, like bed linen. Also, managers aim to be able to provide certificates that public education centres are mandated to give out so that women can put their capital together to establish a business among themselves.

During the fieldwork, I was able to follow the entrepreneurial efforts of two women, Filiz and Melek. These financially better off housewives had never participated in the handicraft courses offered by the women's centres. These two women were also involved in several of the activities of women's praxis. They participated in the training and activities not because they needed money but because they were simply bored at home. They both had plenty of time because Melek's only daughter was already a teenager, and Filiz was a young newly married woman without children. While their husbands had political connections with the Kemalist Republican People's Party (*Cumhuriyet Halk Partisi*, or CHP), Filiz and Melek were active members of the local women's council, which I introduce in the following chapters.

I was usually meeting Melek and Filiz together, but it was always Filiz's business ideas that we were discussing. She had never worked before, except for running a small business of smuggled cosmetic products for a couple of years when she was still in her twenties. She made so much money that she used to send pocket money to her sister, who was studying in another city, and she also bought a dishwasher for her mother. The system was simple: Filiz bought smuggled replicas of well-known cosmetic brands when she was visiting her relatives living in border towns near Syria and then sent them to her relatives living in the western cities of Turkey, such as Istanbul, Izmir and Bolu, to sell them there. All the relatives on the supply chain were investing in the purchase of the products and then they shared the profit equally among themselves. 'It was a lot of fun!' Filiz said. However, when cheaper brands entered the cosmetic market in Turkey, their profits dropped, and she decided to stop the business.

As a teenager, Filiz was never interested in studying, and therefore, she dropped out of school when she was fifteen years old. She grew up in a crowded family and spent most of her time with her sister. After she married and had her own house, however, she got bored. She amusingly said, 'I was going out shopping all the time and walking around so much that I acquired quite a suntan!' She was determined to find an occupation for herself, but things did not go as she planned:

> So, I decided to work at the orphanage, but I did not have a license to take care of children. I learnt that I could get a certificate from the people's education centre. In the end I got the certificate but couldn't find a job there. So, I applied to the hospital, using my relatives as my referees. But that didn't work out either. I applied for one more job but this time I got pregnant. All my friends who got the certificate at the same time as I did have got a job now.

For some time already Filiz had been thinking about owning a café, where she could sell organic biscuits. She thought that university students in Tigris needed a place where they can spend time and study too: 'It is a need throughout the city'. She shared this idea with her friends from the people's education centre. Although everybody liked the idea, nobody was willing to actively involved in it, except for Melek. However, with Melek's involvement the project idea started to be developed.

Filiz and Melek were particularly curious about the potential business opportunities created by tourism in Tigris. They dreamt about establishing and managing a restaurant together. They had innovative ideas about what products to offer and to whom, as well as how to arrange promotion and pricing. For example, one idea that particularly appealed to them was entertaining customers with an animation of a henna night ceremony. They knew that tourists came to Tigris with the expectation of experiencing local culture and learning about local traditions. This was a well-directed point of cultural tourism. However, identifying potential market needs was only one step in business management.

Melek and Filiz believed in themselves and had big dreams. They were ambitious and self-confident, just as any project promoting women's empowerment would want them to be. Why was that? Filiz was relying on the fact that her father had owned a restaurant. Therefore, she thought she was someone familiar with the idea of managing a small business. Melek, on the other hand, believed that her connections would be useful, because she knew important people. Research on women's empowerment in the example of women married to entrepreneurs show that gendered relationship patterns prevail social and private life in Turkey as a reaction to the potential hazards of the free market economy (Akyüz et al. 2019). How does one read the case of Melek and Filiz in light of this observation?

As I spent more time with them, the number of questions they asked me about their entrepreneurial dream increased. Meanwhile, public institutions, such as the Mesopotamia regional development agency had placed advertisements on billboards all over the city, calling for applications for entrepreneurship training. Finally, I arranged an appointment for them with an expert from the development agency and promised I would accompany them during their visit.

The development expert was very friendly and warm. He spent almost one hour with us and shared information about the training provided by the agency. Getting trained was obviously the first step, because sometimes the terminology was too complicated for us to understand, such as 'investment appraisal' (*yatırım değerlendirmesi*) and 'market segmentation' (*pazar bölümleme*). Also, the requirements for establishing a small business were more stringent than we had expected. For example, neither Filiz nor Melek had a proper certificate to run a food business.

The two women were disappointed when we left the agency. Weeks later when we met, they told me that they decided to drop the idea of starting a business. They had not been encouraged: instead, they had been discouraged by the meeting. The available funds and programmes did not target them: instead, they were aimed at those who already have advantages in terms of financial as well as social capital. Soon after, Filiz gave birth to her son, who became her full-time occupation.

Conclusion

In Tigris, education and woman come together in ways that require detaching sexuality from women's subjectivity, as I showed in my opening vignette at the beginning of this chapter in the conversation with middle-aged men. While this is the case, girls' education is desired because of the potential social mobility it could bring about, and therefore, is promoted by different institutions and actors in various ways. There are many meanings attached to the lack of education. Those who believe it is a problem related to poverty have been running campaigns and distributing scholarships for decades in the GAP region. Educational campaigns attach to other issues like traditional honour codes, which people believe can be eliminated via the expansion of progressive ideas and modernity. The problem of girls' education in the region is also discussed in relation to Kurdish nationalism and Islamic values, which are positioned in opposition to Kemalist principles of Turkish nationalism and secularism. The contradictory stance of the AKP on this matter, considering the long-term modernity and Westernization ideals of the country, adds up to this world of meanings that shape the public debate on girls' education in the southeast. In this context, none of the narratives fits directly into one of the explanations, although their trajectories were intermingled with this reasoning, and therefore, with the meanings attached to education.

In this chapter I also focused on employment as the second area of practices in efforts to empower women living in Tigris. As my strategy of writing illustrates, income-generation activities for women are scattered over a large field of investigation, from handicrafts ateliers at ÇATOMs supported by the UNDP to advertisements for entrepreneurship training offered to housewives at the Mesopotamia regional development agency. Although being a housewife is achieved status, especially for women with a migration background, it is not always prestigious and the women I spoke to agree. In this context, meanings and use of the term 'working woman' and money vary according to different social groups.

In her book on the ways that global capitalism is built on the foundation of local understandings of kinship and womanhood in Istanbul's migrant neighbourhoods, Jenny White (2003) points out that although women may actively engage in production activities, they still call themselves housewives. Women in my field site were in a similar situation; however, they knew they could turn their labour into cash. Some of them called themselves 'working woman' (*çalışan kadın*). 'I am working now' was a common statement, which refers to a shift from the previous status of housewife. However, this does not mean that the women had a regular income and the amount they earned, even at the best of times, was far lower than the minimum wage. Moreover, unlike the participants in White's investigation, the women in Tigris were not 'exploited' via kinship relations but via the state. Following Mies (2012), I argue that the state-sponsored women's centres and women's organizations drawing on various kinds of funding constitute an informal sector and mediate global capitalism in the case of southeast Turkey today.

While earning money is one of the main motivations for women to follow a course in a centre, the women show more interest in NGOs training when they get an incentive to participate. The financial benefit they derived from such activities is irregular and too far below the minimum wage. Although the tutors believe that the money is still good enough for these women as they can use it to buy goods for their children and gifts for their friends and cover their household expenses invisibly, the women themselves are not satisfied with the money they earn in return for their time and labour they invested in the centres. As Aylin says, she could earn more elsewhere, instead of spending her time in a ÇATOM.

It is not easy to find a suitable job where women would feel safe, as public safety for women is an issue in Turkey. Besides, they need to convince their husbands about their safety and also fulfil their domestic duties without compromising on the quality of their care. İlknur used the opportunities that the empowerment practices offered her and actively transformed herself from being a housewife to becoming a wage earner. However, she says, it is challenging to find a work–home balance especially with a husband who holds her bank card and receives her salary without İlknur knowing how much she actually earns. In her case, empowerment practices changed her life dramatically.

Not a majority but a sizeable number of participants of women's centres expressed their wish to improve themselves further and become tutors in the centres. Although the opportunities and examples of this are rare, it is not totally impossible to achieve upwards class mobility in this way. In İlknur's case I showed this possibility does exist. This also shows that holding down a job is not easy because women are primarily perceived as housewives. As in the example of daycare centres, state policies are manifestations of this perception. In this context, some of the participants of women's centres involved in piecework production said that they hoped to become wage labourers with a regular income if only the ateliers would turn into artisan workshops. This means that women imagine a workplace where day-care service is provided for their children, women workers can 'improve themselves by acquiring new skills' and their access to state services are improved.

3

Participation without "us"

Receiving a call from Emel, the supervisor of Al ÇATOM, was quite unusual for me. Her voice on the phone was warm and excited, and she told me that finally the governor of Tigris had confirmed he would be visiting the centre, and it would be nice if I would also show up. Emel was spreading the news to gather a crowd, because she thought that a lively atmosphere in Al ÇATOM would convince the governor to provide financial support for the maintenance of the centre building. When I accepted the invitation and arrived on time, I learned that the governor was going to be late to his appointment. The women were angry about it, complaining that they were supposed to be at home where they had lots of household duties waiting for them. Emel was nervous and afraid that the women would leave, but nobody did.

On the day of the governor's visit, the women of Al neighbourhood waited for more than an hour to see him, because they had a lot to say. When he finally arrived, the women surrounded him and listed their demands one by one. Firstly, there was almost no green area in the old town. A park there was urgently needed so that the children could play in safety. Secondly, they needed regular food markets to be held in each neighbourhood. The only marketplace in old Tigris was far from Al and it was hard for women to carry heavy bags home after shopping. Thirdly, they wanted the healthcare centre that had been closed to be reopened. Going to the new Tigris health centre half an hour away was troublesome each time when the women or someone in their family needed medical attention. Finally, they wanted the governor to open the protected historical area of Tigris to public use so that everybody could enjoy the green area for their picnics.

The demanding tone and determination of the women in Al ÇATOM while they were telling the governor what should be done to make their city a better place was remarkable. It was not important that most of the issues they raised were not the governor's responsibilities but came under the mayor. Yet, at that moment, the women had found a local authority official in Al ÇATOM, who happened to be the governor. For women who did not have enough seats in local government, it was a rare opportunity to push forward their demands to be received and responded to by a decision-maker in the city. In 1994, Fatima Mernissi suggested that when women have no voice through elections and party memberships, they do not have much choice other than to create new opportunities to express them, and therefore, she said women are the builders of civil society (CBC Radio 2015). In Tigris, there were also moments when the women organized and demanded a space for themselves in the decision-making process.

Participation (in public life and in decision-making processes) is an important component of women's empowerment practices. It is one of the most widely used words in the policy documents of governments, international development agencies and intergovernmental organizations in phrasal forms, such as the 'participation of all stakeholders' or 'participatory development' (General Directorate on the Status of Women 2008). Meanwhile, as part of the EU accession process, not only in southeast Turkey but also everywhere else in the country, the decentralization of power in the Turkish administration system and 'participatory governance' (Silverstein 2010: 25) was promoted via interventions, such as city councils.

In southeast Turkey, participation is a loaded term because it is linked to the Kurdish question and related problems of political participation. Women's political representation is very low in Turkey, especially in local governments. Because of the strong pressure of the state upon the Kurdish political movement and self-representation, it is a great challenge for anybody to run for political office in the region. Despite this fact, southeast Turkey is an exceptional case. The percentage of women in the Grand National Assembly has never been less than 5 per cent before 2000 and has never been as high as 20 per cent. There were only twenty-six female mayors in Turkey before the 2014 municipal elections. However, the HDP nominated two candidates per position, one male and one female, to assume the role of equal co-mayors. When other parties also introduced more female candidates, the number of female mayors increased dramatically. Similarly, during the general elections in the June 2015 elections, nearly 49 per cent of female HDP candidates ran for parliamentary office, and 40 per cent of all HDP parliamentarians elected were women. In this way, the overall ratio of female parliamentarians in the country has increased from 14.4 to 17.5 per cent, the highest ratio in Turkish history (Tajali 2015). While I was conducting this study in Tigris, however, women's representation in local governments was weak, and there was only one female representative for Tigris in the national parliament.

Although the ruling AKP government claims that it prioritizes women's involvement in politics, the number of women representatives remains limited at every level of public administration. For instance, only one minister in the council of ministers and only one local governor from eighty-one provinces was a woman in 2013 and these numbers have remained the same since then. The possibility of women's participation in decision-making processes offered within women's praxis is thus intermingled with challenges to their political participation in southeast Turkey under AKP rule.

Women's organizations are central to women's participation in public life. However, differences among women's organizations in their perception of AKP's policies influence their access to local funds. They also influence the state's involvement in grassroots women's empowerment efforts via controlling their financial assistance, a state practice already observed in India (Sharma 2008: xxxiv). In some cases, women's praxis makes it possible for the state to work within NGOs. For instance, gendered violence, as one of the areas where small local funds encourage NGOs to substitute and supplement state services, is also an area where the AKP's gender perspective becomes dominant in Tigris. In this way, the state can extend its power and control through civil society organizations in the name of feminist ideas, such as fighting against gendered violence. To illustrate these processes, I focus on three women who work for women's participation in decision-making processes in different ways. When Efsun, an ex-ÇATOM supervisor, could not find a place in electoral institutions, she took her chance in women's praxis and selectively accepted ideas that she came across in politics and projects. Sibel, an ex-representative of Kamer Foundation, utilized her existing knowledge and connections to involve herself in and to inform national and international debates on gender equality and advocacy. Gülşah, a stranger in the city, expanded the ideas of AKP in the name of saving other women.

Efsun's disappointment: Politics without critique

Efsun comes from a wealthy upper-class Arabic family in Tigris. Together with her young and educated cousins, Efsun was an exemplary 'human resource' for the activities that GAP had planned in the 1990s. When the Mor ÇATOM was established in Tigris, Efsun was a good candidate to be trained as its supervisor. She had worked at Mor ÇATOM for five years and developed herself further as a leader in this period. When she realized that the ÇATOM had started to repeat itself, she left her job and Tigris for a university education in Istanbul.

After completing a degree in science, Efsun decided to come back to her homeland. She could easily find jobs in several public institutions, which are not easily accessible for other educated people who lack clientelist relationships. However, Efsun had broader ambitions in life than public service. She was interested in becoming a politician. She engaged with local politics through the party organization of the AKP, with which her family already had relations. For the general elections in 2011, Efsun strove to be elected as an AKP MP to represent Tigris in Ankara. However, the party chose another person as 'the woman candidate of Tigris' for the rally. In this way, Efsun's political journey ended before it had begun.

During our interview, it was clear that Efsun was disappointed not to be chosen as the parliamentary candidate of Tigris. In her opinion, it was primarily because she was a young and single woman, although she was not aware that this was a disadvantage for anyone involved in political activities under the AKP umbrella:

> To begin with, being married is one of the most important prerequisites for going into politics. My main disadvantage was being single. I think [being married] would strengthen my position. The second factor is where I raced. Being a single woman, a working professional with a social life, etc. created a problem in justifying my candidacy. There is an implied meaning when they see me with a man in public [in Tigris], where men and women rarely interact outside romantic relationships. Now when I look back, I can see how [being single] created the problem.

Efsun admitted that she also felt uncomfortable and concerned about people's opinions while having meetings with married men in public without the presence of their wives. She said she felt 'social pressure' as a single woman. Marriage, she said, could be 'empowering' in her case:

> Even though I know that I am capable of doing whatever I want to do on my own, there were times when I wished I had a man beside me. It wouldn't be a burden, but rather an empowerment. A woman who is married has a higher status in this society. It seems that the words spoken by a married woman have a different weight from words spoken by an unmarried one. She gets more credit than I do. I tell you, whatever I say is attributed to my age. In fact, if a married woman of the same age as I said the same things, they would be taken more seriously.

In Efsun's words, I read the traces of the ÇATOM formation, aiming to create independent women, especially when she says that she believes in herself as an individual who can achieve her goals without the support of a husband. She was very sarcastic about the higher value attached to a married woman compared with single ones. However, this perspective was not useful when she wanted to run in an election, and it was clear that the mismatch between what she had learned and what she had experienced was frustrating. Nevertheless, she was still a single woman when I left the field.

Despite her disappointment, Efsun was not openly critical about the AKP. Rather, she had a self-blaming tone, which related the problem to her civil status rather than the political choices of the party primarily because of two reasons. Firstly, she was still a member of the AKP and following its meetings closely. Secondly, she had to be careful to ensure the support of its political power because she was now trying for a career in civil society organizations.

Although Efsun experienced first-hand the difficulties, disappointments and frustrations of being a woman in politics, she continued working to encourage women to become candidates. Immediately after her failure in politics she established an NGO that aimed to support women who are enthusiastic about politics. In this NGO, she coordinated a project that was funded via a grant provided by an ongoing UN gender-mainstreaming programme. For training, she benefited from the material and trainer support of the Association for the Support of Women Candidates (*Kadın Adayları Destekleme Derneği*, KADER), the largest organization in Turkey working to increase women's political representation. On her decision to work in a civil society organization, she said:

> Women's involvement in politics is important to me. They should at least know that they have this right; the right to be elected. And women, including me, always think that 'I should be better, I am not good enough. I cannot'. But when I compare myself with male candidates, I see that I have nothing less than them. The goal of this project is to give women the confidence that they can do much better [than men].

Efsun's friend Yasemin, who was also a ÇATOM coordinator, was well-known and respected in the neighbourhood, where she had worked for years. Her life story inspired me to ask if she had ever considered going into politics. Despite all the offers she has received, however, she does not intend to get involved in local politics because it is corrupt. Nonetheless, she said, if she were to accept an offer, it would be from the AKP. This is not because she shared their ideology: 'Because I do not want to be jailed'. She said, 'I would be imprisoned, if I start talking about my political opinions. Well, I talk a lot', she admitted. The pro-Kurdish party of the time, the Peace and Democracy Party (*Barış ve Demokrasi Partisi*, or BDP - later the HDP), had repeatedly asked her to run for municipal elections, but she always refused. Time proved that Yasemin was right. As of June 2017, more than eighty co-mayors and thirteen parliamentarians, including the co-presidents of the HDP, successor of the BDP, were arrested.[1]

For Efsun, complementing state practices rather than criticizing them was more constructive. While she prefers to claim responsibility for serving the people, the elites of the ruling party have prevented her from doing so:

> How do we [women's organizations] help? Have we done enough? What should we have done? Only by asking ourselves such questions can we find a solution. [Women's organizations complain that the government] doesn't have a gender perspective and doesn't intend to improve women's status. How do I know that? Perhaps it's not a priority. Should it be? Absolutely. You cannot, however, dictate to them what their priorities should be. It is a process. We can't resolve gender issues simply by saying that they should be resolved in ÇATOM project either.

After reminding her of the low level of state service, I asked Efsun once again what she thought of the government's approach to gender equality. In her remarks, she confirmed that global gender equality norms and mechanisms force governments to take gender-related problems seriously, even if they would choose not to:

> Obviously, some effort is being made, but whether that effort leads to greater equality is also open to debate. This is perhaps, I don't want to say populist, as such but ... it is according to the political conjuncture .... I mean there is such an expectation, [coming] from women. Therefore, it [the government] must do something about it. But I think it is an empty gesture.

What is this empty gesture and how is it related to having at least one – preferably married – woman in parliamentary candidate list? To answer this question, it is necessary to understand the relation between the AKP and the women who support it. Here are the words of Meryem İnat, the AKP's women's union representative for a working-class district of Istanbul, talking in a documentary film:

> Until recently, I did not have an opinion on politics. I used to be instructed by my father who to vote for and I would vote accordingly. But then the AKP was founded and Tayyip Erdoğan won my support right away. He always had his wife by his side. She impressed me by everything she did. (Neville Cardinale 2018)

The camera shows her organizing other women like her and visiting potential voters on behalf of her party. The report indicates that no other party in the world has more female members than the AKP, with most of them being housewives. A powerful women's organization, the AKP women's union has four million members. In the same documentary, the camera also turns to a higher level party member, Özlem Zengin, President Erdoğan's chief advisor. While explaining the AKP's popularity Zengin says:

> The AKP aims to change the lives of women, whereas other parties do not. Women are not just encouraged politically by the party, but also in everyday life by improving conditions for them. Therefore, AKP may be the most popular party among women. ... Politics used to be reserved for women who belonged to a particular category. Women in this group are known as 'white Turks'. These women have studied, don't wear headscarves and are very secular. The AKP encouraged all women to become politically active without discrimination, especially housewives with no education. These women have made the AKP so powerful today.

Zengin's use of the term 'white Turks' is similar to that of political scientist Sevda Demiralp (2012), who combines Nederveen Pieterse's (1995) arguments on the making of the whites and Nilüfer Göle's (1996) criticism of the elitism of the Kemalist founders of the republic. Demiralp argues:

> In the context of the top-down, state-led modernization of Turkey, the Islamism–secularism dichotomy constituted the foundation of the state elite's developmentalist discourse, which justified the relations of power. Islam was portrayed as the symbol of the 'primitive', while secularism defined the way to modernisation, development and civilization. Turkish republican elites established a secularist discourse that allowed them to relate themselves to Western modernity and justify their superior status at home. (521–2)

Demiralp focuses on social positioning based on the secular versus pious Muslim dichotomy. The scholarship focusing on early Republican administrations and women's representation agrees that elite women in particular were encouraged to hold professional positions. This not only maintained their class position but also set clear boundaries between the classes by preventing rural men and women from achieving upward mobility (Saktanber 2006). It is true that Islamist women entering politics were kept away from the centre of power for a long time because of the headscarf ban (Arat 2010; Cindoğlu and Zencirci 2008). However, in her research on feminist Islamic women's perceptions of the government's gender politics, Canan Aslan Akman (2013) shows that it is also true that the demand for equal citizenship for religious women wearing headscarves was in conflict with the inherent sexism of the male political elite in the AKP. According to Ayşe Saktanber and Gül Çorbacıoğlu (2008), Turkish Islamist groups justify women's choice to wear the headscarf as a form of freedom of expression and human rights while they are also highly critical of democratic ideals of Western modernity. In a similar vein, in contrast to Zengin's dichotomous approach, Aksu Bora and Koray Çalışkan (2007) draw attention to the similarities between Kemalist conservatism and the neo-Islamist conservatism of the AKP era in their article on the headscarf controversy in Turkey. The authors argue that symbolic representation, which they define as participation in symbolic spaces, such as being addressed by the political discourse, does not make a real difference in people's life unless they participate in the decision-making processes and put forward their social and political demands. Aside from considerable discontent of oppositional voices, many women in the AKP had to content themselves with symbolic representation until 2013, when the law lifted the headscarf ban in public facilities and universities. Some women parliamentarians decided to wear the headscarf immediately after the new regulation (Bianet 2013).

The lifting of the ban, however, did not increase women's representation in the party. In the local elections of 2014, of the 394 AKP candidates in the electoral area there were fewer than 20 women. Moreover, in the AKP's male-dominated cabinet, there was only 1 woman, who was the Minister of the Family and Social Policies or ASAP, from its Turkish name (*Aile ve Sosyal Politikalar Bakanlığı* – later *Aile ve Sosyal Hizmetler Bakanlığı*).

Sibel's objection to family

Established in 2011 by the third single party government of the AKP, the ASAP's mission is stated thus on its website:

> Producing, implementing and monitoring impartial, demand-driven and comprehensive social policies, with a participatory approach aiming to address the whole society but primarily disadvantaged groups, with the aim of increasing welfare of individual, family and the society. (Aile ve Sosyal Güvenlik Bakanlığı n.d.)

As this statement suggests, with its emphasis on social policies the ASAP became an umbrella ministry gathering under existing directorates including the Directorate General of Women's Status (*Kadının Statüsü Genel Müdürlüğü*, or KSGM). Women's status was established as the national machinery defined by the CEDAW and had been functioning under the Prime Minister's Office since the 1990s. Although the KSGM cannot influence policies in a direct manner, it was effective in coordinating the activities of women's work for women by collaborating closely with the women's movement, which grew within civil society organizations throughout the 1990s (Levin and Falk 2007).

An analysis of political and cinematographic elements used in the public service ads of ASAP indicates that only a particular kind of family is approved and idealized by the government (Günaydın and Özdoğan 2014), and the primary objection to the establishment of ASAP focused on the term 'family' in its name. The ASAP not only puts women and children into a category of disadvantaged groups, together with the disabled, the elderly and veterans, but also locates them in the family structure rather than acknowledging their autonomous individuality. Based on this argumentation, women's organizations found the establishment of the ministry as an administrative change 'unacceptable' and released one after the other press statements to that effect (Belge 2011).

This critique also applies to the name of ADEM that I introduced in Chapter 1 in detail. However, not everybody shares this perspective in Tigris. Efsun said that the name change was not important; it was a mere formality because in practice not much changed, except for the perspective. For her, it was a good decision to highlight the 'culture' of the society in the name of the ministry:

> We are talking about a society and this society has a *culture*, a *heritage* from the past. Ignoring this [culture] would only make the task [related to women's status] more challenging. ... [They say] 'When it is named "family and social policies" the ministry disregards woman'. When I look at the performance, I don't see any difference between before and after its name was changed. I mean, there is no loss here, because it is clear from the laws and measures that the new ministry has taken that it is more active than the previous one. Maybe it isn't about the ministry's label, but the minister's position. (emphasis added)

Like Efsun, Sibel was born into a wealthy and politically powerful Arabic family in Tigris. She was the president of one of the women organizations that was involved in the campaign objecting to the name of the ministry at the local level. In her early twenties, she fell in love with and became engaged to a Kurdish man that her family disapproved of because of his ethnicity. She said, although her fiancée was a 'revolutionary man with socialist ideals', he asked Sibel to stop work soon after their engagement. She blamed her husband for being a hypocrite, for presenting himself as a socialist idealist in the presence of other people while preventing his wife from working outside the home. Sibel was disappointed and wanted to leave him but this time her parents did not permit it, as it would be a disgrace to divorce. Sibel told me, 'I remained silent, resigned from work and stayed at home. My life shifted from one path to another'. She used contraceptives during the first years of her marriage because she was considering divorce. However, she finally gave up due to her family's pressure and got pregnant with her daughter at the end of the fifth year. When their child turned four, her husband committed suicide and died. This is how Sibel became a widow and returned to her parents' house.

Sibel started to work and stood up against her parents again, because she wanted to move out with her daughter. Then, she became involved in the Kamer Foundation. She received training to be a trainer for gender awareness workshops, which at that time was called 'awareness raising'. Then she started to work at the Kamer Foundation as a professional, and this enabled her to establish good relations with this regional organization's national and international partners. At the same time, she gained knowledge and experience about running projects. Soon after, Sibel quit Kamer and established her own organization to support victims of gender-based violence and women entrepreneurs. I will call this NGO the Centre for Entrepreneurial Women in Tigris, or TIGIKAM from its Turkish name (*Tigris Girişimci Kadınlar Merkezi*).

As the president of TIGIKAM Sibel coordinates large projects funded by the main funding institutions for women's organizations, such as Prime Minister's Office Undersecretariat of Treasury Central Finance and Contracts Unit and the Swedish Development Agency. During my fieldwork, TIGIKAM was one of the most powerful civil society actors in Tigris that had no relationships with the government but instead taking a critical stance about its policies.

Sibel told me that the most problematic part of the AKP's gender policy is about violence. While corrective measures were not enough, women's shelters fail to protect women who make official complaints. She explained that whenever women apply to her organization for help, she made sure that they understood fully what would happen, how long they could stay there and what the following procedures for divorce would be. She said, state policy targets marriage and prevents divorce, and this policy relies on women's economic dependency:

> [The state] provides a widow's pension to women whose husbands have died but does not provide any aid to women who are divorced. Isn't that discrimination? ... It says 'well, if it is God's will, I'll take care of you, otherwise not. So, don't divorce!' Doesn't it, Zeynep *Hanım*?

Considering the increase in cases of assault, including murder, committed by women on husbands/boyfriends who indulged in systematic violence against the wives/girlfriends, some feminists suggest that the state policies leave women no room for manoeuvre other than killing their abusers. As Sibel's critical remark suggests, women can survive and get state support in this way, if the law does not catch them. Ottoman history is also full of evidence of women poisoning their husbands to have a decent life (Aykut 2011).

According to the Law to Protect Family and Prevent Violence against Women (Law No. 6284) the state is obliged to secure the rights of victims of gender-based violence. The state is responsible to protect their life and obliged to provide them with shelter, food and legal and psychological counselling. Paradoxically, the name of this law is 'to protect family' – like the name of the ministry – while gendered violence usually comes from family members themselves. With a similar logic, Sibel criticized AKP policies, which prioritize marriage over divorce – and therefore, the family over women:

> To what extent do you consider a woman to be an individual within the family? I believe the woman is not perceived as an individual there [in the family]. She has no value or place. Taking our traditions into consideration, a woman is a living creature whose purpose is to perform housework and to facilitate the lives of others. She also has obligations to the outside world. Since birth, she has learned to live for others: for her children, her neighbours, her kin, her tribe, etc. She lives the way she knows best. Therefore, unless she learns how to deal with these obstacles and becomes aware of them, she cannot realise herself and be an individual in the society. What does that have to do with 'family'? Families are the [source of] the pressure that women face. By objecting to the name of the ministry, we argued that those issues would be taken more seriously if it contained the word 'women'.

Although Sibel was very critical of the ministry, her organization's activities benefited from the possibilities it provided. As I show further on, in addition to pro-government women's NGOs, TIGIKAM also functioned as a vehicle for expanding the access and control of the AKP government while cooperating with the ASAP.

The expansion of government in women's praxis

As well as the Directorate General of Women's Status, the ASAP was also responsible for other directorates, such as that of Family and Public Services,

Children Services, Disabled and Elderly Services, Social Aid and Services for Relatives of Causality Victims and Veterans. This makes ASAP the most relevant ministry in the everyday lives of the poor. In other words, through ASAP's aid programmes, the AKP 'improves women's daily lives', as stated by Özlem Zengin, the chief advisor of President Erdoğan I quoted earlier, in visible and tangible ways.

In her book on the AKP's party organization in a working-class neighbourhood of Istanbul, urban sociologist Sevinç Doğan (2016) provides ethnographic evidence that housewives, among other local actors, constitute the social basis and actual strength of the party. Doğan argues that this is because of housewives' capacity to handle the continuous and regular mass activities that the AKP relies on. As the president of the AKP's women's branch in a working-class neighbourhood in Istanbul, who was one of Doğan's informants, explains, women knock on doors more easily. They are more talkative, more active in recruiting new members to the party and more successful in household visits (Doğan 2016: 232).

While the party organization is strong in urban settings, the women's branch cannot access every part of the country successfully. This is the case not only for political parties but also public services and NGOs. During the meeting of the UN joint programme on fostering an enabling environment for gender equality in Turkey in Mardin in June 2013, I've heard how the head of the parliamentary committee on equal opportunities for women and men admitted that they know a lot about women living in the cities but have no idea about the access of women living in rural areas to state services. Therefore, she said, they planned to study this within the committee. A story that Sibel told me shows how NGOs working for women could be handy in such situations.

Sibel's TIGIKAM had a project using funding from a European philanthropy organization to teach women how to use sewing machines. When the project ended, TIGIKAM left the machines to the talented trainees so that they could establish their home ateliers.[2] Having directly benefitted from the project, the villagers welcomed Sibel and others when they came back months later for another project. They needed to survey further to understand the living conditions of women. However, it was still not easy to enter households and get the consent of families to approach young women. The TIGIKAM workers decided to collaborate with two sociologists working for the ASAP. Working at the social aid department, these sociologists agreed to conduct the survey with the promise of registering villagers for relevant social aid programmes. This 'incentive' facilitated household visits. In this way, TIGIKAM identified the exact number of polygamy cases in the village. Sibel concluded her story by saying, 'Look, in this work we need a little bit of camouflage. If you want to examine the situation fully and see the reality behind the closed doors, you need to work undercover'.

AKP's success and durability are based on establishing, maintaining and developing an extensive network of privileges and dependency among the population through public procurement contracts for the rich (Çeviker Gürakar 2016) and distributing aid for the poor (Adaman and Akbulut 2021). Çeviker Gürakar (2016) says that the AKP maintains its ties both with private sector firms and with voters by using new methods to create and allocate resources to them. Municipalities and pro-government NGOs are two of the main actors for distributing these resources. Sibel was not a supporter of the AKP government's gender policies. However, she found it useful to work with the ASAP and use the tool of social aid to help her to establish a relationship between the villagers and her organization. Her primary aim was not to spread the state service to remote places. Yet her activities facilitated the AKP's access to households even though it was not her intention to support political power.

The project feminism debate of the 1990s, which I discuss in Chapter 5, specifically focuses on such unexpected and undesired outcomes of the alliance between the state or political power and women's organizations. However, there were also women's organizations, which were knowingly and willingly tied to the central government in Tigris, and the Association for the Prevention of Honour Crimes or NACIDER (an acronym of *Namus Cinayetlerini Önleme Derneği*) was one of them. NACIDER was established to fight against honour crimes in 2008 by a group of women who were not locals of Tigris. Most of its members and its president had more than one affiliations, the one to the AKP and the other to NACIDER. Coming from other cities in the region, these women were educated and had a working or activism background in political circles that claim public Muslim identity against the secular state in Turkey.

The timing of the establishment of NACIDER was telling, as it was two years later when the government established a research commission and issued a notice on the specific measures to be taken against honour crimes and violence against women and children. This coincides with the times when suicide cases in Batman became nationally known, as I narrated at the beginning of the book. The organization prepared many reports on honour crimes and other social problems, including the migration from Syria after the war. They also organized vocational training in tourism for young women and undertook surveys with the financial support of the EU and the help of *muhtars*.[3]

The president of NACIDER was Banu, who had received training from KADER in the past and actively participated in women's work for women in Tigris during my fieldwork. In the promotional film shared with me, Banu explains the motivation to establish an organization on honour crimes in the southeast with women coming from other regions of the country as follows:

> We will be 'the seeing eye and the holding hand', as stated in our slogan. In terms of morals, it would be disrespectful to not extend a helping hand to those who [need help] and ignore the events taking place in this region when we have the means to do so. Therefore, [we choose to] take part into any kind of activity for women, regardless of what group they belong to, and demonstrate that especially women from conservative circles are interested in such issues.

Despite her charismatic leadership and full commitment to the party, Banu was never a parliamentary candidate herself. People around her told me that she did not want to compromise her headscarf for politics when there was a ban. Later I learned that she had to stop her studies because of the headscarf too. When the headscarf ban was lifted, she finally became a candidate in 2015.

When I asked for an appointment with Banu, she refused saying that she has not enough time even to spend with her children. Hence, I talked to Neslihan, who was a representative of NACIDER. Neslihan was the second in command and worked closely with Banu both in the party and the association. Like Banu, Neslihan was an outsider with a university degree, married to a bureaucrat working in Tigris. She was running her own accountancy bureau, where we conducted the interview while her children were sleeping on chairs in the next room. She said that she was lucky to have this office, because she was one of the very few working women who had the privilege of organizing their time according to her family's need.

Neslihan was a professional woman running her own business in Tigris since the early 2000s. Although she came from a traditionally social democrat family that supported the CHP, she became involved with political Islam during her university years when she also met her husband. She was the only person in her family to wear a headscarf.

During our interview, I asked Neslihan about her involvement with civil society organizations. She framed women's praxis in NACIDER as a political activity but not necessarily a feminist one. In general, she took a sarcastic tone, especially when talking about men and politicians who degrade her organization's efforts: 'Oh sure, we have heard [everything] including "what are you doing here? Why you are not at home taking care of your children?"' According to her, the state did not fully defend equality between men and women because women were still not represented equally. For her, violence against women in the name of honour was not punished seriously because of the underrepresentation of women's perspective in parliament. She said it was because men felt good about the gender status quo, and they did not bother to push for change:

> Even policemen, who witness [such crimes] at first hand, stay away, thinking that it is a family matter. Similarly, prosecution office and the courts do not conduct thorough investigations thinking that it is an ordinary suicide case. The local health authority, hospitals, and community clinics all see, know and identify what happens but they rarely report it. For some reason it is or it might be perceived as something to hide and keep as a secret.

Neslihan had to stop the interview because she had to rush to a lunch party for the AKP's mayoral candidate given for the women's organization. She invited me as well, and I accompanied her. I described this lunch party and the candidate's speech in Chapter 1. However, before the mayoral candidate spoke, Banu also addressed the audience as the president of AKP's women's branch in Tigris.

In her talk, Banu said that it was the AKP's political decisions to facilitate the establishment of civil society organizations that had led to reforms in the Criminal Code and the Civil Code. Then she asserted that the government proved its determination to end violence against women by establishing the parliamentary committee on equal opportunities for women and men, where government representatives cooperate with any 'marginal, feminist or ideological groups'. Because women are the most important 'governesses' of the society, she said, the AKP had introduced social aid targeting women. For instance, financial support for children's education had been transferred to the mother's bank account. The health system had been changed; patients were no longer held hostage in hospitals for not paying the medical fees. Moreover, women were being paid for the care that they provide to the elderly and disabled people at home.

Banu's speech summarized the mission statement of the Ministry of Family and Social Policies. More than that, her speech was a paraphrased version of the description of her organization's aim that I referred to under the subchapter 'Sibel's objection to family'. The common point of all these statements was the way that they position women as caregivers in an extended family, including children, the elderly, the disabled and sick members. This extended family model conflicts with the ideal family model in the Republican vision, which was a nuclear family. Although both models asked women to be primarily good housewives and mothers, the AKP's policies more aggressively demand that women replace the welfare services. Moreover, it seems as if politically active women in the AKP, such as Banu, also promote their public identity primarily by reference to their domestic duties. However, they simply do not have any time to take care of their children because of their party work and do not believe in the idea that women should 'stay at home and take care of their children', that Neslihan criticized.

This inconsistency resonates with the Özlem Zengin's controversial statement made in in September 2017: 'Good ideas always come to my mind when I do the dishes' (*Cumhuriyet* 2017). Oppositional media shared critical opinions blaming her for defining women in terms of their domestic duties. Zengin replied to these criticisms on her official Twitter account, saying, 'Women who wash dishes decide the future of this country. Either wake up to this fact or ... shut up!' Moreover, the online campaign she started was successful and '#Iwashdishes2 (*#bulasiktayikarim*)'[4] became a top trend in a short time, supported by the twitter accounts owned by women supporting AKP, including Banu and Neslihan.

The way that Zengin claimed political space in the name of women who were expected to commit themselves to household work is remarkable.

However, the rhetorical twist Zengin makes does not explain why women – and not men – commit themselves to household duties. Far from criticizing the inequalities derived from the gendered division of labour, the women engaged in politics in the AKP who, most of the time, also involve themselves in women's praxis in civil society organizations, have appropriated these inequalities.

Women's organizations of the post-80 coup d'état feminist movement had close connections with departments and research centres working on gender and women's studies. Accordingly, feminist scholars were actively involved in the efforts of the movement to build civil society. They brought their knowledge of legal and social matters to their involvement in policymaking, such as the reform in the Civil Code and the Criminal Code. These organizations defended the separation of civil society and the government and criticized any kind of involvement with financial and political pressure groups (İlkkaracan 2010). On the other hand, the civil society field merged with the government during the AKP era as a result of people's multiple identities of people. If one example of this is Banu, the other one is Özlem Zengin.

Besides being an active politician in the AKP and a television producer, Özlem Zengin is the founder of an NGO called the Women's and Democracy Association (*Kadın ve Demokrasi Derneği* or KADEM) that was established in 2013 by a group of elite women, including Sümeyye Erdoğan, the daughter of President Erdoğan. This national organization has many local branches and runs projects in cooperation with UN Women, the United Nations entity for gender equality and the empowerment of women. KADEM also produces a peer-reviewed academic journal of women's studies.[5] In this way, the women's branch of the AKP was channelled into civil society organizations through pro-government women's organizations, which mimic the post-1980s feminist movement. These organizations connect to political and academic circles, and also they engage in gender projects using third-party funds. KADEM is a national organization and the front runner of such women's organizations together with the Istanbul-based Hazar Education, Culture and Solidarity Association (*Hazar Eğitim Kültür ve Dayanışma Derneği*) that visited Diyarbakır in 2013 during my fieldwork.

With or without 'us'?

In the large conference room, I was sitting next to Iknur from the Mor ÇATOM. She squeezed my hand and smiled. She was happy because she had been given permission from her husband to come to Diyarbakır with her friends from Tigris. We were listening to speakers in the conference room of a hotel in Sur. This old neighbourhood of Diyarbakır was becoming popular and being visited by more and more tourists ever since March 2013, when the ongoing peace process started to end the conflict between the PKK, the armed organization of the Kurdish national movement and the Turkish army.

It was a time when women were referred to as the mothers of martyrs (soldiers or guerrillas), as in the slogan 'Mothers Shouldn't Cry!' (*Analar Ağlamasın!*)[6] However, there was no platform in the peace process for discussing the role and opinions of women. Therefore, the aim of the diverse group of people at the Diyarbakır meeting was to demand a space in the peace talks. At the end of the meeting, women cooked *helva*, a sweet dish traditionally distributed at funerals. In this way, women remembered the soul of the dead from both the Turkish and Kurdish sides during the decades-long war (Tahaoğlu 2013). Remembering the *#Iwashdishes2* protest of Özlem Zengin that I discussed earlier, reclaiming the kitchen represents a similar political act here. However, in this example, women claim the position of 'suffering motherhood' and turn it into a demanding political subject position without using populist simplifications of victimhood.

Originally part of a series of visits to cities in northern Kurdistan, the gathering in Diyarbakır was initiated by the Hazar Education, Culture and Solidarity Association. When women from Hazar announced that they would pay a visit to Diyarbakır, the Kamer Foundation, the well-known women's organization working in the region, offered to co-organize the event. While Kamer was rather critical of certain policies of the AKP government, the Hazar supported the government. At the meeting women from different socioeconomic, religious and ethnic groups observed each other carefully. There was tension, but it was under control.[7] Moreover, its outspoken claim to celebrate diversity and pluralism marked the 'Diyarbakır Visit'. For this event women from different parts of the society came together to raise a voice for peace. For example, a Kurdish folk singer, an Armenian author, a Turkish parliamentarian, a conservative journalist, an Islamist activist and a feminist scholar made speeches in the same panel. The audience was responsive and interactively engaged in the discussions. All these women coming from different backgrounds agreed upon the importance of women's place at the negotiation table: 'Let's get involved and be a part of the process. Otherwise, men will mess it up, as they always do whenever they do something without us'.

Two years after the meeting in Diyarbakır, the UN Commission on the Status of Women[8] was hosting accredited NGOs in New York. However, women's organizations, including the Kamer Foundation, which had already been working in the commission for many years, were not accredited by the Turkish government. Instead, the ASAP of the AKP government accredited the Hazar Education, Culture and Solidarity Association, which had never previously been involved in the commission's activities or advocacy. The ASAP did not respond to the complaints made by the women's organizations (Kadın Koalisyonu n.d.). In this way, the New York meeting showed that governmental relations cannot be considered separate from non-governmental spaces and processes. On the contrary, NGOs 'came to exist in continuity with the state' (Bernal and Grewal 2014: 8) and this has increasingly been the case in Turkey.

Conclusion

Women have a lot to say on political issues, from how to provide urban services to how to end a war. In this chapter I presented the complicated ways in which women challenge the barriers that stand between them and their participation into decision-making processes at every level of politics. First, I presented the example of Efsun, who had her first professional experience as the supervisor of a ÇATOM in Tigris. Influenced by the ideas she developed in the ÇATOM, she transformed herself into an independent woman. Coming back to Tigris after completing her higher education in Istanbul did not help her to find a husband but encouraged her to try her chance in politics under the auspices of the AKP. However, being single was the primary obstacle to her political career. I show that Efsun decided to go back to the women's praxis with which she had been familiar from her ÇATOM years. Without raising an overt criticism against the gender policies of the AKP, she had devoted herself to train women for politics in the hope that more women will enter politics in the future.

As Efsun's friend Yasemin's words show, participation in the southeast is not only a gendered problem: it is also related to ethnicity and nationalism. Because the pro-Kurdish party programme has clear goals for gender equality and prioritizes women's representation more than any other political party in Turkey, the most common claims to gender equality are mingled with Kurdish identity political claims. Local women's organizations are very sensitive and responsive to national politics. The competition and cooperation between different groups say a lot about this responsiveness. To contextualize women's support for the AKP, I show how symbolic representations and everyday activism in the form of the political labour of housewives are connected at the national-level party organization.

Then, as a second figure from a civil society organization in Tigris who was involved in the women's praxis, I introduced Sibel. As a person who had built herself a second life after the death of her husband, Sibel created space for herself to manoeuvre in Tigris to transcend the position of a widow. Utilizing her powerful family's existing relationships in the city and relying on the knowledge and experience that she had gained in the Kamer Foundation, she established her own organization to work for women. This organization functioned to extend state control in remote places in the region, although she did not directly support but even bluntly criticized the AKP. Sibel's main criticism was of the AKP's social policies that deny women's individuality outside their family relationships. However, the activities that she organizes necessitate her using the tools offered by the very same policies.

I show that civil society organization are not only an alternative to party politics but also an extension of the government control over women. Thus, the AKP extends its power over households and family life in the southeast primarily with the help of pro-government NGOs. Moreover, women like Banu or Özlem Zengin who engage in politics in the AKP find it hard to steer a path through their multiple identities: striving for a political position yet are also expected to have their own family. However, their controversial ideas about women's position in the society does not allow these politically active women to form a political alliance with other women's organizations who are committed to gender equality. Any deviation from the neoconservative Islamic discourse of the AKP can be a reason for being excluded from the party's resources and the political field that is accessible to NGOs. Therefore, although their everyday lives conflict with the party's political agenda, as in the example of domestic duties, the women working in pro-governmental NGOs rarely criticize it.

4

Streaming Mainstreaming

It was just another weekday afternoon in Tigris. Twenty people, including me, had gathered in a massive provincial government building for the gender mainstreaming programme of the UN meeting. Notably absent, however, was the *Hanımefendi*, or the wife of the governor (*vali*). This was disappointing, particularly for Oya, the local coordinator of the UN programme and the host of the meeting. The programme was designed to ensure women's political representation in local policymaking processes. Civil servants working in the local public institutions under the provincial government had been invited to the meeting via an official letter from the governor (which is to say their attendance was compulsory). There were also participants who represented other public institutions, such as the municipality, as well as representatives of NGOs. Their attendance was not compulsory; they were there because the UN programme interested them. Emel, the supervisor of Al ÇATOM, and Neslihan from NACIDER were also present. All the participants were in different ways involved in women's empowerment projects in the city and together they constituted the Tigris local women's rights coordination committee. But I noticed that some people left after the first ten minutes because they got unexpected calls. I knew from my other encounters with a professor at the local university that these 'unexpected calls' were fabricated, and I had heard the criticisms of some public officials who said that these meetings were a 'waste of time' or full of superficial talk.

In this chapter, I present an ethnography of the meeting, with a focus on precisely this kind of superficial talk that addresses women's already known problems without offering any concrete policy suggestions, instead focusing on activities that reproduce gender stereotypes. This kind of discussion produces detailed descriptions of everyday life, together with anecdotes, personal experiences and encounters. They thus sometimes allow the ethnographer to observe a group's stream of consciousness. A careful examination of these conversations reveals how gender mainstreaming as an international strategy for gender equality operates in a particular locality.

Gender mainstreaming is a policy term frequently used in gender and development context – and more recently has also been used in humanitarian programmes ever since it was developed in 1995 in Beijing as a feminist strategy to intervene in governments. Differing from the 'add-women-and-stir' method, which means simply including women in every aspect of life by redesigning existing organizations (Win 2004: 1), gender mainstreaming is supposed to analyse and integrate the gendered needs of women and men differently in planning and policymaking processes. Within the past decade it has been embraced internationally and has become the official bureaucratic strategy of various organizations, including agencies of the UN and EU institutions (European Institute for Gender Equality n.d.). In EU's gender equality strategy, for example, gender mainstreaming goes hand in hand with legal and institutional actions for eliminating gender-based violence, fighting against gender stereotypes and empowering women economically.

The foundations of the nation-state are inherently resistant to the larger feminist political project for an equal society (Connell 1987). Because mainstreaming depends on existing legal structures, the organizations, institutions, experts and bureaucrats of the state, who already hold the power of policy and decision-making, are able to contain the strategy of mainstreaming using their norms, knowledge and expertise on gender (Rawłuszko 2019). My contribution with the case of Mrs Governor addresses challenges to gender hierarchy and how void spaces for policymaking and application within the bureaucratic structure are filled by a female authority figure emerged through the institution of marriage.

In this chapter, I show how local actors navigate legal and institutional ambiguities of the state, and make use of available resources to implement an international strategy for gender equality on the ground. They use several different discourses to do this. Primarily, there is development and corporate social responsibility jargon, with an emphasis on women's empowerment. While these ideas are born within the structures of international organizations, they are filtered by state structures and travel at times of gender backlash. This chapter contributes to the ongoing discussions of the relations between the state and feminism by situating these discourses within a local gender mainstreaming project. It focuses on top-down approach of empowerment that is ideally combined with bottom-up approach of awareness building on gender, which I will discuss in the next chapter.

To fulfil this aim, I focus on a meeting. Schwartzman defines meetings as rituals of governance: 'communicative events' where relations, perspectives and knowledges are ordered or structured (1989: 5). They 'are not just instances that exemplify broader issues, but key sites through which social, political, temporal, spatial, and material circumstances are constituted and transformed' (Brown, Reed and Yarrow 2017: 14). The objects of communication are produced during these events, where participants of a meeting 'bring the world into the committee room' through their performative actions and discursive strategies (Abram 2017: 41). Following these ideas, I scrutinize the encounters and negotiations that took place during the meetings of the Tigris local women's rights coordination committee introduced earlier on. I introduce and explore what Pedersen calls the brief events, or moments 'saturated with qualities of immediacy, abruptness and the faltering of expectations' (2008: 58).

The problems addressed, such as gendered violence or lack of employment opportunities for women, are not solved during the committee meetings, with concrete and effective policy recommendations. In this sense, as members of the committee recognize, meetings are empty gestures to please the donors and high-level bureaucrats in Ankara who initiate and support the project. Another way of thinking suggests, however, that 'meetings are spaces for the alignment and negotiation of distinct perspectives, and are constituted through the contextual interplay of similarity and difference' (Brown, Reed and Yarrow 2017: 14), that is, the means itself can be the aim. Thinking through this perspective, I argue that committee meetings have a strong potential for being used as a platform for exchanging and negotiating political ideas as well as for criticizing others' opinions and self-reflection – a space for doing discursive politics even for a closed audience.

'Legitimate but not legal' grounds

Gender has never been a priority area of politicians in Turkey, most of whom are male, as I have noted in Chapter 3. Political activity in this area of policy is not very stable, and support for gender equality depends on the needs of the day (Kardam and Acuner 2002: 103). In the 1980s, the feminist movement of Turkey put pressure on government to demand a stable space in the political field – a position from which individuals might make, implement and monitor policies on gender (Tekeli 2010). In contrast to these wide-ranging demands, the state's response to this feminist intervention was confined to project-based efforts and a lack of coordination and coherence in plans and strategies, if not exactly resistance to them. The single-party government terms of Recep Tayyip Erdoğan's AKP merely follows this pattern, adding a twist of hyperpolarization of feminism, women's and queer rights.

The AKP came to power in 2002 promising to break from the ultra-secularist norms and values of the past and make a series of reforms and regulations in legislative and bureaucratic structures. In this spirit, for instance, Turkey became the first country to sign the Istanbul Convention in 2011. However, the AKP started to show authoritarian tendencies towards the end of 2000s primarily in, but not limited to, its political discourse (Acar and Altunok 2013; Cindoğlu and Ünal 2017; Coşar and Yeğenoğlu 2011). For example, in 2015, a male parliamentarian was elected as the spokesperson of the parliamentary committee, although most members were women. The result led to a controversy about the parliamentary committee. While some AKP MPs defended the view that a man could represent women' interests better than a woman could, others from the parliament like Filiz Kerestecioğlu were openly critical of it. In her press statement, Kerestecioğlu argued that the election of a male spokesman only confirmed the fact that the AKP government had established the parliamentary committee as an 'empty gesture' (*usulen*) and displayed neither a gender perspective nor respect for gender equality (*Evrensel* 2015a). Coming from an activist feminist background and as an outspoken feminist MP of the pro-Kurdish party HDP, Kerestecioğlu objected both to making the parliamentary committee ineffective and its appropriation by the AKP. It was instead an achievement of women's decades-long struggles to have a place in the Parliament of Turkey, the highest level policymaking institution.[1]

The parliamentary committee is a political field within the state that has been opened by feminist activists in Turkey and is transnationally connected and capable of putting pressure on earlier governments. Aiming to be a part of the international community, Turkey has been a party to CEDAW since 1985. The bill has a higher status than Turkish laws and regulations, because Article 90 of the Turkish Constitution states that the international treaties to which Turkey is a party have the force of law. In this connection, the Turkish Parliament agreed to establish this parliamentary committee to be the 'national machinery for gender equality' during the 1995 UN World Conference on women in Beijing. The aim was to create the foundation for parliamentary processes to make institutions, policies and plans more gender-sensitive and to strengthen the dialogue between governmental and non-governmental bodies on gender-related issues. Turkey established this central unit only in 2009, over a decade later. As Efsun explains in the previous chapter, neither Erdoğan nor any other AKP representatives explicitly defend gender equality but there is pressure on them to do so. Therefore, the national machinery of this parliamentary committee is part of the bureaucratic structure within which they are consigned to operate.

The UN programme I focus on in this chapter shares this legacy of the women's movement that shows its determinism to work within the state. It also confirms the important role played by the UN in the women's movement in Turkey, and its representatives have been involved in the movement for decades as activists, reporters, policymakers or experts and critics (Aydın et al. 2017). Although there is no direct connection or legal tie between the local women's rights coordination committee in Tigris (henceforth 'the committee') and the parliamentary committee, the former mimics the latter. However, if followed through chronologically, this link might be missed: while the parliamentary committee in Ankara was established in 2009, the ministry had been developing quasi-legal and local (provincial) gender equality committees ever since 2006. At that time, the Ministry of Interior of Turkey, in collaboration with UN agencies and the financial support of the Swedish Development Agency, started the UN programme that adopts a gender mainstreaming strategy. The programme aimed to bring a gender perspective to local administrations by creating gender equality units (called gender desks) in all governmental departments and demanding gender budgeting, as well as training their personnel in gender-sensitive governance. In each pilot city, a local coordinator was hired by the UN to work directly with the city's governor, the highest provincial administrator assigned by the central government, and with the mayor, the elected provincial authority. Together with representatives of women's NGOs, the gender desk officers made up the local gender equality committees. The committee shape, implement and monitor local gender action plans that address the gendered needs of women in everyday city life.

The local committees, action plans and gender desks were all designed by the experts in the UN programme, but they were not independent initiatives of the UN. Instead, they were centrally coordinated by the government in Ankara but were also tied to the global gender mainstreaming strategy following CEDAW. However, they were not necessarily connected to the national economic and political strategy of the central government in Ankara. On the contrary, the committee and the action plan were only short-term instruments. They had no legal basis other than a circular order issued by the Ministry of Interior referring to Article 90 of the Turkish Constitution, stating that international treaties to which Turkey is a party have the force of law – I already mentioned about this document in the preface. The bureaucratic structure that the UN programme aimed to build within the local administrations was 'legitimate but not legal' (*meşru fakat yasal değil*) as a governor explained to me. Local coordinators, committees, action plans and gender desks were all project-based with no permanent legal basis. Therefore, it was up to the initiative of respective governors to establish these bodies and ensure their operation. Moreover, the personnel at these gender desks were tenured civil servants who do not necessarily have any expertise in the field of gender and are appointed directly by the governor. This implies that in addition to their existing duties, they were responsible for issues related to gender equality in their institution. Needless to say, they were not always content with this extra work. These bodies in the local administration were extensions of a hypothetical or presumed gender equality mechanism to be implanted by the state – or its civil servants from the top to the bottom of the hierarchy.

The UN project was in process in twelve cities during the year 2013 when I conducted my research. At the same time, the GAP RDA launched another mainstreaming project ('the EU project') with the object of 'upgrade women's status in the least-developed regions of Turkey with a view of reducing disparities' (European Commission n.d.). Putting weight on capacity building for women's advocacy skills, the project aimed to empower women's NGOs (Delegation of the European Union to Turkey 2012). Having successfully obtained the grant of €5 million from the EU, the project proposal directly referred to the priorities set by the Council of the EU. The EU project is also linked to the National Development Plan of Turkey where 'some gender inequality problems are addressed as priority problems to be solved' (European Commission n.d.). Similar to the UN project, the EU project aimed to develop committees and local equality action plans. However, it placed stronger emphasis on the empowerment of local women's NGOs.

In my field site, the EU and the UN projects used to cooperate until the former was completed before my arrival and the latter took over the coordination. The committee in Tigris had been working in line with the local equality action plan of Tigris. I had a chance to attend two of the meetings of the committee, which gather twice a year. The meeting's purpose was to share information about the execution of the local equality action plan and to address issues that NGO workers encounter while carrying out projects that are funded by a variety of sources, including the UN project.

'Add-women-and-stir' tourism

Oya opened the session by listing two specific items on the agenda. These were finding a place to sell women's handmade products, which includes claiming a public place for women and children and combating gender-based violence by training men about it. I follow her agenda on the committee's role in mediating women's demands about a place in urban transformation, to integrate women to the local tourism sector.

It was never easy to find a market where women could sell their products, and this was an ongoing topic of these meetings. It was also not clear whose responsibility it was to solve this problem. There were many players in the game. Not only ÇATOMs and ADEMs but also women's cooperatives, several women's organizations and public education centres were producing handmade goods for sale. While the local government was promoting the ADEMs and sending their goods to national fairs organized in big cities, others had to rely on their own resources and networks. Talking about this unequal treatment by the local government had created tensions in the previous meeting. Realizing that the very same tension was hovering on the horizon, Oya intervened in the discussion and gave the floor to her friend Münire.

Coming from Istanbul, Münire was not particularly happy about living in Tigris because of the lack of cultural activities that she used to engage in. She was dreaming of moving back to Istanbul where she would make more money from her specialization on trade law. However, it was not possible to convince her husband, who was from Tigris. Münire did not have many friends in Tigris, although she was a cheerful and interesting woman who liked reciting Nâzım Hikmet's poems and talking about art. She met Oya while volunteering as a lawyer in women's organizations' activities. She also invited me to dinner at her house once, where I watched her serving food to her in-laws, washing the dishes and taking care of her new-born child, while her husband was nonchalantly watching TV. When I asked how she managed to do everything at the same time, she said: 'Somehow you find the *power within*' (emphasis added).

I knew that Münire had been extremely disturbed by the proposal to build a large mosque in Tigris city centre lately, and this was the focus of her speech. The project was spelled out by the prime minister of the time, Recep Tayyip Erdoğan, on his visit to Tigris months previously. Münire interpreted this as a manifestation of the pro-Islamist tendencies of the AKP government as it triggered her 'secularist anxieties', which envisages an Islamization project that expands religion's scope to all aspects of life (Kocamaner 2017: 677). She was in favour of a complex for joint worship, inspired by the short-lived turn to pluralism in the mid-2000s (Dağtaş 2018). A space that contained both a mosque and a church would be a better and more respectful gesture to respond to the cosmopolitan character of Tigris. She said that it would also be possible for women to have permanent shops in this religious cultural attraction site, to sell their handmade products. In this way, just like other examples elsewhere in the world, women could have a public place to spend time safely in the centre of Tigris. However, objections rose immediately after she ended her enthusiastic presentation.

Underlining her own authority as a pious woman, Neslihan from NACIDER said that men are very unlikely to welcome women to mosques. Therefore, it was not realistic to imagine women claiming a space at a religious site, let alone selling their products there. Moreover, it was not clear why Tigris needed a church while most of its residents were Muslim. Münire said that this was merely her opinion, and she invited everybody to share their opinions on the matter. However, some members of the committee were displeased and even told her that she should keep her opinions to herself.

Other attempts to point to Tigris's multicultural character were greeted with similarly furious reactions from the natives of Tigris. However, those who were eager to speak up and demand the most basic urban services had very few platforms for airing their views, as I explained in the example of governor's visit to Al ÇATOM in Chapter 3. Debate on the mosque/church proposal was pointless in terms of the aim of the committee, because such large-scale urban planning issues in general were both secondary and difficult to intervene in due to the existing relations of power. Therefore, it failed to address such daily problems, which effect women's daily lives dramatically and directly. However, the debate was useful for Münire as it allowed her to share her political opinions with an audience – even though she was silenced. So, Oya dropped the subject and brought another option for creating a marketplace for selling women's products: 'What about having a street of our own, I mean, for instance having an 'Art Street' in Tigris?'

In 2014, the provincial government of Tigris launched an infrastructural renewal project funded by the EU to improve the urban façade of old neighbourhoods that attract tourists most. The eastern provinces of Turkey were a destination for cultural tourism because of their cultural heritage and archaeological sites but they never attracted as many tourists as the government wished for. This was due to its limited infrastructural facilities and weak hospitality sector (Tosun, Timothy and Öztürk 2003: 158). However, domestic tourists were interested in the GAP region because of its cuisine, which had become a brand of its own as in the examples of *Urfa Kebap, Diyarbakır Ciğercisi, Yöresel Mardin Lezzetleri and Antep Sorfası*. Moreover, stories about the authentic lifestyle of the region in soap operas screened on national TV channels have contributed to the promotion of locally produced tastes (Kuijpers 2015). The GAP had also invested in developing cultural tourism and protecting the cultural heritage in the region. The GAP regional development administration sponsored archaeological excavations, opened new museums and organized various events including film festivals, youth festivals and international contemporary art exhibitions. Tourism businesses, such as boutique hotels, museums, fine dining restaurants, concept cafes and nightclubs, were opened by local and national private investors. Compared with other eastern provinces, the GAP provinces had the most attractive stands in the travel and tourism exhibitions I visited in Turkey.

While local administrators were hopeful that the EU-funded urban renewal project would make the city more attractive, Oya, the local coordinator of the UN programme, was preoccupied with the question of how to include a gender component into it. A trained sociologist from the western coast of Turkey and a self-identified feminist, Oya was new in Tigris and her knowledge of the local social dynamics was limited. We became friends in time, and I observed how dedicated she was to her job and defending the values that the UN programme stands for. After lengthy research, she had become convinced that women in Tigris would benefit significantly from an Art Street, a marketplace in one of the newly renovated parts in the old town for women to sell their handmade souvenirs.

When Oya introduced the idea of the Art Street during the committee meeting, an NGO representative named Roza was enthusiastic about the proposal. She was the director of a women's cooperative which had been producing handmade goods for years. Because she was also involved in the tourism sector through her Kurdish family's businesses, she expressed herself with confidence while talking. Roza supported the idea but asked for a more concrete plan and urgent action because planning and production were serious issues and required time. 'To be honest', she said, 'we all have a lot of work; it should be worthy if we will put an effort to make it real. Our plates are already full. We have high tempo lives with family, children and housework'. She knew that not only her cooperative but many other women's organizations and state-sponsored women's centres were producing souvenirs. Therefore, she made it clear that the committee should urgently start planning who would produce what goods and in what quantities because the tourist season was approaching.

Following up on Roza's argument, Emel, the supervisor of the state-sponsored women's centre, said that she had been involved in an Art Street project in Tigris a couple of years previously. However, it had failed because of poor planning and research. Without clear goals, Emel said, Oya's proposal would do nothing more than create 'false hopes' for women producing handicrafts, no matter how exciting this idea was:

You can't just come up with the idea and say, 'OK ladies, knit some socks'. You need to know who will produce how much. Also, you need to modernize the design of the products according to the customers' taste. You need branding, attractive packages and standardisation in production … First, you need to survey how many tourists will come and when. And you must make sure that the tourist guides include this location in their sightseeing tours.

Having been involved in empowerment projects of the regional development project in Tigris at an early age, Emel's contribution was based on her fifteen years of experience and the knowledge that she gained at various training courses and workshops that she had attended on tourism and regional development. Moreover, because she was from a local Arab family, she knew the everyday problems of people and her words were taken seriously. Nodding heads signalled that Emel had impressed the audience with her talk, peppered with management terminology. Oya also valued her comments, saying that the committee needs the exchange of ideas on previous experience more than anything, although she seemed disappointed by the negative feedbacks to her proposal.

At this point, Ayla, the representative of the regional development agency, took the stage with her proper Turkish and elegant gestures: 'Earlier mistakes are golden opportunities to develop better strategies'. A well-educated development expert coming from the capital city, Ayla had moved to Tigris for work as a young single woman a couple of years previously. She said that branding, marketing and promotion were vital points that should be considered. However, learning about them and gaining skills were not very difficult if people would take advantage of the training provided by the development agency where she worked. As if sharing a secret, she also stated that Tigris was a 'shining star' in the region in terms of cultural tourism. Therefore, a site for selling handmade products would eventually be created in Tigris. 'Why not by women, by the committee?' Thus, with her rhetorical skills and amplification strategy, Ayla convinced the audience, including Roza and Emel, to work together to realize the Art Street project.

Yakup, a representative of the Labour Agency, took the floor while Ayla and Emel were discussing further collaboration in whispers. He repeated what had already been said as if they were his unique opinions. I caught Roza rolling her eyes and exchanging glances with Oya, Emel and Ayla – signals that they were getting irritated with this hijacking of her arguments and presenting them as his own thoughts. They then ended the discussion quickly with the decision to permit Oya to explain the Art Street project to the governor, so that he would demand that women's handmade souvenir shops should be added in the plan of a specially designated area in the city.

Developing an Art Street to sell handmade goods in a highly competitive souvenir market was a risky investment in the relatively modest tourism sector of the city, particularly considering the fact that making handmade souvenirs does not always generate an income for women. Instead, it naturalizes their gendered role as 'traditional' homemakers and their domestic duties of care that rely on feminine skills (Harris and Atalan 2000). Also, it has been shown worldwide that these income-generating activities support the exploitation of women in the informal sector (Pearson 2007), as they do not earn a regular income and the amount that they do earn, even at best, is unlikely to exceed the minimum wage in handicraft production. Finally, the decision of the committee was in line with the good old 'add-and-stir' approach, in contrast to what mainstreaming strategy urges.

Then, why did the committee not demand a substantial revision of Tigris's tourist action plan with a gender lens? And why did it not address the structural conditions that prevent women from participating in formal waged employment in Tigris?

The answer is that constrained by its structure, the committee was intended by the local government to be an empty gesture even though it was built upon legitimate but not legal grounds. This prevented both members of the committee and the moderator, Oya, from intervening in local politics in any substantial manner. However, going beyond their assessment of the project, my observations demonstrate how agency operates within this structure. In the end it is the *superficial talk* that keeps the wheel of gender projects running. These projects enable figures like Roza and Emel to demonstrate their expertise. Although they did not address the points I spotlighted earlier, their objections were valuable as experienced local experts in terms of showing how to work with the community. This goes hand-in-hand with their benefiting from the UN programmes and establishing themselves as officials, elites, experts and businesswomen. In the end, owing to Ayla's support, Oya could tick the box of 'women's employment' in the Tigris gender equality plan, when the committee ended up planning a couple of market stands that may in future turn into small shops for women to run.

'Social responsibility' of Mrs Governor

The other topic discussed in the committee meeting was gender-based violence in the city. Oya shared figures from a recent survey that she had conducted, according to which only a quarter of the women who are subjected to physical violence had applied to the authorities for help. Raising a point specific neither to Tigris nor Turkey, the officer from the Police Department stated that women often withdraw their complaint soon after reaching out to the authorities. 'Of course, this does not mean that the violence has stopped', Oya replied.

Emel said that women were aware of their rights and willing to take the necessary actions to live a better life. Despite their best efforts, however, the police had failed to protect women, she noted. In most cases when a police officer is needed to safeguard the woman in danger, she said, the police require a court order, which is very difficult to obtain in emergency situations. Therefore, she added, it was not realistic for women to work up the courage to oppose their husbands, other male relatives or household members, let alone to break up with them and leave home. Then, she referred to a case in which she had personally been involved – 'Even though it was not even part of my job!' In this specific case, Emel had asked *Hanımefendi*, or Mrs Governor, to make *some calls* to facilitate the process of providing police protection to a regular participant of the women's centre that Emel manages. Thanks to Mrs Governor's mediation, police protection was provided quickly. 'She is very attentive over such *social affairs*, luckily' (emphasis added), Emel said.

Emel knew what tools that the police can employ, such as the emergency barring order defined by the Article 52 of the Istanbul Convention.[2] She therefore criticized the department's unwillingness to implement the law. While doing so, however, she reduced gendered-based violence to a *social affair* and displayed her dependence as a social worker on the moral judgements and voluntary engagement of Mrs Governor. In fact, Emel's framing was in line with those at the top of government. On her webpage, Mrs Erdoğan, the wife of President Erdoğan, lists projects that are financially supported by or come under the aegis of the presidency among her interests and initiatives, calling them 'social responsibility projects'. Some of the projects focus on girls' and women's empowerment, which were previously run by third-party funding. Accordingly, in cities like Tigris, the governors' wives – and their equivalents – find themselves conducting 'social affairs' by representing the state in fields like gender, which remains external to public and political affairs.

Governors and their wives, who usually come into a province from another part of the country and leave for yet another destination after their term of office ends, are temporary actors in local administration. However, they are powerful figures and being on good terms with them might be useful. Governors' wives decide whom to support and whom to keep out because their role is not defined or written down in the Constitution or the by-laws. It is up to them whether to engage or not and in what capacity to do so. This means that they can be also open to innovation and experiments. For instance, when I first met Mrs Governor in Tigris, she was baking biscuits at the women's centre for Kurdish women producing handicrafts, as a goodwill gesture from the state. She also used to show up at various activities of local civil society organizations. In the case Emel referred to, she had convinced Mrs Governor to take personal initiative and inform the governor himself about a matter that required immediate action.

In fact, to coordinate interventions against similar cases of gender-based violence, a local women's organization had been running a special project in Tigris. Funded by a grant distributed by the UN programme and provided by the Sabancı Foundation, the philanthropic arm of one of the largest industrial and financial groups in Turkey, the project was based on close cooperation between women's organizations and all relevant state institutions. However, the responsibilities for the project implementation were not equally divided among the team. While ensuring a citizen's safety is a state duty, it was delegated to women's organizations, which mostly rely on voluntary work and activism or, as in this example, to the ethical values of a corporation. Emel initially had an issue of reaching Mrs Governer, as I wrote about the first time I met her in Chapter 1, under the subchapter 'Managers'. What would happen if Emel had not had access to Mrs Governor? What if Mrs Governor did not care about – or was utterly incapable of dealing with – gender-based violence? And what if the Sabancı Foundation stopped giving financial support to the UN programme's grant scheme for local women's organizations to establish an immediate action centre for women at risk of violence? Would First Lady Emine Erdoğan take over the sponsorship of this 'social responsibility project' too?

Underlining the contrast between the actual lives of urban women with socioeconomic vulnerabilities and the political rhetoric of the government, Berna Yazıcı (2012) shows that the celebration of the classical patriarchal family is a discursive tool used by the AKP to excuse the state from its social care responsibilities. The neoconservative and neoliberal framework mobilized by this political party results in its failure to implement laws to provide state support to women who do not fit their definition of the ideal family and need shelter, money or protection for themselves and their children (Yazıcı 2012: 128). Instead, their arbitrary workings and legal practices, as in the example of the police protection, necessitate case-specific solutions that are attempted by dedicated women's organizations as well as by the top-down interventions of authorities – or their wives.

The mechanism for gender equality that the committee aimed to establish in the local administration is currently embodied by the *Hanımefendi*, an ambiguous but well-established institution within the state bureaucracy. In Turkey, where the family is the central reference point for having a secure social position, wives of state officials and bureaucrats can be very autonomous and influential in shaping state practices towards gender equality. Yet, it would be misleading to explain the dominant position of these women in local bureaucracy only by the status that they gain through marriage. They also hold the authority for 'social issues' because there is no other public body that can claim power over issues of gender equality. In other words, the *Hanımefendi* exists because the state will not build a legally defined local gender equality mechanism, which demands experienced local bureaucrats specialized in gender equality to work within local governments. In return, project-based interventions, such as the women's centre programme or the UN programme, support this ambiguity within the state structure by relying on the normatively legitimate but legally undefinable positions held by random women who happen to be married to high-level bureaucrats. Although our *Hanımefendi* left the seat offered to her in the meeting empty, she was still referred to as a problem solver and a legitimate actor. Yet, the final decision maker is Mr Governor. At the end of the day, 'he' defines the limits of 'her' power and autonomy.

'Rowing against a tsunami': Gender backlash in Turkey

Oya continued speaking over the survey on domestic violence. She said while women were getting intensive training thanks to the projects run by various women's organizations and public institutions, there were no awareness projects targeting men or at least couples. The representative of the Higher Education Loans and Dormitories stressed the importance of 'educating women'. He added that, for example, educators from the Police Department regularly visited university dormitories in the region. They not only give talks about victim's rights in cases of gender-based violence but also inform women about other *important issues related to the region*, such as counter-terrorism and national security.

As a solution to the problem, Oya suggested organizing gender equality training in coffee houses, where men can be reached, and women can be invited. However, the idea was controversial for the members of the committee because coffee houses were exclusively male places and did not welcome women – either as trainees or as trainers.[3] The representative of the Labour Agency came up with an alternative suggestion and said:

> Places where women *naturally* gather are more suitable for such an activity.
> For example, neighbourhood furnaces, where women gather to bake bread
> for their households, were perfect locations. (emphasis added)

Almost everybody objected to this idea by reminding him that the point was to train couples together. Besides, together with the group of middle-aged men I introduced at the beginning of Chapter 2, this was just another attempt to equalize women with tradition and fix them in the past with a nostalgic gesture, instead of talking about or at least developing a curiosity about their present-day concerns. Therefore, participants of the meeting rightly said there is no such a practice anymore; why would women collectively make bread in furnaces in the middle of the city when bread is available in markets and bakeries?

Roza said that working for gender awareness in coffee houses has been tried out in the past. However, no improvement had been observed in the neighbourhoods where this training had taken place. On the contrary, she said, the number of violence cases increased. She believed that unless the central government took more severe action to fight against violence and unless courts stopped protecting perpetrators and started to make decisions that embraced women's rights, projects targeting raising awareness among women or men would remain 'useless' and would never reach their goal. Following her, Emel used the opportunity to say that the UN dismisses the aim of protecting women by putting more emphasis on activities targeting visibility, such as training at coffee houses. In her opinion, a better idea would be to make training not separately as a single activity but rather embedded in the system.[4] Offended by objections raised by Emel and Roza, Oya stopped for a moment, took her glasses off and tensely said:

> If training does not have any point, then this committee meeting is nonsense too. In the end, we are rowing against the current [*akıntıya karşı kürek çekiyoruz*], as you all know. Especially nowadays, we are rowing against a tsunami!

Oya's words can be taken as an expression of her exhaustion with the pressure and resistance she had encountered from the committee members. She could keep her temper only until this honest confession came out in the form of a self-critique directed towards the paradoxes of the UN programme. Relying on a series of earlier conversations I had with Oya, I understand her outbreak as a sign of frustration expressed by an ordinary citizen with a particular political opinion about more recent developments in the country. By rowing against the tsunami, she meant the ideological and institutional resistance of central government to the normative political project of gender equality in Turkey. Indirectly, the anti-Kurdish and openly sexist statements of the public officials attending the meeting merely mimicked those in power. For example, words about educating women in dorms were problematic because delivering nationalistic speeches to university students who have spent their childhood under the state of emergency is a demonstration of militaristic state power, and therefore, anti-Kurdish. Even during the peace process, it is hard not to imagine that these speeches were full of notions that deny the rights and freedoms of Kurdish citizens of Turkey. These discriminating and harassing acts targeting young and curious minds enthusiastic to explore new ideas and discover their identities were simply celebrated by the representative of the Higher Education Loans and Dormitories. Another example is that defining homemaking activities as women's natural duties, such as baking bread, simply reinforces biological determinism, and therefore, sexism.

Oya used the tsunami metaphor, denoting a disaster with an unpreventable destructive power pushing things back, to refer to the backlash in gender politics in Turkey. For instance, the then prime minister Recep Tayyip Erdoğan stated on numerous occasions that he did not believe in gender equality but rather in 'equal opportunities' and *fıtrat* (Kandiyoti 2011). Denoting the Islamic doctrine of creational differences between women and men, the prime minister used the term *fıtrat* to refer to women's maternal roles (Özyeğin 2015). In response to this statement, feminist activists and scholars had criticized his usage of the term, leading to a public debate.[5]

Conclusion

I decided to dedicate this chapter to one single meeting because it was like an unguided focus group discussion that nicely ties up the main pillars of empowerment I introduced in the previous three chapters. Local women who are members of the committee refrain from allowing the state to regulate local power relations, including the one between men and women, and therefore, between different women. However, it is at the same time true that the bureaucratic structure does not allow women's interests to be represented. For example, while the Tigris women's rights coordination committee is not visible in law regulating Turkey's administrative structure at the local level, provincial coordination committees have real power in planning in local policies, yet most of the time not a single woman bureaucrat can be found among their number. The local coordinator Oya cannot join these meetings, as she is neither a public officer nor a high-ranking one. While *hanımefendis*, or wives of high-level local bureaucrats, fill the gaps created by project-based efforts, such as the UN project, they have no official mandate in the bureaucratic structure of the state. In this way, the committee is like an island in the state structure with no connection to any policymaking processes. At the same time, it is tied to the larger global strategy of gender mainstreaming, which is mainly recognized in the European countries, to open a space for feminist discourse and gender equality within the state structure.

Scholars have already identified the paradox resulting from gender mainstreaming's dependence on existing norms, actors and structures.

However, the strategy has a dialectical promise, which implies that the inconsistencies and ambiguities in the institutions of the state will be resolved in the long run through gender mainstreaming. Short-sighted initiatives, however, face greater legal and institutional resistance. The problems addressed, such as gendered violence or lack of employment opportunities for women, are not solved during the committee meetings by concrete and useful policy recommendations. Thus, as argued both by the feminist parliamentarian and by the members of the committee, these meetings are empty gestures designed to appeal to donors and the high-level Turkish bureaucrats who support the UN programme.

Turkey's feminist movement and its dedication to establishing and expanding international gender equality norms are well known and dominate discourse about women's issues. Despite the progress made so far in the legal framework, this feminist project needs to win more battles in restructuring the organization of the state, particularly against prevention of legitimate but non-legal entities from making meaningful change. Project-based efforts to build gender equality mechanisms within the state merely weaken those working on the ground. In the example I presented, public officers, such as the representative of the Police Department or the Labour Agency, who were hired according to their qualifications for a specific profession, are expected to function as gender equality officers without any relevant skills, only because the governor has assigned this role to them and for which they get no additional payment. It is not a title that one can pursue as a career because it does not exist in the bureaucracy. Actors involved in women's work are quicker than public officials in pointing out gendered experiences and in thinking about the consequences of some of the plans made on behalf of women. Field workers with an experience in poorly planned projects, such as Emel and Neslihan, can provide crucial warnings about the false hopes that poorly planned projects can create. In general, however, these interventions by local gender experts do not evolve into more significant claims in power relations. This weakness of the project-based gender mainstreaming initiatives in the absence of government support is the point I aimed to illustrate in this chapter.

Legally, because they have no permanent basis, these projects rely on initiatives civil by servants who follow the neoconservative central government's political agenda. Local authorities tend to be unwilling to implement international laws, such as the Istanbul Convention let alone to show initiative in supporting gender mainstreaming. Thus, preconceived practices and techniques, such as add-women-and-stir, are reproduced. This ensures the continuity of gendered inequalities and their project-based answers. The obsession of members of the committee with the handmade souvenir productions, which served state-sponsored forms of exploitation of female labour and the reproduction of women's traditional roles, exemplifies this point. In this setting, the problem was how to meet the actual needs of women to have secure jobs and earn a regular and decent income. Actors who were new in the research site, such as Oya and Ayla, were unwilling to respond to criticisms of their ideas by experienced people who had been working in the field but were eager to fulfil their task in the best way possible. Experienced old actors, on the other hand, were too comfortable with the position that they held and the career they had made within the existing structure as gender elites of their locality to address the problem.

Institutionally, where gender expertise is not available in the local bureaucracy from the top to the bottom of the hierarchy, burning issues are reduced to social affairs. As the case of gender violence illustrates, providing protection to a woman in danger is left to the initiative of a Mrs Governor. She occupies a seat in the bureaucratic structure that the women's movement has been demanding for decades. The position is accompanied by the state budget at higher levels of the administration, as in the case of the president's wife mentioned earlier.

By representing women's concerns in policymaking, the women's policy committee raises the possibility that policies will be infused with a gender perspective. But to achieve actual gender equality, the organization lacked the political and legal backing to implement its plans. However, it has created a platform for members to make clear their political positions and negotiate boundaries between members who have multiple belongings, as demonstrated in the example of Oya's outbreak. In this sense, the means can be the ends. Meetings offer opportunities to practice political engagement and collaboration with the state for activism and advocacy, but they also expose the quality and limits of their power. Women's organizations and experienced gender workers push hard to unveil transnational organizations' obscurity and to vocalize the critique. The diversity among the participants at meetings of the committee has the potential to imagine the category of women as a subject of policy. This imagination is closely tied to the external political and economic contexts defined by nationalism and development in southeast Turkey.

5

A Project of One's Own

'Jump in, Zeynep!' Aliye said, from the front seat of a truck, with a big smile on her face. It was a few days after she started to wear a headscarf, following the abolishment of the headscarf ban for civil servants.[1] Her completely new look was strange to my eyes, but I was starting to get used to it. We were heading to the awareness workshop that she was coordinating as part of a larger gender project. Aliye seemed proud of having organized a vehicle and a driver, which were needed because the workshop was taking place in a neighbourhood far away on the outskirts of the city. When we arrived at the state-sponsored women's centre, the housewives were working busily in ateliers to produce labour-intensive handmade souvenirs, which were going to 'empower them' by being sold to tourists. The women had already been informed that there was going to be some sort of training on women's rights. Aliye gathered them and briefly explained the day's programme. Then, she quickly hung up posters for the project and prepared biscuits and soft drinks as offerings for each workshop participant – these incentives were effective in ensuring 'participation and project ownership by beneficiaries', as grant proposal guidelines state. She also took some photos that were to be used later as evidence of the event, as demanded by the funding institution's progress reports.

The moderators then grouped us and ushered us into separate rooms, and the workshops started behind closed doors. Our moderator was a psychologist working at the state-funded women's shelter. She introduced herself and then asked us to find a name for our group. 'What about "snowdrops"', somebody said quickly. Another proposed, 'Aren't we women all "two-legged demons?"' Everybody laughed. Then, a woman offered 'desperate housewives' but her neighbour rejected, stating firmly: 'Of course not! What is the point of attending this workshop if we are "desperate"?' Finally, one of the participants ran out of patience and said that we had spent enough time on this: 'Just cut the discussion!' Then, the moderator interrupted and asked softly: 'Have you ever thought about why we have such different ideas?' One woman replied that they are not aware of each other's thoughts because they avoid having sincere conversations out of fear of giving cause for gossip, 'which is very common among us Kurds', she said. Perhaps gossiping was not about being Kurdish, but about their level of education, another woman argued. They all agreed that educated people also behave badly, but that the damage caused by gossip varies between different groups. In the end, the group deemed that there was an enormous difference between the place of educated and uneducated girls in their society. One woman explained bitterly that her parents had not allowed her to study, and added, 'I wish I had been born male'. To which another woman added: 'Then my parents wouldn't have forced me to marry at an early age'.

'Gender awareness' workshops, such as this one, are designed to guide participants to reflect critically on their personal experiences and to shed light on the ways in which gender inequalities operate in their everyday lives. These are the primary activities of women's organizations in the context of the 'NGO-ization of feminism', or the 'shift away from experience-oriented movement politics toward goal- and intervention-oriented strategies' in separate and isolated projects (Lang 1997: 116). Together with skill-building training courses, and incentives to initiate entrepreneurship and schooling, gender awareness workshops are the main tools that women's NGOs use in their projects and towards the larger goal of women's empowerment.

In this chapter, I focus on one gender awareness project to show women's responses to, and engagements with, the empowerment discourses and practices that surround them, in addition to other normative political projects. I look not only at women's organizations and their relationships to public institutions, but also at the participants' perceptions of gender projects and the differences among women more generally. I aim to contextualize project feminism in this particular locality, which has already been addressed in the literature at national feminist activist/scholarly circles (Coşar and Özkan-Kerestecioğlu 2013).

Gender awareness workshops I observed were similar to the self-help groups observed in other development contexts, where feminist scholarship defend organically emerging initiatives based on shared concerns and reflecting women's priorities (Thorp, Stewart and Heyer 2005). However, diverse power relationships and different interests among women can undermine the idea of solidarity in these groups (Ward and Mouly 2013). Therefore, an intersectional approach is needed to expose the ways in which oppression is perceived and experienced from different subject positions with multiple belongings. The gender awareness workshops in Tigris do not adopt an intersectional approach, which is particularly relevant to the everyday lives of women in southeast Turkey, where multiple forms of oppression get linked over women. While there was a clear focus on gendered identifications and related differences, as well as inequalities, other identifications, such as ethnic belonging or class, were not questioned and discussed during the workshops. Instead, these differences were reduced to homogeneous and abstract dichotomies. Moreover, the gendered power structures embedded in governmental bodies were already visible when women started working to organize events for empowerment. The tools provided by the state and various women's organizations for those who want a life outside the family are neither sufficient nor powerful. Particularly in southeast Turkey, the state is not open to claims for more rights and freedoms – let alone women's objections to gendered structures. Consequently, women who have gender awareness mostly prefer to make small modifications to their lives and focus on self-improvement or their individual careers, all of which holds them back from politicizing private spheres in a collective fashion.

Funding 'we are women!'

In Turkey, the state is the key mediator, or filter, between global ideas and practices and within their local footprint. Whether they are national, international or supranational, all organizations and bodies must act through the laws, regulations, institutions or offices of the state. Thus, women reflecting on state-sponsored empowerment projects in southeast Turkey were stuck between feelings of alienation in terms of integrating their empowerment practices into state practices and marginalization in terms of their understanding of themselves as part of a larger feminist movement (Savran

1998: 3). Externally funded projects are essential for women's movements in Turkey to sustain themselves and for lobbying (Tekeli 2004). However, within the limits of project-based activism, or project feminism (Bora 2006), feminists had to give up on more comprehensive and long-run political claims. On the one hand, because the state provides financial assistance only to projects and organizations that are in line with governmental ideologies and interests, women's organizations define and limit their activities accordingly. On the other hand, due to the selective funding of projects and organizations, the job market created by the project-based development industry is not open to everyone with a good idea.

On a sunny afternoon in autumn, Aliye, Nalan and I were sitting in the kitchen of Nalan's new office. We were watching the noisy machines outside the window drilling into the earth as they began construction on yet another multi-storey apartment house, of a type that was being erected everywhere in the modern part of Tigris. These modern structures were neither bizarre nor surprising. But we viewed them as unfortunate in relation to the charming old town area of Tigris. In fact, tall buildings and unplanned urbanization are a shared pattern in both big and small settlements across Turkey. The government has been encouraging them and people call it 'development'.

The rhythmic sound of the construction machines was filling the room while Nalan's volunteer, Hazal, was serving us tea. Nalan and Aliye were having an intense conversation on the form, content and approach of the awareness workshops that they were organizing together. Nalan was not providing full support to Aliye. 'I am not officially involved in this project. I cannot lend you my handbook for your workshops because it is copyright material, you know. It would be illegal to share it with you', explained Nalan. Aliye was disappointed but stopped insisting.

Aliye is the daughter of one of the most powerful families of Tigris and has an Arabic ethnic background. She started to work for the municipality, the elected local government, after she had graduated from university and returned to her hometown. Since then, she had shown a genuine interest in women's organizations as well as the meetings and events of ongoing gender projects in Tigris. As a worker for the AKP municipality, she also enthusiastically took part in the party's regular visits to recruit party members from the households she visited. I never heard her define herself as a feminist although I knew she was curious about feminist ideas. Her main impulse was to do something for other women who 'needed to be saved'. Her inspiration was the president of the AKP's women's branch in Tigris, who coordinated many projects aimed at women's empowerment, and who received financial backing from local governments through state funding.[2]

Aliye's enthusiasm towards building a career in civil society was welcomed by Oya, the local coordinator of the UN's gender mainstreaming project. According to the UN project objectives she was working for, Oya was supposed to establish a gender equality office in the Tigris municipality and find suitable personnel to run it. Aliye was the perfect candidate for this office, and therefore, Oya had invested in training her. Oya had also designed a project with the purpose of developing the municipality's 'capacity' for gender equality activities. The project was based on awareness-raising workshops moderated by psychologists and targeting women living in disadvantaged neighbourhoods, that is, where Kurdish people with rural to urban migration backgrounds usually reside.[3] She encouraged Aliye to apply for financial support on behalf of the municipality from the project grant that the local government distributes. This is how the 'We Are Women!' project came into being, and how Aliye's career began.

Oya carefully formulated Aliye's project proposal in the way that the local government would accept and fund. The workshops were defined as psychological support groups aimed at helping women develop a stronger sense of self-worth, rather than spaces to reflect on the structurally disadvantageous positioning of women in society due to their gender. Moreover, Oya established a local cooperation between the municipality and an openly feminist organization by avoiding certain unwritten rules precluding them from local funding. She first convinced Aliye about the benefits of getting external and unofficial support from someone more experienced in coordinating a project, like Nalan. Nalan has been working for the Kamer Foundation and could ensure that the project would be run more in line with the objectives of the UN's empowerment approach. Both Aliye and Nalan agreed to work together in We Are Women!

Oya knew that Nalan's official involvement would put the financial support of Aliye's project at risk because state officials in Tigris perceived Kamer to be a pro-Kurdish organization.[4] The Kamer Foundation is a well-established regional women's organization that had been working against violence – and especially gender-based violence – in the southern and eastern provinces of Turkey since the early 1990s (Arat and Altınay 2015). Until the 2000s, the word 'organization' (*örgüt*) in Turkish connoted the armed organization of the Kurdish movement, the PKK,[5] and was therefore criminalized, especially in southeastern Turkey. However, the establishment of civil society organizations was facilitated and encouraged after legal amendments to expand freedom of association were passed by the Turkish Parliament in accordance with Turkey's EU candidacy. Turkey's EU accession process enabled women's organizations in the region to become established and to increase in number (Keysan 2019). Kamer was established in this context and opened offices in all eastern provinces. The foundation also launched 'awareness workshops' which were transformed over the years to adopt a non-hierarchical philosophy between the moderator and participants (Belge 2012). The Kamer Foundation's feminist political stand resonates well with the gender perspective of the pro-Kurdish HDP. Moreover, due to the fact that Kamer operates in provinces with majority Kurdish populations, most of the women working for the organization have organic ties with the Kurdish political movement. This proximity enabled state officials to come to rapid conclusions about the Kamer Foundation and to criminalize the women who work for them on these grounds. Although neither Nalan nor the previous Tigris representative of Kamer had a Kurdish background, civil servants and military officials has accused them both of supporting terrorism on various occasions and had tried to prevent their activities. In such situations, Nalan usually reminded officials that her brother was a well-known scholar who sympathized with the ruling party.

Resisting male resistance

Aliye and Oya were also facing differing forms of resistance from local state officials to gender-oriented activities and projects. Aliye experienced challenges while organizing her workshops, especially when trying to arrange a space to gather participants. For instance, on one occasion Aliye wanted to hold a meeting in one of the Quran schools regulated by the state. However, this time she could not get permission from the *müftü*, the provincial authority of the central government's Directorate of Religious Affairs (*Diyanet İşleri Başkanlığı*).[6] The *müftü* used to allow her to use Quran schools for the municipality's other activities, but this time he opposed it because he did not want to support a project run in cooperation with the UN. His rationale was that 'UN agencies were serving alcohol during their events'. The project had nothing to do with the UN, except for Aliye's unofficial cooperation with Oya.

On another occasion, Aliye repeatedly complained about a particular *muhtar*, the lowest level governmental administrator elected directly by the residents of a neighbourhood. Aliye was organizing one of her workshops in the neighbourhood where she resided with her family. She said that when she asked for a space for women to gather for the workshop, the *muhtar* refused her request for unexpected reasons. He said that he would never allow her to gather women together to teach them how to disobey their husbands at home. This was a serious problem because the *muhtar* is the one through whom welfare benefits are distributed.[7] These social benefits are crucial for women to provide for their households. Therefore, afraid of losing their access to these benefits, the women living in the neighbourhood hesitated to participate in Aliye's project.

In both cases, Aliye could ask for help from the municipality where she worked as a salaried officer. However, it was not clear whether she could reach someone higher than the *müftü* or the *muhtar*, who were both directly connected to the central government. Therefore, Aliye decided to ask for help from her male kin. For instance, to change the *muhtar*'s mind, she relied on her brothers, who are powerful and influential men in Tigris. After they had become involved, the *muhtar* stepped back on his threats of preventing her project. However, Aliye still had to find another space for her workshops. Angry and frustrated by such problems, she later told me, 'I learned that one has to be able to move through a very tiny hole in order to achieve something in this city when it comes to gender-related work. And one has to be persistent'.

However, this also means that it is more difficult for an outsider to be flexible or fit through 'the tiny hole'. For instance, when Oya offered to give gender training to the Diyanet personnel of Tigris, her offer was rejected by the same *müftü* who had denied Aliye a place to meet. As I learned from Oya, her proposal was turned down because she was not veiled, although wearing the veil is not an official requirement for anything. Besides, according to the state hierarchy, the *müftü* was expected to provide the necessary assistance to Oya because she was technically working at a higher level than him, being attached directly to the Ministry of the Interior. Her link with the most powerful agent of central government was supposed to give a legal basis to Oya's bureaucratic authority and protect her project in the face of difficulties with local governments. However, neither Oya's authority nor that of her project was clearly defined by the public administration, so that too left much open to local interpretation. After facing so many blockades, the planned training never took place because the *müftü* refused to negotiate further. The proposed gender training reached a dead-end because Oya, unlike a local organizer like Aliye or Nalan, was unable to develop a solution.

As her indeterminate position demonstrates, Oya's project represents a perfect example of the lack of commitment by the state, as well as the absence of government coordination and coherence, to gender equality. Working with governments requires creativity, flexibility and alliances between women's organizations. Alternative solutions demand greater flexibility from some of the parties involved in alliances compared with their partners and co-organizers. Nalan's unofficial but personal involvement in Aliye's project illustrates this point. While partnerships are short-term for project-based activities that do not aim for structural change, women in this process accommodate existing power relations. An example of this is Aliye's utilization of the power of male kin to create a space of manoeuvre for local women working in NGOs. Therefore, the link between awareness and collective action is broken at the very beginning of the organizational stage of the workshops. Nevertheless, the core feminist ideas promoted by various transnational feminist networks do not totally melt away, but continue to haunt women in different ways. While Aliye, for instance, was ambitiously holding onto the dream of having a project of her own and thus a seat among the women who define civil society in Tigris, she found herself transcending her career goals and reflecting on the gendered roles and expectations in her personal life.

Aliye's 'life and words'

When Aliye had left Nalan's office, Oya entered the door. Nalan started to complain about Aliye's lack of feminist socialization: 'She believes that being subjected to violence is about women's *fitrat* [nature]!' When I heard Nalan, I too thought to myself what an unfortunate choice of word that was. Denoting the Islamic doctrine of creational differences between women and men, the Arabic word *fitrat* created public debate[8] after it was used to emphasize women's maternal roles by the prime minister at the time, Recep Tayyip Erdoğan (Özyeğin 2015). As the head of Kamer's Tigris office, Nalan's experience working with women was based on various workshops and meetings planned by her organization, which has organic ties with feminist circles critical of the government's gender policies. Therefore, she was familiar with this debate.

Soon after I learned about Aliye's faux pas, she told me that she did not believe in natural differences between women and men. Therefore, I understand that *fitrat* was a popular word of the day and that she used it just as a figure of speech. Aliye was not familiar with these feminist circles, and she was not familiar with the feminist jargon or debates. Her experiences were based on the activities of local women's organizations that did not necessarily define themselves as feminists defending pro-choice arguments. Aliye initially started to work on gender projects within the AKP, as well as with pro-government state officials and local bureaucrats, who were quick to adopt Erdoğan's language.

Aliye supported Erdoğan and his government; however, this did not mean that she defended all the ideas behind his and his followers' discursive performances. After one of the awareness workshop sessions, Aliye and I were having lunch downtown. She was complaining about Oya's and Nalan's bossy behaviour in return for the scant help they had given to her project. When I said that I could sympathize with Oya, as I used to work for the UN just like her, I could at last sense Aliye's attention and respect. She wanted to learn more about me and my research. I explained to her my interest in gender and power in reference to what had been discussed during the workshop. Aliye said, 'Well, I experience similar things with my boyfriend all the time'. She was involved in a long-distance relationship, but she confessed she had felt it emotionally distant from him for some time. He had seemed like an easy-going person at the beginning of their relationship but had become more intrusive in her life as time passed. After hearing this, I asked:

Z: In what ways, do you mean?

A: For example, he says, I should not work extra hours, you know, for the project …

Z: Perhaps his job doesn't demand working extra hours. Is that so?

A: No, he works a lot and all the time! Even at nights.

Z: Then, why doesn't he want you to work as much as you want?

A: Because of his religious beliefs, [according to which] 'women don't work!' [Muttering]

Z: But you are religious too, and you want to work hard, right?

A: Exactly. I don't share his opinion. When he sends me *hadiths* [the sayings of the prophet Muhammad, intended to support his argument], I tell him that it is his misinterpretation. But then, he tells me that 'certain things cannot be questioned in religion'.

Z: I understand the difficulty of arguing against holy sources … but perhaps you can explain to him that religious views and women's rights belong to separate fields of discussion.

A: I am aware of that. I tell him that conditions were different in the prophet's time. Now we live in a different world.

I knew that Aliye's boyfriend would not be convinced by a non-religious argument – especially a feminist one. However, I was not knowledgeable enough about the Quran to build an argument that would win him over, and besides, the gender equality discourse that Aliye was using against him did not belong to religious reasoning but to a secular one. She had learnt these arguments while she had been organizing workshops for others. However, Aliye made a distinction between the participants of the workshops and herself, which was inherently contradictory to the aim of building group identity through gender awareness.

Nalan had explained to me once that empowerment was a process, and therefore, she did not assume that she was in a position to teach others. In this way, she rejected the idea of saving others. In the workshops that she moderated, there was no hierarchy. For her, it was an opportunity to share and acknowledge common problems so that everybody could learn from each other. She did not view herself as teaching Aliye either, although Aliye found Nalan's behaviour domineering. Meanwhile, Aliye herself treated women in workshops in an authoritarian way. At times I witnessed that she acted as though she was above everyone, including the moderators and participants. For instance, during one of the workshops when the moderators were introducing the confidentiality rule, Aliye took the floor and authoritatively said: 'I do not want things we talk about here to go out of this room. Never! I forbid you to gossip with your neighbours after these workshops!' When Nalan or Oya told her that she should behave differently, Aliye did not comprehend on what grounds they were criticizing her. As a result, she became bitter and distant from them.

On the one hand, Aliye perceived herself not as a victim but as a saviour. On the other hand, in our private conversations she was eager to talk about how close she felt to women who complained about their husbands because she had very similar and unresolved conflicts with her boyfriend. Her identity as a Muslim woman conflicted with the way that her boyfriend was positioning her. Additionally, the more she heard other women talking about their gendered experiences, the more convincing feminist arguments became for her – even although she was not yet able to reflect upon the emerging mismatch between her life and words. She was adopting new values, and her in-betweenness was confusing both for herself and for others, who relied on her despite her apparent contradictions.

Differences negotiated (or not)

Here I narrate my observations from a particular session that Nalan organized and moderated in a project that the Kamer Foundation had run with the help of third-party funding in the beginning of November 2013. As I observed this workshop and others, I was interested in hearing answers to questions including: how do women learn from each other? How do they discuss the most serious topics in their lives open-heartedly with strangers? How do they claim autonomy about gender relations and how do they resist their 'sister's' claims? By this I mean, how do they deal with tension while negotiating their conflicting values? And finally, where does gender awareness lead? In general, within the workshops that I witnessed, the women's stories and their reactions to the facilitator's answers were very similar to each other, although the individual workshops, their content and the composition of their participants varied. Usually, the moderator introduced themes step by step and asked the women to share and reflect on their personal experiences. Most of the time the discussion flowed spontaneously. Another important aspect was that sometimes the participants had previously attended similar workshops, and these women tended to stimulate the debate for those who had attended for the first time. Interestingly, while listening, I found that the Kamer session greatly resembled sessions of Aliye's project We Are Women!

The session started at the large room of Kamer's office precisely on time. We were a dozen women sitting in a circle, and some of the women's children were playing in the next room, without interrupting us. After we introduced ourselves to each other, Nalan began the first theme, which was childhood. She asked why clothes and toys for boys and girls were different from each other. The women started to discuss the topic freely, giving examples from their own lives. One woman remembered that she had never been given a gun because she was a girl, although she had liked toy guns a lot when she was a child. Others gave similar examples. Highlighting the differences between girls and boys evolved to a discussion of their parents' attitudes to their daughters and boys. A woman said that she never felt she was loved as much as her male siblings. She said her parents loved her brothers more only because they were boys. It was clear that this remark made the women reflect on their own childhoods. They were suddenly deeply sad, and this created a cold silence in the room. Moments of cold silence, such as this, recurred frequently after other difficult discussions during the session. A woman broke the silence by remarking on her desire to have a male child, and that she had a lot of children for this very reason. Another woman supported her by saying, 'and we all know that this is especially the case here, in the east'. She was referring to a national divide within Turkey. Other women nodded that 'the east' was different from 'the west' of the country in terms of parents' gender-based discrimination against their own children.

We moved from talking about childhood to marriage. Somebody said that while a man could marry again after divorce, it was not easy for women to do so because of the moral judgements of the society. 'Yet ... there is a double-edged exception!' one said with a bitter tone. 'Widowed women are forced to marry their deceased husband's brother'. Another woman reminded us that men also could have more than one wife, although it was not legal. She said, 'Whereas, a woman can never have two husbands!' A woman with big blue eyes reacted with an exaggerated expression: 'Oh! I can't deal with one, what I would do if I had two husbands? May God forbid!' Everybody laughed at this joke and the sombre air in the room finally dissipated.

The name of the blue-eyed woman was Nazmiye. Nazmiye was a Kurdish woman in her thirties. This was her first time to be in at an awareness workshop and Hazal, the volunteer from Kamer, had invited her. Nazmiye was not shy, in fact she was very vocal, and from time to time a challenger. She made jokes to entertain people but, at the same time, her statements were provocative and opposed to Nalan's inputs. She came from a well-off family and was married to a successful local businessman.

Nazmiye was also a mother of two adolescents, whom she admitted that she treated unequally. While her son, who was the younger child, had a cell phone and spent most of his time on the Internet, Nazmiye did not permit her daughter to have a cell phone: 'I also don't allow her to spend time on the Internet because I am afraid that she might find a boyfriend or something. Then she would stop studying. I want her to study'. But an experienced participant named Hale confronted Nazmiye. When she had been a teenager, Hale had a complicated relationship with her mother, who also forbid her to use the Internet. However, Hale always found a way to connect, and she met her husband via a friend-making website. As Hale explained:

> My mother still doesn't know this. When we finally decided to marry, I asked my husband to ask my father for my hand but we arranged things so that it looked like an arranged marriage. We hid the fact from our parents. Believe me, your daughter will also find a way if she really wants to break your rules ... [Pause]. Oh, for a moment, I felt as if it was my mother sitting in your chair.

As she said, not only this experience but also many other things in her relationship with her mother made Hale feel weak and even insecure. The awareness workshops that she attended made her feel powerful, but she was still hesitant to tell her mother the secret about her choice of spouse. For her, to meet a strange man on the Internet, establish a romantic relationship based on trust and eventually have a family were important achievements – mainly because she did them all on her own, with consciously taking steps to do so, and without harming her honour. Confirming the findings of Elisabetta Costa on the use of social media in southeast Turkey, Hale's example also 'shows that social media and these new forms of communication and romance have not eliminated "ideal" forms of traditional arranged marriage, which continue to remain rooted and strong' (Costa 2016: 33).

Hale continued the discussion by saying that it was difficult for her to express herself, not only to her mother but also to others. She shared a story about how she felt terrible about sharing her opinions in public. Once, during a family dinner at her in-laws' home, she mentioned her desire to go back to high school. Her husband mocked her, saying, 'So I should hire a Russian nanny for the kids'. Because migrant women from Russia are stigmatized as immoral, the husband was implying that he might also have an affair with the nanny. Hale had replied in a rage: 'Fine by me, but then, you'll be OK when I'll hang out with boys at school'. While Hale's husband found her reply amusing, others at the dinner took a dim view of her remark. According to Hale, those who judged her for her remark preferred to take her joke seriously rather than her wish to study. In this way, they questioned her morality and punished her for wanting something for herself. Again, Nazmiye broke the sombre atmosphere in the room: 'There are no Russians here, only Syrians, don't worry!' Female migrants escaping from the war in Syria were also stigmatized in Tigris in the same manner. Then, this time, she directed her criticism to Hale:

> But you said that you were flirting with men on the Internet rather than studying. So, I don't understand your ambition to go back to school now, what's the point?

Hale explained that she had a difficult family life, and that she had agreed to marry only if her husband would allow her to continue her studies. Although distance education was always an option, things had not gone as planned and she had to postpone studying. She did not want to postpone her education any longer.

The emphasis on education and on getting a degree made a woman who had been silently listening speak for the first time. As I learned from others, she was the second and unofficial wife of a married man who did not allow her to have a paid job. She said, 'You know what I've been through but please, also know that all this time I have been educated. I mean, education does not always protect you'. However, Hale defended the importance of education. She gave the example of how her father lied to her mother about what is written in the Quran:

> Mother was illiterate and believed him when he said that the Quran forbids girls to own or inherit property. This is why she did not invest in me; she did not even prepare a dowry for me. When it came to my brothers, however, she agreed to get a loan from the bank. It still hurts me. It is nothing other than discrimination. I will never treat my own daughter the way my mother treated me!

Hale's comparison between herself and her brothers demoralized the women again; the air was heavy. Nazmiye, on the other hand, was thankful for small blessings: 'Thank God that we are not living in the prophet's time. Back then men were burying their daughters alive'. The women laughed again when somebody asked Nazmiye: 'So you mean, we should be grateful that they don't bury us alive?'

Nalan then switched to a 24-hour exercise that aims to make women realize how much unpaid work they do during the day in comparison to men. During the exercise, the moderator divides the women into four groups, each of which is given the empty schedule of an imaginary couple. The differences between the four imaginary couples are primarily based on their class background, where they live and the number and age of their children. The women are asked to fill the couple's daily schedule in a realistic manner and later reflect upon it. Nalan also participated in this exercise. She then asked her audience to tell the group what their imagined everyday lives looked like. This strategy led women to reflect upon each other's lifestyles, which led to judgmental assessments, instead of inspiring full reflection on their own experiences. For example, when a newly married woman said that her husband also prepares breakfast on the weekends, somebody said, 'My husband would push me out of the door [*kapının önüne koyar*] if I were a wife like you'. With some intrusive guidance from Nalan, the women finally reached a point where they complained about carrying all the responsibility of the household on their shoulders. Only Nazmiye was absurdly filled with gratitude, once more:

> Thank God that we all are healthy and can do all the housework. My sister has been in a permanent vegetative state for years, she can't even move her fingers. What if we were like her?

The conflict between Hale and Nazmiye was unexpected and entertaining to the participants of the session. In general, women were respectful of each other's stories, and they were aware that they couldn't talk about these topics freely in the presence of their husbands. In fact, one of the participants stated, 'If I told my husband what we talk about here, he would never let me join you again'. Another one said, 'My husband would be angry if he found out that you have opened my eyes here [*burada benim gözümü açtığınızı fark ederse*]. You should organize similar workshops for our husbands too'. For this reason, Nalan advised women not to talk about what happened during the workshops to others.

'Burning anger'

Hale was impatient. She urged women in the room to 'act together and do something!' But her urge remained unanswered. In such moments Nalan tended to talk about 'the society' that existed out of the room. This almost transcendental being called 'the society' regulated women's lives in many ways. 'We aim to change it', Nalan was repeating, without saying exactly how. Once she told me that awareness alone was not enough to make women's lives easier: 'If you inform them about gender-based violence, for instance, and do not tell them how to fight against it, you leave them with burning anger within. It harms them more'. It was true that the workshops generated anger when women reflected on their everyday life from a gender perspective. One participant was particularly hurt because her in-laws did not treat her with respect:

> Our freedom is restricted. As an individual, I know when I should be at home. However, they constantly remind me of it. It is not my husband but

his father who puts his nose into my business. We live in separate houses but eat together. Now, I wonder, to whom is a married woman accountable?

When other participants of the workshop said that she should respect her in-laws, the woman replied furiously: 'But who will respect me? Then, I want to be respected too!'

Nalan once told me that she had not been aware of the violence that she had experienced as 'a perfect housewife, a dedicated mother and a good wife' before going through years of awareness-raising workshops. She says that it was extremely challenging for her to strip herself away from her previous self. She was proud of being a professional woman working for other women's well-being. Yet this linear story does not apply to every participant, mainly due to unaddressed structural boundaries drawn by the unequal access to resources and social exclusion that some ethnic or religious groups experience.

Surely awareness is a step forward. It could be the start of a process, where women go through stages of anger and frustration until they finally decide to face the power imbalances between women and men in society and accept its dominance in their lives. However, the lack of an intersectional approach to power relations, which is highly relevant to women in southeast Turkey, disconnects gendered experiences from others. Class positions and ethnic identifications, which divide not only Hale and Nazmiye but also 'the east' and 'the west' that all workshop participants imagined and referred to, were not a part of the discussion. In the same vein, women were able to discuss what kinds of state services were available, but they did not discuss what else was needed and how existing support systems could be developed. However, as the case further on illustrates, building oneself into an independent individual with gender awareness in and beyond the household is bounded by state policies, some of which specifically target specific cultural and political biographies.

Hazal's pieces: Afterlife of workshops

'You know what? If I had studied, I would be someone like you!' Hazal said. I froze, surprised. We were in a café in the town. The waiter came to our table too often. I was not sure whether he could hear us. I told her to speak a little more quietly if she did not want to be overheard. I asked this because we were talking about her life and she was giving intimate answers to my questions, such as 'he literally rapes me every day'. She was talking about her husband, whom she was almost forced to marry at an early age. Her motivation to accept his proposal, she told me, was primarily because he promised her to send her to school. Her parents would not let her go to school, 'because I was too beautiful', she said, and added, 'I hated being beautiful'. And at that moment, I realized that I wished I were as beautiful as she was.

This moment during the interview with Hazal, where two women sit down and crave for the other's life experience, preoccupied me for a long time, even after the fieldwork was completed. At first, I thought she was angry with me due to my privileges that enabled me to study. Then, I came to realize that her aim was different, and it was not about me, it was about her. She was emphasizing her potential. She was surrounded by people like me living and working abroad. Her cousin was a film director and working in London. Her brother was living and studying in the United States. He was getting the financial support of her father; she said, 'because he is a man'. Hazal was comparing herself to them just as she did with me. The gap between her existing self and the person she would like to be was troubling her.

Hazal was born in a large town primarily populated by Kurdish people. She went to school until fifth grade, but her father took her out of school when she reached puberty. Her father was an influential figure in the Kurdish national movement. As Hazal explains:

> In people's eyes, my father was a modern [*çağdaş*] man, and this was why women in the movement were surprised when they heard that he wasn't sending me to school. I said, 'My father behaves like a modern man to outsiders, not to us'. I mean, he is authoritarian at home. For him, women have a different place [in society] than men have, and this is not open to discussion.

Like her father, Hazal was supporting the struggle for Kurdish identity politics. However, her father's vision of Kurdish politics did not match her own. In fact, in Hazal's view, her father's behaviour contradicted the ideals of the Kurdish political project, which was supposed to promote gender equality, and therefore, also to encourage girls to study and become independent individuals. This critique of the movement suggests that women like Hazal, as members of Kurdish community living in Turkey, could initiate structural changes. In fact, the gender awareness workshops that she attended had the potential to help create the grounds for political participation and collective action. Yet, even if Hazal's father had allowed her to engage in politics, the state would put her obstacles. While state practices always rejected Kurdish political demands in Turkey, this became more severe as the movement got stronger. After successfully crossing the 10 per cent election threshold in 2015, the HDP came under attack by the ruling state power. During this time, a number of MPs, co-mayors, district heads and party members were arrested and jailed. Women were especially, if not exclusively, targeted. Therefore, the contradiction lay not only in Hazal's father's behaviour but also in state practices, which oppose women's participation in politics and self-representation – and eventually their empowerment.

Despite her father, Hazal never gave up on her dream to study. She even accepted a marriage proposal from an *imam* (a Muslim preacher) eleven years older than herself after he had promised to send her to school, although she had disliked him from the beginning. When she changed her mind, it was too late. Her mother cried for hours thinking that it would be dishonourable to break the engagement. In the end, Hazal had to give up and agree to marry him to please her mother. Because she married young, she compares herself with the children she sees on TV. Specifically, she found the promotional film directed by Çağan Irmak (2010) for the social responsibility project 'Dad, Send me to School' heartbreaking. The film opens with a classroom scene where the teacher calls the roll. When it comes to girls, the camera leaves the classroom and travels to the various places where girls actually are to be found: in the fields, the greenhouses, the gardens and the houses, where we see school-age girls working and shouting, 'Here I am!' The final scene is in a bedroom where a girl in a wedding dress with a red belt sits on the bed. She looks into the camera with her heavily made-up face and repeats the same words in a close-up shot from a high angle (Irmak 2010). Referring to this last scene, Hazal said, 'that's me'.

Her husband kept his promise and registered Hazal to attend school a week after their wedding. After she had given birth to two children, she started university and earned her diploma. However, Hazal never really liked her husband and defined every sexual intercourse as marital rape. The violence in her marriage was so intense that Hazal decided to see a psychologist. Regular therapy sessions worked, and she felt better. Although her husband got jealous and insisted that she stopped the therapy, she continued seeing her psychologist, even secretly.

During the interview, Hazal defined herself as the victim of her parents' decisions. However, she was not a victim per se. It was also clear that she had developed a sense of belonging to a group of women who found the power within to change their lives after following gender awareness workshops. Perhaps she married at a young age, but this enabled her to get an education. She found shortcuts to earn a diploma and managed to experience a full student life while raising her children. She was interested in having a career outside home and her volunteer job at the Kamer Foundation was her first step towards this aim.

During the time we met, Hazal had already started negotiating with her husband to find a work in a paid job. Her husband wanted her to work in a public institution so that they could have another baby, because the government provides many childcare benefits to public officials. Hazal was interested in the job but not in having another child, as she explains:

> He says the state provides all the necessary support: milk money, maternal leave, etc., in such circumstances you could easily bring [up another] child, he says. He also says, even if you were appointed to [work] somewhere else, you could stay here only because you are pregnant. Imagine! He tells me all these things ... And I say, yeah, right. He thinks that he can fool me with all this. Too late, it's gone!

The legislation regulating rights and duties of state officials defines extensive maternity benefits that include paid maternity leave up to six months and part-time temporary leave afterwards. In contrast, however, paternity rights are rather limited – such as five days paid leave – and in exceptional cases like the death of mother during the birth (Resmi Gazete [Official Gazette] – 29882 2016). While many professional women have a positive take from this legislation, it indicates a pro-family rather than pro-women policy considering also discursive attacks at women's production rights in general and abortion in particular – besides the pronatalist prescription for women to have at least three children (Kandiyoti 2016). Therefore, the state policy has placed Hazal in the situation where she ought to submit to the path designed for her as a mother and a housewife by retreating from the emancipated self that she built for herself during the awareness workshops. What she wanted was to work, not to take paid maternity leave. Yet, the way in which she utilized state policies that idealize women primarily as mothers while negotiating with her husband to get a job is similar to the way in which she used marriage to bypass her parents in order to have access to education. Considering the fact that the cost of having access to education through marriage was marital rape and unhappiness, however, it is not certain that she would be able to convince her husband to allow her to work outside home and not have to pay him back for the opportunity of being employed by giving him another child.

Conclusion

In the 1990s, southeast Turkey has been used as an object for reflection by national-level women's organizations based in western cities, such as Istanbul or Ankara, and has been at the centre of the 'project feminism' debate. Since the mid-2000s, however, women's organizations based in the region have been involved in activities that conceptualize empowerment within the frame of externally funded projects. In this way, these projects also create employment opportunities for women, most of whom belong to the local elite. Not only regional women's organizations but also local organizations on provincial, and sometimes neighbourhood levels, compete for funding. Until recently, organizations acting on the transnational level dominated the field of financial assistance. With more accessible local funding mechanisms, however, the state responded to the dynamism of civil society organizations and became a significant player with the power to dictate indirectly the content and form of these activities. The We are Women! project is an example of how the state took over the role of giving financial support to local NGOs from transnational development actors and national NGOs.

The local funding enabled Aliye, who was an officer of the municipality and also a member of the AKP, to coordinate a gender project. As a young, educated woman, she observed others and understood the potential of the civil society organizations in the city. Running her own project could be a potential jump-off point for a position in the women's branch of the party or a similar powerful position. While Aliye gained experience in the field within which she wants to pursue a career, Oya ticked the box in the 'planned activities' list of the UN project she worked for. In this way, Oya could write in her report that she had supported an emerging 'woman leader' in Tigris, and also that a project on 'gender awareness' was designed and organized with the 'technical assistance' of UN agencies and in cooperation with 'local bureaucratic partners'. Furthermore, We are Women! was the product of a burdensome alliance between the municipality and an 'objectionable' NGO like the Kamer Foundation. Although Oya managed to bypass selective funding, she failed to navigate the local power structures as an outsider.

The plans for women's empowerment that had been carried into Turkey from other parts of the world and filtered through the national – and almost totally male – bureaucratic structures to the Tigris locality – do not fit within local power configurations for the most part. Being local enabled Aliye and Nalan to work within the structural confines and act according to the mind-set of the men who represented the state and created obstacles to women's empowerment work. However, both women justified their activities by requesting the help of powerful men behind them. These types of actions contradict the normative ideas of empowerment, which suggests challenging power structures rather than simply accommodating to them. Nevertheless, the feminist ideas that circulate through short-term project-based activities found a place in Aliye's understanding of her own gendered subjectivity. Aliye's self-perception as a career-pursuing Muslim woman conflicts with her boyfriend's world view, which, as her language suggests, she used to agree with prior to running the gender workshops. While she was in the process of making sense of all the new confrontations to her prior world view, Aliye's differences of opinion were challenging to Nalan and Oya.

Women who joined the awareness workshops often went through a similar process. For Nalan, her perception of Aliye's confusion, Nazmiye's sarcastic resistance to change and Hale's impatient demand for more autonomy were expected outcomes. In any case, gender awareness is a challenging process during which anger and impatience hit women hard mainly because they do not have the means to transform their lives by using the knowledge that they gain during the workshops. After the workshops, inequality becomes crystal clear, but the rest becomes more blurred. I argue that this is because women often do not speak publicly about differences, such as the gap between household incomes among participants, which was a totally untouched topic.

The category 'woman' signifies motherhood and family in state policy, and women from southeast Turkey can be understood through the lens of the government as divided into a few generic social categories: the 'innocent' housewife to be 'empowered', the 'criminal' political subject to be punished. An unexpected outcome of the discourses and practices operating behind these categorizations is the angry and disappointed women navigating silently but steadily through their individual lives, owing to the reflexive exercises during the awareness workshops I narrated. Going through a self-reflexion process, Hazal, as a proud Kurdish woman, both volunteered in women's struggles in a regional organization that is outspoken about women's human rights and also challenged gender structures at home. Despite what is visible at first glance, however, the theme underneath her narrative spoke volumes about the burdens women experience that are created by a state policy that targets women in the southeast.

Hazal obtained the 'skill' of critical reflection on her own experience starting from her childhood and a deconstruction of the meaning of education in her life. This was because she had gone through a series of awareness workshops organized by Kamer Foundation. Like Aylin, whom I introduced already in Chapter 2, Hazal was not happy about where she had ended up in life and she also became an adult via marriage at a time when she was rather interested in schooling. She interpreted her father's decision not to send her to school as a contradiction to his political consciousness as a Kurdish socialist. For her, educating girls was supposed to be a part of the progressive values that the Kurdish movement promises to women. She continued studying to find a regular paid job and did not miss any Kurdish-language classes. She chose to remain in an unhealthy and unfulfilling marital relationship instead of divorcing, but she did not want to compromise her well-being and self-improvement. After I completed my fieldwork, I learned that she started to work for the new administration at the municipality. There were many chairs emptied by the old administration after the elections that ended with the victory of the pro-Kurdish party – including the one left by Aliye.

Conclusion

Ethnography takes time, both as a research method and also as a form of writing. This is why in their concluding chapters ethnographers usually introduce an update about developments that have taken place in the research context since the actual fieldwork was conducted. It took me precisely a decade to publish this book, which is close to the average time it takes in anthropology. However, the time between when I completed my fieldwork and left Tigris and the time I finished the book was too dense in terms of political developments in Turkey – and in the southeast. I could not go back to Tigris and visit people again until 2021. In the meantime, I lost most of my connections with women's work for women. This includes a tutor in Dargeçit ÇATOM named Sabahat Kılıç, who was murdered during the urban clashes between the Turkish army and the pro-Kurdish armed urban militia in December 2015.

The 'Kurdish–Turkish peace process' collapsed in the summer of 2015, following the general elections when the HDP, the pro-Kurdish party, won numbers of seats in the parliament that was enough to prevent the establishment of yet another one-party government of the AKP. Following the insurrection spearheaded in support of the defence of the Syrian city of Kobanî in November 2014 and declaration of self-governance by the PKK-affiliated groups in August 2015, the youth wing began digging ditches and building barricades around urban areas (Ercan 2019). As a result, authorities imposed 24-hour curfews and held military operations in both cities. Public campaigns calling for a return to peace talks were rather weak but loud enough to be criminalized (Baser, Akgönül and Öztürk 2017). According to the report of the Human Rights Foundation of Turkey, 1,642,000 people were affected by the 63 curfews implemented in 7 provinces and 22 districts between 16 August 2015 and 18 March 2016, and 310 civilians lost their lives (Bianet 2016). In this context, while pro-government news agencies said that the tutor Kılıç 'had lost her life' during a PKK attack, pro-Kurdish news agencies reported that she was killed during an attack on her house launched by the Turkish police (Bianet 2015).

I heard from Oya, who quit her job in Tigris and moved back to Izmir shortly after I left the field, that Kılıç had been murdered. I thought that I might have met Kılıç, but only once and very briefly during my preliminary research in 2012. I also remembered the high iron gate of Dargeçit ÇATOM that I had found ridiculously cold and aggressive at the time. Kılıç's death brutally showed me that protection that a state institution intends to offer to the women in the region does not really respond to the actual conditions that the violence can create. Considering the controversy about the source of violence, in fact, this claim to protection becomes even more problematic. In his analysis of official propaganda of military operations during the urban warfare, Eray Çaylı (2016) demonstrates how the state frames itself as an actor that mostly invests on economic and infrastructural development of the region although it is the one that entangles with multiple conflicts including international ones. In a similar vein, I aimed at highlighting this very controversial issue in this book by asking what the state does for women in southeast Turkey.

A female death would not be my choice to finish this book – a gender stereotype in fiction. However, since I finished my research, numerous women have died in (southeast) Turkey due to military conflicts, poverty and femicide. Neither did I design my research or write my book with the aim of producing a restudy of women's suicides. However, I see now that it has the potential to be considered a restudy of Müjgan Halis's book on women's suicides in the early 2000s. In contrast to Halis's journalistic endeavour and its precise focus, my ethnographic research aimed to look at larger questions about the lives of women living in the same area almost two decades after hers. Since the early 2000s, the lifting of the state of emergency has enabled researchers to engage in the everyday lives of people living in the region. Like Halis's study, at the time I conducted my research there was a ceasefire, without violent conflicts but with a longing for a 'permanent and honourable peace'.[1] The call for peace remains valid for many groups in Turkey even today. However, in terms of a violence-free atmosphere, the year 2013 was an exceptional time. For this reason, I have often found it difficult to make the connection between stories I told that belong to another time lost in the past and the violence that I followed on media in despair and from afar.

This study contributes to a limited number of long-term ethnographic studies conducted in southeast Turkey on women's perceptions and practices and to scholarship on gendered citizenship in Turkey with an anthropological account on the rhetoric of empowerment. Instead of a policy analysis or political science perspective, this book aims to offer an analysis of the multitude of daily experiences of ordinary people discussing the forces that shape the conditions of their lives. Since the GAP was one of the dominant forces in the region, I directed my attention primarily to the ways in which women's empowerment was situated in development projects. This enabled me to go beyond a nationally bounded analysis to look at the transnational ties of ideas that are connected to local ones.

Tracing the historical constructions of women's place in international development plans shows that women's empowerment has close ties to first, women's human rights discourse, and second, culturalist arguments that can offer only a limited understanding of the agency of women. Practices informed by the assemblage of these ideas seek out *innocent* targets or *victims* of poverty or local culture to *empower* or *save*. I showed that women in the GAP region were suitable candidates for directing these efforts. 'The good news', as Yakın Ertürk (2012: 274) announced earlier, is that these intrusions have not been silently accepted by women. I used the term 'women's praxis' precisely to emphasize this dual (the subject and the object) position of women in these practices.

In my analysis I directed my attention to the sites of contestation manifested in empowerment, women's human rights and the modernist idea of 'progress' that surface in many of the narratives, activities and discussions of women. These tensions underline the multiplicity and fluidity of notions of women's rights in southeast Turkey articulated at the nationalism in Turkey. In this way, I have contributed to analyses that have examined the circulation and reception of multifarious feminisms across ethnicity and class-based differences by considering the conflicts and alliances rooted in different experiences of life. While such discourses and practices reproduce and maintain differences, they also offer new insights into conditions that surround and create feminisms. Enlarging my focus on women to include those with privileges and challenges, I showed their varying efforts to adopt and engage with these ideas.

I made a claim about the ideologies that have dominated state practices since the establishment of the republic and said that there was continuity in the gender policy of the state. Accordingly, I showed that serving their purpose of defining a special location for women and reproducing their home-based activities and establishing women's centres is an outcome of the masculinist state repertoire of Turkey that goes back to the late Ottoman era. While developmentalist understanding aims at a modified version of empowerment in women's centres, today neoconservative AKP's Islamism is establishing women's centres in the southeast in order to expand state control. AKP policies define the ideal Kurdish woman as a housewife who spends her time at centres, instead of home, to improve her feminine skills and to serve her family in the best way possible, without becoming attracted to the Kurdish movement dominant in the region. In this way, ADEMs successfully replace the empowerment rhetoric of ÇATOMs with rehabilitation that has open connections with assimilation practices.

Building upon this historical framing, I discussed three main pillars that the empowerment practices in women's work for women rely on in Tigris. I used the power of ethnography to show ambiguities and contradictions in women's words and actions, in response to the structures that maintain their housewifery role in the society. In the following two chapters of the book, I showed how women negotiate their position in their intimate relations by utilizing the discourses that surround them and the tools offered to them by women's praxis.

In 'Alternative Opportunities', firstly I focused on education, as a tool for social mobility and self-improvement. The narratives about education that I derived from the interviews helped me to understand and present the link between the meta-narratives on women in the southeast and the ways in which women perceive themselves and other women. To highlight this point, I said that my positionality as an educated woman from the western part of the country influenced the tone and content of narratives during the interviews. Secondly, I introduced the income-generating activities that empowerment practices offer women. Although I named this second pillar 'employment', I showed that considering the larger framework of economic development that shapes liberal development practices, women do not engage in the labour force in formal ways but instead remain in the informal and underpaid sector. I quoted women who do not consider working outside their homes because they do not feel safe in public space, as other scholars already pointed out. However, the women who are involved in women's work for women in different ways are able both to have and to pursue various careers including entrepreneurship. Therefore, I included entrepreneurial efforts, as they are part of the scattered field of paid employment.

In 'Participation without "us"', I focused on the third pillar of empowerment, and I presented the strategies that women develop to participate in decision-making processes. Mainly following the statements of three women involved in civil society organizations in Tigris, I showed the sensitivity and responsiveness of local women's organizations to national-level politics and how the government expands its control through NGOs and the political labour of women with multiple identities. With the focus on participation, I also presented feminist critiques of the AKP's ideal family construct and the obstacles behind alliances among women to speak as 'we women' due to their political positionings in relation to the dominant agenda, which is neo-Islamic conservatism.

After discussing education, employment and political participation, I looked at the response these ideas find in the bureaucracy. Focusing on interactions in the setting of a quasi-official meeting, I showed that bureaucracy cannot respond very well to demands of professionals and volunteers in women's praxis in Tigris, due to their lack of expertise and institutional capacity. The 'solution' that the state bureaucracy found to this was a woman who is not an insider of the inner circle of kinship relations but is instead attached to them through their marriage. While pressing *hanımefendis* into the service of empowerment practices, once again, the masculinist state defines women in relation to a man and within the family unit, rather than as autonomous individuals.

Finally, I put the emphasis on negotiations among women with a focus on women's awareness workshops. A careful reader would notice that the name of traditional needlework that women make in Tigris and the name of the UN employee are the same: Oya. This is not a coincidence but a conscious choice. I wanted to emphasize both the transnational links of the women's work for women in Tigris and also the fact that *oya* (lace) is a construction made of careful work. I showed that women's organizations find innovative solutions to create awareness with the hope of altering power relations tirelessly. I narrated individual stories and encounters of women under the conditions defined by overlapping regimes of power – both those who dedicate themselves to 'open the other's eyes' and those who want to be better like two mirrors facing each other.

I trust various critical readers of earlier versions of these pages that I gave a just account of what I have seen and heard from people who generously allowed me into their lives and accepted to be my mirror. Within the last ten years since I conducted my research in Tigris, not only me as a researcher and Turkey as the country of my focus but the whole world has gone through intense phases and experienced serious challenges from wars to pandemics and disasters. During all this time, women's empowerment has been a very relevant topic, and projects aiming to achieve it have been welcomed by international donors in almost all fields despite the criticisms of empty gestures, as I presented in this book with various examples. As I come to the end of this adventure for myself, there is only one thing I trust, and that is change – and, of course, the ability of women to turn even the most ridiculous things into something useful and beautiful.

Notes

Preface

1 From the line of the poem 'The Probability of Being Able to Live' (Erdoğan 1996).
2 The armed conflict continued in the region after 2015 in different forms, and the state of emergency resumed.
3 Turkey also accepted the optional protocol in 2002.
4 This webpage is no longer active. Since I started this research, the GAP Regional Development Administration (GAP RDA) has renewed its website many times and some of the texts has been changed.

Introduction

1 Other major groups were children and youth, indigenous people, NGOs, local authorities, workers and trade unions, business and industry, scientific and technological community and farmers. In the report that Turkey prepared as a follow up in 1997 only the women's section was filled, among other major groups.
2 I am aware of the discussion on the rhetoric of systematic discrimination against Kurds in Turkey on alternatives like 'Turkish question'. My rhetorical choice follows the existing literature on the topic.
3 Among many incidents of assaults, the most striking story is the murder of a 21-year-old man named Sedat Akbaş. According to news reports, Akbaş was murdered by six members of the Grey Wolves, a youth organization of the far-right nationalist party National Action Party, because he was talking on the phone in Kurdish (*Evrensel* 2015b). After a two-year-long trial, the murderers got a remission for good conduct and were released in 2017 (Dihaber 2017).
4 I mainly refer to scholarship in higher education institutes in Turkey but acknowledge exceptional critical scholars, like İsmail Beşikçi.
5 Preventing smaller parties from being represented in the parliament, the 10 per cent threshold was introduced after the coup d'etat took place on 12 September 1980. With the amendment in the election law in March 2023, the election threshold was lowered to 7 percent.
6 Both these attacks are still under investigation.

1 Second Home

1 The Kamer Foundation claims to be a centre for women in earlier versions of its name, which is *Kadın-Merkezi* (Women's Centre). I omit Kamer in this chapter where I discuss state ideology, simply because Kamer is not a state-sponsored organization.

2 For Ayşe Saktanber this dichotomy is debatable because Republican reforms did not reject gender roles in the private sphere, and they continued to be based on Islamic religious life. See Saktanber 2002.

3 The Dersim uprising took place in 1937–8 and was suppressed by the military action of the Turkish state, which claimed thousands of lives. The Dersim massacre, also referred to as genocide, is a taboo topic in Turkish politics. See van Bruinessen 1994; Ayata and Hakyemez, 2013.

4 Kurdish women's movement keeps challenging feminisms in Turkey and worldwide. For a discussion, see Al-Ali and Käser 2020, and its repercussions.

5 Other partner organizations were the International Labour Organization, UNICEF, the AnaKültür Cooperative (Turkish Children's Rights Coalition for General Coordination), the Izmir Turkish Women's Council, the Mother Child Education Foundation and the Turkish Family Health and Planning Foundation.

6 The first phase of the cooperation between the GAP RDA and the UNDP, 'The GAP Sustainable Development Program' (TUR 95 004) ended in 2003 (1996–2003). In 2004, a new project entitled the 'Reduction of Socioeconomic Differences in the GAP Region – GAP Phase 2' was started with a narrowed focus and with specific interventions (2004–8) (UNDP 2006). In 2008, a project called 'Innovations for Women's Empowerment: A Workable Model for Women in Southeast Anatolia' was launched with the financial assistance of the Swedish Development Agency (2008–10). In 2013, ÇATOMs were supported by the 'Innovations for Women's Empowerment in Southeast Anatolia – Phase 2' (2011–15) (UNDP 2012).

7 Among the many examples of social responsibility projects are Eureko Sigorta (2015), 'Çermik ÇATOM Projesi' [Çermik ÇATOM Project], http://www.gar antisigorta.com.tr/tr-tr/content/details/sosyal-sorumluluk-anlayisimiz/topl uma-destek/4877/cermik-ÇATOM-proje-si (accessed 17 November 2015); Payda Platformu (2015), 'Oya Projesi/Payda Projeler' [Oya Project, Payda Projects], http://paydaplatformu.org/projects/9 (accessed 17 November 2015).

8 Two in Adıyaman, three in Batman, seven in Diyarbakır, two in Gaziantep, two in Kilis, eight in Mardin, four in Siirt, eight in Şanlıurfa and six in Şırnak.

9 Social assistance and solidarity foundations (SYDV) are under the control of Ministry of Family and Social Policy and are found throughout Turkey. They provide social assistance in terms of the policies that are produced by central government. The

amount they receive depends on the population size of the province, unemployment rates, its contribution to GDP and development ranking. Each SYDV has its own board of trustees that are responsible for the evaluation of applications for social assistance. For a discussion on the role of SYDV in ethnic identity-based targeting of social assistance towards the Kurdish minority, see Yörük 2012.

10 I preserved the wording and meanings rather than syntax while translating this poem.

11 For a critical assessment, see Donaghy 2017.

12 During my fieldwork, I heard rumours that Aygül Fazlıoğlu had cooperated with the Ministry of Family and Social Policies for the establishment of the ADEMs after she had quit her job at the GAP RDA. It is not clear to where Fazlıoğlu was affiliated with after leaving the GAP.

13 During my visit to the Diyarbakır branch of the Development Foundation of Turkey, I found that the foundation had shrunk dramatically over the previous decade, and there was only one person in charge of the ÇATOMs. Monitoring is mainly based on the registration and calculation of the numbers of participants attending the different courses. The number of beneficiaries, such as people involved in courses and other activities and girls receiving financial support for their education, also indicates the success of the ÇATOMs.

14 There was only one exceptional case of a male director, and this was explained to me by the people in the GAP headquarters as a temporary solution to a shortage of personnel.

15 In Turkish provinces, there are two local authorities: the provincial governor (*vali*) and the mayor (*belediye başkanı*). While the governor is assigned by the central government, the residents of a city elect their mayor. In the administrative system, the province is both the local organization of the central government and the local government unit. Governors are the superiors of all public institutions in a province and are responsible to ministers. A lower level of public administration is the city and is ruled by a district governor (*kaymakam*) assigned by the central government. Both cities and provinces elect mayors. The lowest level of public institution is the neighbourhood, and this is administered by a neighbourhood head (*muhtar*) elected by the people.

2 Alternative opportunities

1 Materials used in this chapter partly appeared in a previously published journal article (Sarıaslan 2020).

2 Although this was a simple statement, it was also a quote (apophthegm) from Kemal Atatürk from a speech he made on 31 January 1923 in Izmir (Cunbur 1997). Later, in November 2014, Prime Minister Erdoğan again made the same statement but with an emphasis on Islam: 'Our religion [Islam] has defined a position for women: motherhood' (Agence France-Presse 2014).

3 Together with Abkhazian, Adyghe and Laz. However, the demand for these elective language courses cannot be met because there is a lack of teachers. There are still obstacles for university language departments that would train teachers for these courses (Göçer 2018).

4 On 28 December 2011, the Turkish Armed Forces killed thirty-four Kurdish civilians near the border between Turkey and Iraq, in a village named Uludere in Turkish and Roboski in Kurdish in the province of Şırnak, Turkey. The civilians, who were smuggling goods, were attacked under the suspicion that they were militants of the PKK. The government spokespersons announced that this was a mistake made by the officials involved. However, the state prosecutor decided not to take the issue to court. For a legal analysis of the case, see Altıparmak 2020.

5 I was surprised to learn that it is very easy in Tigris to receive certificates or diplomas without even attending classes or taking exams for those who have government officials as acquaintances.

6 In Turkey there are no legal restrictions about pregnancies outside marriage. However, according to a new regulation in the registration process for newborn children, the state records whether the child was born outside a marriage or not.

7 Referring to an event that was covered by the mainstream media for weeks and created a public discussion about motherhood (*Milliyet* 2013).

3 Participation without "us"

1 The report prepared by the Union of Southeast Anatolia Region listed the twenty-nine municipalities where trustees were appointed by the central government and sixteen female co-mayors were arrested in the region. HDP Europe, 'Report on Local Governments and Appointment of Trustees to Municipalities' (2016). Two months after the report was released, the central government appointed a trustee to the administration of the Union of Southeast Anatolia Region too (*Evrensel* 2017). A later report notes that trustees were appointed to forty-eight municipalities, seventy-two co-mayors were arrested and thirty-seven elected mayors were imprisoned (HDP 2021).

2 Leaving behind materials used during a project to participants is not permitted, according to the rules of many funding institutions, including the EU.

3   The *muhtar* acts as a source of information and is also a facilitator of benefit distributions. In the brochure for the Ministry of Family and Social Policies, various kinds of social support are listed under the headings: 'family support', 'education support', 'health support', 'disability support' and 'supports for extraordinary situations'. *Muhtars* have been becoming more important political actors since Erdoğan began organizing monthly meetings with them, beginning in October 2015. He has invited them to become close collaborators with the higher administrative bodies in the central government. For additional information, see Çetingüleç 2015.

4   According to the grammar rules of Turkish language, the consonant of the conjunction 'da' does not agree, but in this usage, it became 'ta', and this was a mistake. In web discussions, speakers of Turkish language are particularly attentive to mistakes made in the use of this particular conjugation. In her article on the polarization in the society, literary critic Nurdan Gürbilek (2016) says that because mayors from the ruling party, presidents, scholars and columnists make this mistake, the opinion that the people who rule the country cannot write correctly is widely shared.

5   The organization also puts on academic events and produces scholarly works to introduce new conceptualizations. 'Gender justice' instead of 'gender equality' is one of the concepts that was introduced by the president of the organization Sare Aydın Yılmaz (Güralp 2015). Pınar Ilkkaracan, a woman's rights activist and researcher in Turkey, wrote an article criticizing the KADEM for using this concept and reminded that the term 'gender justice' was first proposed by the Vatican to replace 'gender equality'. In response, Sümeyye Erdoğan, the daughter of the president Erdoğan as well as the co-founder of KADEM, had filed a complaint for 'insult'. However, the case was dismissed (Istanbul Convention Monitoring Platform 2017).

6   The prime minister of the time, Erdoğan, first announced the peace process during a party speech in January 2012. He said, 'We took this path saying that mothers shouldn't cry and that mothers have neither ideology nor a political position' (Ak Parti 2012a). Other politicians used the same phrase to support or oppose Erdoğan's position.

7   For example, in one corner of the large meeting room, young women wearing headscarves were laughing at the cartoons on the wall that illustrated the systematic discrimination that veiled women experience in Turkey. In the other corner of the room, many other women were looking at this crowd and talking about the same cartoons in a different way: 'They should stop assuming that everybody is Sunni Muslim in this country'.

8   The commission is 'the principal global intergovernmental body exclusively
    dedicated to the promotion of gender equality and the empowerment of women'
    (UN Women n.d.).

4 Streaming Mainstreaming

1   Although the political system in Turkey changed after the 2017 Constitutional
    Referendum, and an executive presidency replaced the parliamentary system, the
    Parliament is still in charge of making laws. For a discussion of the constitutional
    change process, see Esen and Gümüşçü 2017.
2   The emergency barring order is one of the most important novelties of the
    convention intended to underline the responsibility of the state in preventing
    domestic violence. See Logar and Niemi 2017. Also, According to Law No. 6284
    on the Protection of Family and Prevention of Violence against Women, which
    refers to the Istanbul Convention, protective measures apply to those who are at
    risk. These measures include providing shelter, financial aid, day-care for children,
    guidance and counselling in a variety of topics as well as police protection. Either
    the civilian authority – meaning the governors or district governors – or a judge
    can give the decisions of protective measures. However, 'in cases where the delay
    is considered to be risky' law enforcement chiefs, that is, the police, can also take
    these measures.
3   Previously in Tigris, a trainer was insulted for being a woman and talking in
    front of a group of men during gender training. The trainer, who did not want to
    make this public, told me the story in a personal conversation. In 2016, a similar
    incident was covered in national media. In Of district of Trabzon, the mayor
    interrupted a female trainer saying, 'We don't need training from female trainers'
    (*Cumhuriyet* 2016).
4   The committee decided to organize coffee house training after I left the field.
5   In 2014, when Erdoğan repeated his views on gender equality, feminist groups
    released public statements criticizing his remarks (Bianet 2014).

5 A Project of One's Own

1   Materials used in this chapter partly appeared in a previously published working
    paper (Sarıaslan 2019). Turkey lifted rules banning women from wearing the
    headscarf in state institutions (except for the judiciary, military and police) in
    2013.

2 This funding body is named SODES. It was first initiated in the southeast Anatolia region in 2008 with the aim of supporting public institutions and local NGOs in the development of human resources in the region. However, it later became very popular and spread to other cities across Turkey. Currently, the source of Social Support Program's (SODES's, or *Sosyal Destek Programı*) funds is the Ministry of Development in the central government. For more information, see sodes.gov.tr.

3 Towards the end of my fieldwork, 'Syrians,' or people running from the civil war in Syria and moving to the outskirts of Tigris, replaced 'Kurds' in this tacit definition of target groups.

4 In other cities, Kamer's local projects enjoyed access to local grant schemes.

5 This was the case in the judgement of youth political organizations after the coup d'état of 12 March 1971.

6 The Turkish Directorate of Religious Affairs is a government body that provides and regulates official Islamic activities in Turkey. All mosques belong to the directorate, and all *imams* in those mosques are life-long civil servants assigned by the central government. After the 1980s, the directorate became the largest transnational network of Islam in Europe as well. For more on this subject, see Sunier and Landman 2014.

7 About the political functions of *muhtars* in Erdoğan administration, please see the footnote number 16 in Chapter 1 and footnote number 3 in Chapter 3.

8 In 2014, when Erdoğan repeated his views on gender equality, feminist groups released public statements criticizing his position (Bianet 2014).

Conclusion

1 Here I refer to the parliamentary oath that Leyla Zana took in Kurdish in 2015. Previously in 1991, Zana had also spoken in Kurdish at her oath-swearing ceremony in the parliament and she received a prison sentence for this act.

Bibliography

Abram, Simone. 2017. 'Contradiction in Contemporary Political Life: Meeting Bureaucracy in Norwegian Municipal Government'. *Journal of the Royal Anthropological Institute* 23 (S1): 27–44. https://doi.org/10.1111/1467-9655.12592.

Abu-Lughod, Lila. 2008. 'Writing against Culture'. In *The Cultural Geography Reader*, edited by Timothy Oakes and Patricia Price, 1st edn, 50–9. London: Routledge.

Abu-Lughod, Lila. 2013. *Do Muslim Women Need Saving?* Cambridge, MA: Harvard University Press.

Acar, Feride, and Gülbanu Altunok. 2013. 'The "Politics of Intimate" at the Intersection of Neo-liberalism and Neo-conservatism in Contemporary Turkey'. *Women's Studies International Forum* 41 (1): 14–23. https://doi.org/10.1016/j.wsif.2012.10.001.

Adaman, Fikret, and Bengi Akbulut. 2021. 'Erdoğan's Three-Pillared Neoliberalism: Authoritarianism, Populism and Developmentalism'. *Geoforum* 124 (August): 279–89. https://doi.org/10.1016/j.geoforum.2019.12.013.

Agence France-Presse. 2014. 'Recep Tayyip Erdoğan: "Women Not Equal to Men"'. *The Guardian*, 24 November. http://www.theguardian.com/world/2014/nov/24/turkeys-president-recep-tayyip-erdogan-women-not-equal-men (accessed 8 March 2023).

Aile ve Sosyal Güvenlik Bakanlığı [Ministry of Family and Social Security]. (n.d.). 'Misyon ve Vizyonumuz [Mission and Vision]'. (Aile ve Sosyal Güvenlik Bakanlığı). https://www.aile.gov.tr/bakanlik/hakkinda/misyon-ve-vizyonumuz (accessed 31 October 2021).

Aile ve Sosyal Politikalar Bakanlığı [Ministry of Family and Social Policies]. 2016. '"Terör Operasyonlarının Sürdüğü Şehirlerde Psikolojik Restorasyon ve Rehabilitasyon Çalışmalarımızı Bütün Hızımızla Sürdürmekteyiz" [We Carry Out Psychological Restoration and Rehabilitation Work in Cities Where Counter-Terrorism Operations Are Going On]'. http://www.aile.gov.tr/haberler/teror-operasyonlarinin-surdugu-sehirlerde-psikolojik-restorasyon-ve-rehabilitasyon-calismalarimizi-butun-hizimizla-surdurmekteyiz (accessed 9 November 2021).

Ak Parti. 2012a. '24 Ocak Tarihli TBMM Grup Toplantısı Konuşması [24 January 2012 Party Group Meeting Speech]', http://www.akparti.org.tr/site/video/19319/basbakan-erdogan-grup-toplantisi-konusmasi (accessed 20 December 2017).

Ak Parti. 2012b. ' "Doğu ve Güneydoğu Anadolu Bölgesi'nde Kadın Sorunları ve Çözüm Önerileri" Konulu Çalıştay Raporu [Report of the Workshop "Woman's Problems and Their Solutions in East and Southeast Anatolia"]'. https://www.akparti.org.tr/upload/documents/10.doc (accessed 9 November 2021).

Akcan, Esra. 2009. 'Civilizing Housewives versus Participatory Users: Margarete Schütte Lihotzky in the Employ of the Turkish Nation State'. In *Cold War Kitchen: Americanization, Technology and European Users*, edited by Ruth Oldenziel and Karin Zachman, 185–207. Cambridge: MIT Press.

Akdoğan, Yalçın. 2004. *Ak Parti ve Muhafazakar Demokrasi [AK Party and Conservative Democracy]*. Istanbul: Alfa Yayıncılık.

Akıncı, Zeynep S., Arda Bilgen, Antònia Casellas and Joost Jongerden. 2020. 'Development through Design: Knowledge, Power, and Absences in the Making of Southeastern Turkey'. *Geoforum* 114 (August): 181–8. https://doi.org/10.1016/j.geoforum.2020.06.011.

Akşit, Bahattin. 1993. 'GAP Sulama Sistemlerinin İşletme-Bakım Yönetimi Projesi Sosyo-Ekonomik Çalışma [Irrigation and Project Design or Irrigation Methods Project: A Socioeconomic Survey]'. Ankara: GAP Bölge Kalkınma İdaresi Başkanlığı.

Akşit, Bahattin. 1994. 'GAP Bölgesi Nüfus Hareketleri Araştırması' [GAP Region Population Movement Survey]'. Ankara: GAP Bölge Kalkınma İdaresi Başkanlığı.

Akşit, Elif Ekin. 2011. 'Harem Education and Heterotopic Imagination'. *Gender and Education* 23 (3): 299–311. https://doi.org/10.1080/09540253.2010.491788.

Akyüz, Selin, Feyda Sayan-Cengiz, Aslı Çırakman and Dilek Cindoğlu. 2019. 'Married to Anatolian Tigers: Business Masculinities, Relationalities, and Limits to Empowerment'. *Turkish Studies* 20 (2): 297–321. https://doi.org/10.1080/14683849.2018.1524710.

Al-Ali, Nadje, and Isabel Käser. 2020. 'Beyond Feminism? Jineolojî and the Kurdish Women's Freedom Movement'. *Politics and Gender* 18 (1): 1–32. https://doi.org/10.1017/S1743923X20000501.

Alkan, Hilal. 2018. 'The Sexual Politics of War: Reading the Kurdish Conflict through Images of Women'. *Les Cahiers Du CEDREF. Centre d'enseignement, d'études et de Recherches Pour Les Études Féministes*, 22 (October): 68–92.

Alnıaçık, Ayşe, Özlem Altan-Olcay, Ceren Deniz and Fatoş Gökşen. 2017. 'Gender Policy Architecture in Turkey: Localizing Transnational Discourses of Women's Employment'. *Social Politics: International Studies in Gender, State and Society* 24 (3): 298–323. https://doi.org/10.1093/sp/jxx007.

Altan-Olcay, Özlem. 2014. 'Entrepreneurial Subjectivities and Gendered Complexities: Neoliberal Citizenship in Turkey'. *Feminist Economics* 20 (4): 235–59. https://doi.org/10.1080/13545701.2014.950978.

Altan-Olcay, Özlem. 2016. 'The Entrepreneurial Woman in Development Programs: Thinking through Class Differences'. *Social Politics: International Studies in Gender, State and Society* 23 (3): 389–414. https://doi.org/10.1093/sp/jxv013.

Altınay, Ayşe Gül. 2004. *The Myth of the Military-Nation: Militarism, Gender, and Education in Turkey*. New York: Palgrave Macmillan.

Altiparmak, Kerem. 2020. 'Roboski and Procedural Rules: How the Truth about a Massacre Was Buried in the Pages of History'. *New Journal of European Criminal Law* 11 (4): 489–503. https://doi.org/10.1177/2032284420913950.

Arat, Yeşim. 2000. 'From Emancipation to Liberation: The Changing Role of Women in Turkey's Public Realm'. *Journal of International Affairs* 54 (1): 107–23.

Arat, Yeşim. 2010. 'Religion, Politics and Gender Equality in Turkey: Implications of a Democratic Paradox?' *Third World Quarterly* 31 (6): 869–84. https://doi.org/10.1080/01436597.2010.502712.

Arat, Yeşim, and Ayşe Gül Altınay. 2015. 'KAMER, a Women's Center and an Experiment in Cultivating Cosmopolitan Norms'. *Women's Studies International Forum* 49 (March): 12–19. https://doi.org/10.1016/j.wsif.2015.01.001.

Arat, Zehra. 2010. 'Turkish Women and the Republican Construction of Tradition'. In *Reconstructing Gender in Middle East: Tradition, Identity, and Power*, edited by Balaghi Shiva, 57–80. New York: Columbia University Press.

Aretxaga, Begoña. 1997. *Shattering Silence: Women, Nationalism, and Political Subjectivity in Northern Ireland*. Princeton, NJ: Princeton University Press.

Aslan Akman, Canan. 2013. 'Islamic Women's Ordeal with the New Face(s) of Patriarchy in Power: Divergence or Convergence over Expanding Women's Citizenship'. In *Gendered Identities: Criticizing Patriarchy in Turkey*, edited by Rasim Özgür Dönmez and Fazilet Ahu Özmen, 113–45. Lanham: Lexington Books.

Ayata, Bilgin. 2011. 'Kurdish Transnational Politics and Turkey's Changing Kurdish Policy: The Journey of Kurdish Broadcasting from Europe to Turkey'. *Journal of Contemporary European Studies* 19 (4): 523–33. https://doi.org/10.1080/14782804.2011.639988.

Ayata, Bilgin, and Serra Hakyemez. 2013. 'The AKP's Engagement with Turkey's Past Crimes: An Analysis of PM Erdoğan's "Dersim Apology"'. *Dialectical Anthropology* 37 (1): 131–43. https://doi.org/10.1007/s10624-013-9304-3.

Aydın, F. Çiğdem, Kamile Yılmaz Arsoy, Özlem Küçükyılmaz, Selma Acuner, Sunay Karamık, Yasemin Bektaş and Yasemin Öz. 2017. *Birleşmiş Milletler Kadının Statüsü Komisyonu Rehberi ve 60. Oturuma İlişkin Notlar [Guidelines of the*

*United Nations Commission on the Status of Women and Notes on the 60th
Session]*. Istanbul: Kadın Adayları Destekleme Derneği (KA.DER). http://ka-der.
org.tr/wp-content/uploads/2020/12/Birlesmis-Milletler-Kadin-Statusu-ve-Komisy
onu-Rehberi.pdf (accessed 8 March 2023).

Aydın, Delal. 2009. ' "Dağ Çiçekleri"Ni Vatandaş Yapmak! [Making Citizens out of
Mountain Flowers]'. *Toplum ve Kuram* 2: 257–61.

Aykut, Ebru. 2011. 'Alternative Claims on Justice and Law: Rural Arson and Poison
Murder in the 19th Century Ottoman Empire'. Unpublished Doctoral Thesis,
Istanbul: Boğaziçi University. http://ata.boun.edu.tr/ebru-aykut-alternative-cla
ims-justice-and-law-rural-arson-and-poison-murder-19th-century-ottoman.

Babül, Elif. 2015. 'The Paradox of Protection: Human Rights, the Masculinist
State, and the Moral Economy of Gratitude in Turkey'. *American Ethnologist* 42
(1): 116–30. https://doi.org/10.1111/amet.12120.

Babül, Elif M. 2017. *Bureaucratic Intimacies: Translating Human Rights in Turkey*.
1st edn. Stanford, CA: Stanford University Press.

Baser, Bahar, Samim Akgönül and Ahmet Erdi Öztürk. 2017. ' "Academics for
Peace" in Turkey: A Case of Criminalising Dissent and Critical Thought via
Counterterrorism Policy'. *Critical Studies on Terrorism* 10 (2): 274–96. https://doi.
org/10.1080/17539153.2017.1326559.

Batliwala, Srilatha. 2010. 'Taking the Power out of Empowerment – an Experiential
Account'. In *Deconstructing Development Discourse: Buzzwords and Fuzzwords*,
edited by Andrea Cornwall and Deborah. Eade, 111–22. Warwickshire: Practical
Action Publishing.

Batliwala, Srilatha. 2014. *Engaging with Empowerment: An Intellectual and
Experiential Journey*. New Delhi: Women Unlimited.

Behar, Ruth. 1997. *The Vulnerable Observer: Anthropology That Breaks Your Heart*.
Boston: Beacon Press.

Belge, Burçin. 2011. 'Kadın Bakanlığı Kaldırıldı, Kadın Örgütleri Öfkeli [Women's
Ministry Was Abolished, Women Organizations Are Angry]'. Bianet – Bağımsız
İletişim Ağı. 8 June. http://www.bianet.org/bianet/kadin/130585-kadin-bakanl
igi-kaldirildi-kadin-orgutleri-ofkeli.

Belge, Ceren. 2012. *Ohal'de Feminizm: Nebahat Akkoç Anlatiyor* [Feminism in the
State of Emergency: Nebahatt Akkoç Narrates]. Ankara: Ayizi Kitap.

Bernal, Victoria, and Inderpal Grewal. 2014. 'The NGO Form: Feminist
Struggles, States, and Neoliberalism'. In *Theorizing NGOs: States, Feminisms,
and Neoliberalism*, edited by Victoria Bernal and Inderpal Grewal, 1–18.
Durham: Duke University Press Books.

Berry, Marie E. 2015. 'When "Bright Futures" Fade: Paradoxes of Women's Empowerment in Rwanda'. *Signs: Journal of Women in Culture and Society* 41 (1): 1–27. https://doi.org/10.1086/681899.

Berry, Maya J., Claudia Chávez Argüelles, Shanya Cordis, Sarah Ihmoud and Elizabeth Velásquez Estrada. 2017. 'Toward a Fugitive Anthropology: Gender, Race, and Violence in the Field'. *Cultural Anthropology* 32 (4): 537–65. https://doi.org/10.14506/ca32.4.05.

Beşpınar, F. Umut. 2010. 'Questioning Agency and Empowerment: Women's Work-Related Strategies and Social Class in Urban Turkey'. *Women's Studies International Forum* 33 (6): 523–32. https://doi.org/10.1016/j.wsif.2010.09.003.

Bianet. 2013. 'Ve Başörtülü Vekiller Mecliste [Headscarved Parliamentarians Are in the Parliament]'. 31 October. https://www.bianet.org/bianet/siyaset/150 953-ve-basortulu-vekiller-mecliste (accessed 8 March 2023).

Bianet. 2014. 'Kadin ve LGBTI Örgütleri: Fıtrat Değil Anayasa: Kadınlar Ve Erkekler Eşit Haklara Sahiptir [Women and LGBTI Organizations: Constitution, Not Fitrat: Women and Men Have Equal Rights]'. 27 November. https://www.bianet. org/bianet/kadin/160287-fitrat-degil-anayasa-kadinlar-ve-erkekler-esit-haklara-sahiptir (accessed 8 March 2023).

Bianet. 2015. '2 Civilians Killed in Dargeçit'. 24 December. http://www.bianet. org/english/human-rights/170473-2-civilians-killed-in-dargecit (accessed 8 March 2023).

Bianet. 2016. 'TİHV: 7 İl, 22 İlçedeki 63 Sokağa Çıkma Yasağında 310 Sivil Öldü [HRFT: 310 Civilians Died in 63 Curfews in 7 Provinces and 22 Districts]'. 22 March. https://www.bianet.org/bianet/toplum/173228-tihv-7-il-22-ilcedeki-63-sokaga-cikma-yasaginda-310-sivil-oldu (accessed 8 March 2023).

Bilgen, Arda. 2019. 'The Southeastern Anatolia Project (GAP) in Turkey: An Alternative Perspective on the Major Rationales of GAP'. *Journal of Balkan and Near Eastern Studies* 21 (5): 532–52. https://doi.org/10.1080/19448 953.2018.1506287.

Billaud, Julie. 2015. *Kabul Carnival: Gender Politics in Postwar Afghanistan.* Philadelphia: University of Pennsylvania Press.

Biner, Zerrin Özlem. 2007. 'Retrieving the Dignity of a Cosmopolitan City: Contested Perspectives on Rights, Culture and Ethnicity in Mardin'. *New Perspectives on Turkey,* 37: 31. https://doi.org/10.1017/S0896634600004726.

Biner, Zerrin Özlem. 2020. *States of Dispossession.* Philadelphia: University of Pennsylvania Press. https://doi.org/10.9783/9780812296594.

Bora, Aksu. 2005. *Kadınların Sınıfı: Ücretli Ev Emeği ve Kadın Öznelliğinin İnşası*
    [Women's Class: Paid Domestic Labour and Construction of Subjectivity].
    Istanbul: İletişim Yayıncılık.

Bora, Aksu. 2006. 'Eyleme Güvenmek [Trusting to Action]'. Istanbul: Amargi.

Bora, Aksu, and Koray Çalışkan. 2007. 'What Is Under a Headscarf? Neo-Islamist vs.
    Kemalist Conservatism in Turkey'. *The Arab Studies Journal* 15 (2): 140–55.

Boserup, Ester. 1970. *Woman's Role in Economic Development.* 1st edn. Sterling,
    VA: Routledge.

Bozdoğan, Sibel. 2001. *Modernism and Nation Building: Turkish Architectural
    Culture in the Early Republic.* Washington, DC: University of Washington Press.

Brown, Hannah, Adam Reed and Thomas Yarrow. 2017. 'Introduction: Towards
    an Ethnography of Meeting'. *Journal of the Royal Anthropological Institute* 23
    (S1): 10–26.

Bruinessen, Martin M. van. 1994. 'Genocide in Kurdistan? The Suppression of the
    Dersim Rebellion in Turkey (1937–8) and the Chemical War against the Iraqi
    Kurds (1988)'. In *Conceptual and Historical Dimensions of Genocide*, edited by
    George J. Andreopoulos, 141–70. Pennsylvania: University of Pennsylvania Press.

Butler, Judith, Zeynep Gambetti and Leticia Sabsay. 2016. *Vulnerability in Resistance.*
    Durham: Duke University Press.

Çağlayan, Handan. 2013. 'Anne Çocuk İlişkisi Üzerine Milli Politika Üretmek
    [Producing National Policy on Mother-Child Relation]'. Bianet - Bağımsız İletişim
    Ağı. 23 February. https://www.bianet.org/biamag/kadin/144607-anne-cocuk-ilisk
    isi-uzerine-milli-politika-uretmek (accessed 8 March 2023).

Çağlayan, Handan. 2019. *Women in the Kurdish Movement: Mothers, Comrades,
    Goddesses.* Translated by Simten Coşar. 1st ed. 2020 edn. New York: Palgrave
    Macmillan.

Can, Başak. 2019. 'Caring for Solidarity? The Intimate Politics of Grandmother
    Childcare and Neoliberal Conservatism in Urban Turkey'. *New Perspectives on
    Turkey* 60 (May): 85–107. https://doi.org/10.1017/npt.2019.4.

Çarkoğlu, Ali, and Mine Eder. 2005. 'Developmentalism à La Turca: The Southeast
    Anatolia Development Project (GAP)'. In *Environmentalism in Turkey: Between
    Democracy and Development*, edited by Fikret Adaman and Murat Arsel, 238–49.
    London: Ashtange.

Çavdar, Gamze, and Yavuz Yaşar. 2019. *Women in Turkey: Silent Consensus in the
    Age of Neoliberalism and Islamic Conservatism.* 1st edn. London: Routledge.

Çayır, Kenan. 2014. '*Biz*' Kimiz? *Ders Kitaplarında Kimlik, Yurttaşlık, Haklar* [Who
    'We' Are? Identity, Citizenship and Rights in Schoolbooks]. Istanbul: Tarih Vakfı
    Yayınları.

Çaylı, Eray. 2016. 'Bear Witness: Embedded Coverage of Turkey's Urban Warfare and the Demarcation of Sovereignty against a Dynamic Exterior'. *Theory and Event* 19 (1). https://muse.jhu.edu/article/610225.

CBC Radio. 2015. '"Women Are Builders of Civil Society": A Speech by the Late Fatima Mernissi'. 30 November. http://www.cbc.ca/radio/asithappens/as-it-happ ens-monday-edition-1.3343703/women-are-builders-of-civil-society-a-spe ech-by-the-late-fatima-mernissi-1.3343714.

Çelebi, Elifcan. 2022. 'How Do Women's GONGOs Influence Policymaking Processes in Turkey?' *Journal of Civil Society* 18 (3): 326–48. https://doi.org/10.1080/174486 89.2022.2125417.

Çelik, Kezban, and Demet Lüküslü. 2010. 'Spotlighting a Silent Category of Young Females: The Life Experiences of "House Girls" in Turkey'. *Youth and Society* 44 (1): 28–48. https://doi.org/10.1177/0044118X10391636.

Çelik Levin, Yasemin. 2007. 'The Effect of CEDAW on Women's Rights'. In *Human Rights in Turkey*, edited by Zehra F. Kabasakal Arat, 202–14. Philadelphia: University of Pennsylvania Press. http://www.jstor.org/stable/j.ctt3fhr4w.16.

Çetingüleç, Tülay. 2015. 'Orwell's 1984 Comes to Life in Erdogan's 2015 Turkey'. Al-Monitor. 24 August. https://www.al-monitor.com/pulse/originals/2015/08/tur key-erdogan-intelligence-support-from-headmen.html.

Çeviker Gürakar, Esra. 2016. *Politics of Favoritism in Public Procurement*. New York: Palgrave Macmillan. http://www.palgrave.com/us/book/9781137592750.

Çınar, Kürşat, Selin Akyüz, Meral Uğur-Çınar and Emine Öncüler-Yayalar. 2021. 'Faces and Phases of Women's Empowerment: The Case of Women's Cooperatives in Turkey'. *Social Politics: International Studies in Gender, State & Society* 28 (3): 778–805. https://doi.org/10.1093/sp/jxz032.

Cindoğlu, Dilek, and Didem Ünal. 2017. 'Gender and Sexuality in the Authoritarian Discursive Strategies of "New Turkey"'. *European Journal of Women's Studies* 24 (1): 39–54.

Cindoğlu, Dilek, and Gizem Zencirci. 2008. 'The Headscarf in Turkey in the Public and State Spheres'. *Middle Eastern Studies* 44 (5): 791–806. https://doi. org/10.1080/00263200802285187.

Connell, Raewyn. 1987. *Gender and Power: Society, the Person, and Sexual Politics*. Cambridge, UK: Polity Press in association with B. Blackwell.

Cornwall, Andrea, Elizabeth Harrison and Ann Whitehead. 2007. 'Gender Myths and Feminist Fables: The Struggle for Interpretive Power in Gender and Development'. *Development and Change* 38 (1): 1–20. https://doi.org/10.1111/j.1467-7660.200 7.00400.x.

Cornwall, Andrea, and Jenny Edwards. 2015. 'Introduction: Beijing+20 – Where Now for Gender Equality?' *IDS Bulletin* 46 (4): 1–8. https://doi.org/10.1111/1759-5436.12149.

Cornwall, Andrea, and Karen Brock. 2005. 'What Do Buzzwords Do for Development Policy? A Critical Look at "Participation", "Empowerment" and "Poverty Reduction"'. *Third World Quarterly* 26 (7): 1043–60. https://doi.org/10.1080/01436590500235603.

Coşar, Simten, and İnci Özkan-Kerestecioğlu. 2013. 'Feminizmin Neoliberalizmle İmtihanı [Feminism's Test with Neoliberalism]'. *Doğu-Batı* 64: 21–36.

Coşar, Simten, and Metin Yeğenoğlu. 2011. 'New Grounds for Patriarchy in Turkey? Gender Policy in the Age of AKP'. *South European Society and Politics* 16 (4): 555–73. https://doi.org/10.1080/13608746.2011.571919.

Costa, Elisabetta. 2016. *Social Media in Southeast Turkey*. London: UCL Press. https://doi.org/10.14324/111.9781910634547.

Crewe, Emma, and Richard Axelby. 2012. *Anthropology and Development: Culture, Morality and Politics in a Globalised World*. Cambridge: Cambridge University Press.

Cronin-Furman, Kate, Nimmi Gowrinathan and Rafia Zakaria. 2017. 'Emissaries of Empowerment'. New York: Colin Powell School for Civic and Public Leadership, The City College of New York.

Cumhuriyet. 2016. ' "Kadından Alacağımız Eğitime Ihtiyacımız Yok" [We Don't Need Training from Women]'. 3 April. http://www.cumhuriyet.com.tr/haber/siyaset/509377/_Kadindan_alacagimiz_egitime_ihtiyacimiz_yok_.html (accessed 9 November 2021).

Cumhuriyet. 2017. 'Erdoğan'ın Başdanışmanı Özlem Zengin: "Fikirlerim Hep Bulaşık Yıkarken Aklıma Gelir" [Erdoğan's Cheifadvisor Özlem Zengin: "Good Ideas Come to My Mind When I Do the Dishes"]'. 26 September. http://www.cumhuriyet.com.tr/haber/turkiye/832186/Erdogan_in_basdanismani_Ozlem_Zengin___Fikirlerim_hep_bulasik_yikarken_aklima_gelir_.html (accessed 9 November 2021).

Cunbur, Müjgan. 1997. 'Atatürk ve Kadın Eğitimi [Atatürk and Woman's Education]'. *Atatürk ve Kadın Eğitimi [Atatürk and Woman's Education]* 8 (23): 259–72.

Dağtaş, Seçil. 2018. 'Nationalism, Displacement, and Ethnoreligious Differentiation in Turkey's Southern Borderlands'. *Dialectical Anthropology* 42 (4): 359–72. https://doi.org/10.1007/s10624-017-9481-6.

Dedeoğlu, Saniye, and Adem Yavuz Elveren. 2012. 'Introduction: Gender, Society and Welfare State in Turkey'. In *Gender and Society in Turkey: The Impact of Neoliberal Policies, Political Islam and EU Accession*, edited by Saniye Dedeoğlu and Adem Yavuz Elveren, 3–14. London: I. B. Tauris.

Delegation of the European Union to Turkey. 2012. 'Türkiye'nin Az Gelişmiş Bölgelerinde Kadınların ve Kadın STK'larının Güçlendirilmesi - Hibe Programı Açılış Töreni [Empowerment of Women and Women's CSOs in Less Developed Regions of Turkey – Grant Scheme Opening Ceremony]'. 12 May. http://avrupa. info.tr/tr/bilgi-kaynaklari/haber-arsivi/news-single-view/article/tuerkiyenin-az-gelismis-boelgelerinde-kadinlarin-ve-kadin-stklarinin-gueclendirilmesi-h.html (accessed 25 January 2015).

Demiralp, Seda. 2012. 'White Turks, Black Turks? Faultlines beyond Islamism versus Secularism'. *Third World Quarterly* 33 (3): 511–24. https://doi.org/10.1080/01436 597.2012.657487.

DiAngelo, Robin. 2018. *White Fragility: Why It's so Hard for White People to Talk About Racism*. Reprint edition. Boston: Beacon Press.

Dihaber. 2017. 'Sedat Akbaş Davasında "Indirimli" Ceza' ['Good Conduct Remission' in Sedat Akbaş's Trial]. http://www.dihaber.net/TUM-HABERLER/content/ view/6939 (accessed 12 December 2017).

Dihaber. 2017. 'Sedat Akbaş Davasında "Indirimli" Ceza ["Reduced" Sentence in Sedat Akbas Case]'. 12 December. http://www.dihaber.net/TUM-HABERLER/ content/view/6939 (accessed 8 March 2019).

Diner, Cağla, and Şule Toktaş. 2010. 'Waves of Feminism in Turkey: Kemalist, Islamist and Kurdish Women's Movements in an Era of Globalization'. *Journal of Balkan and Near Eastern Studies* 12 (1): 41–57. https://doi.org/10.1080/19448950903507388.

Doğan, Sevinç. 2016. *Mahalledeki AKP: Parti İşleyişi, Taban Mobilizasyonu ve Siyasal Yabancılasma* [AKP in the Neighbourhood: Party Structure, Grassroots Mobilization, and Political Alienation]. Istanbul: İletişim Yayıncılık.

Doğanay, Ülkü. 2007. 'AKP'nin Demokrasi Söylemi ve Muhafazakarlık: Muhafazakar Demokrasi ve Eleştirel Bir Bakış'. *Ankara Üniversitesi SBF Dergisi* 62 (01): 65–88. https://doi.org/10.1501/SBFder_0000002009.

Donaghy, Ryan J. 2017. 'Pedagogies of Neopatriarchy: Critical Reflections on Occupational Courses and Women's Economic Mobility in Turkey'. *Women's Studies International Forum* 61 (March): 28–37. https://doi.org/10.1016/j.wsif.2017.01.001.

Düzel, Esin. 2018. 'Fragile Goddesses: Moral Subjectivity and Militarized Agencies in Female Guerrilla Diaries and Memoirs'. *International Feminist Journal of Politics* 20 (2): 137–52. https://doi.org/10.1080/14616742.2017.1419823.

Düzkan, Ayşe. 1998. 'Devletin Eli Uzanıyor Mu Kalkıyor Mu? [State's Hand, Reaching or Threatens?]'. *Pazartesi*, 37: 2–3.

Elyachar, Julia. 2005. *Markets of Dispossession: NGOs, Economic Development, and the State in Cairo*. Durham: Duke University Press Books.

Ercan, Harun. 2019. 'Is Hope More Precious Than Victory?' *South Atlantic Quarterly* 118 (1): 111–27. https://doi.org/10.1215/00382876-7281636.

Erdoğan, Aslı. 2017. Asli Erdogan: 'It's My Country, Too'. Interview by Ceyda Nurtsch. *Deutsche Welle*. http://www.dw.com/en/asli-erdogan-its-my-country-too/a-39766882.

Erdoğan, Yılmaz. 1996. *Kayıp Kentin Yakışıklısı [Handsome of the Lost City]*. Istanbul: Sel Yayıncılık.

Erensü, Sinan. 2018. 'Powering Neoliberalization: Energy and Politics in the Making of a New Turkey'. *Energy Research and Social Science* 41 (July): 148–57. https://doi.org/10.1016/j.erss.2018.04.037.

Ertürk, Yakın. 2007. 'UN Human Rights Council: Addendum to the Report of the Special Rapporteur on Violence against Women, Its Causes and Consequences, Mission to Turkey. A/HRC/4/34/Add.2.' UN Human Rights Council. http://www.refworld.org/docid/45fea1812.html.

Ertürk, Yakin. 2012. 'Culture versus Rights Dualism: A Myth or a Reality?' *Development* 55 (3): 273–6. https://doi.org/10.1057/dev.2012.25.

Escobar, Arturo. 1988. 'Power and Visibility: Development and the Invention and Management of the Third World'. *Cultural Anthropology* 3 (4): 428–43.

Esen, Berk, and Şebnem Gümüşçü. 2017. 'A Small Yes for Presidentialism: The Turkish Constitutional Referendum of April 2017'. *South European Society and Politics* 22 (3): 303–26. https://doi.org/10.1080/13608746.2017.1384341.

Eureko Sigorta. 2015. 'Çermik ÇATOM Projesi [Çermik ÇATOM Project]'. http://www.garantisigorta.com.tr/tr-tr/content/details/sosyal-sorumluluk-anlayisimiz/topluma-destek/4877/cermik-catom-projesi (accessed 2 December 2015).

European Commission. 2004. 'Recommendation of the European Commission on Turkey's Progress towards Accession. Communication from the Commission to the Council and the European Parliament'. https://eur-lex.europa.eu/legal-content/EN/TXT/?uri=CELEX%3A52004DC0656 (accessed 8 March 2023).

European Commission. n.d. 'Standard Summary Project Fiche IPA Decentralised National Programmes Project Number: TR 07 01 04: Empowerment of Women and Women NGOs in the Least Developed Regions of Turkey'. https://ec.europa.eu/neighbourhood-enlargement/sites/near/files/pdf/turkey/ipa/tr_07_01_04_empowerment_of_women_en.pdf (accessed 30 April 2017).

European Institute for Gender Equality. n.d. 'Gender Mainstreaming'. http://eige.europa.eu/gender-mainstreaming.

Evren, Erdem. 2022. *Bulldozer Capitalism: Accumulation, Ruination, and Dispossession in Northeastern Turkey*. New York: Berghahn Books.

Evrensel. 2015a. 'İlk Fırsat Eşitliği Erkeklere Oldu! [Eqality in Opportunity After Men]'. 1 December. http://www.evrensel.net/haber/266461/ilk-firsat-esitligi-erkekl ere-oldu.

Evrensel. 2015b. ' "Telefonda Kürtçe Konuşuyor" Diye Öldürüldü' [Murdered for 'Talking in Kurdish on the Phone']. 7 September. https://www.evrensel. net/haber/260129/telefonda-kurtce-konusuyor-diye-olduruldu (accessed 12 September 2017).

Evrensel. 2017. 'Güneydoğu Anadolu Belediyeler Birliği'ne de Kayyım Atandı' [Trustee Appointed to Union of Southeastern Anatolia Region Municipalities]. 27 January 2017. https://www.evrensel.net/haber/305786/guneydogu-anadolu-bele diyeler-birligine-de-kayyim-atandi (accessed 6 January 2018).

Farris, Sara R. 2017. *In the Name of Women's Rights: The Rise of Femonationalism*. Durham: Duke University Press.

Fazlıoğlu, Aygül. n.d. 'Women Writing Their Own Stories in Development: Biographical Examples from South-Eastern Anatolia Region, Turkey'. http:// www.gewamed.net/share/img_documents/51_gender-bari.pdf (accessed 15 December 2012).

Fazlıoğlu, Aygül, Nilüfer Dersan, Ahmet Katıksız, Emine Eken, Gülpınar Er, Enver Cerit and Gönül Sulargil. 2010. *Güneydoğu'nun Işığı Kadınlar: Öyküleri ve Fotoğrafları İle Güneydoğu Anadolu Kadını'nın Varoluşu [Women, the Light of the Southeast: The Existence of Southeastern Anatolian Women with Stories and Photographs]*. Istanbul: T.C. Başbakanlık GAP Bölge Kalkınma İdaresi, UNDP.

Feldman, Ilana, and Miriam Ticktin. 2010. *In the Name of Humanity: The Government of Threat and Care*. Durham: Duke University Press.

Ferguson, James. 1990. *The Anti-Politics Machine: 'Development,' Depoliticization, and Bureaucratic Power in Lesotho*. Ann Arbor: University of Minnesota Press.

Ferguson, James. 1997. 'Anthropology and Its Evil Twin: "Development" in the Constitution of a Discipline'. In *International Development and the Social Sciences. Essays on the History and Politics of Knowledge*, edited by Frederick Cooper and Randall Packard, 150–75. Berkeley: University of California Press.

Ferguson, James, and Akhil Gupta. 2005. 'Spatializing States: Toward an Ethnography of Neoliberal Governmentality'. In *Anthropologies of Modernity*, edited by Jonathan Xavier Inda, 105–31. Malden, MA: Blackwell Publishing. https://doi. org/10.1002/9780470775875.ch4.

Freire, Paulo. 2000. *Pedagogy of the Oppressed*. 30th Anniversary edn. New York: Continuum.

Friedan, Betty. 2013. *The Feminine Mystique*. 50th anniversary edn. New York: W.W. Norton.

GAP. 2014a. *ÇATOM Tanıtım Filmi [Promotional Film]*. https://www.youtube. com/watch?v=wQtAJdwNKrQ&feature=youtube_gdata_player (accessed 2 December 2014).

GAP. 2014b. 'History of GAP'. 27 April. http://www.gap.gov.tr/about-gap/hist ory-of-gap (accessed 2 December 2014).

GAP ÇATOM. 2004. 'Çok Amaçlı Toplum Merkezleri 2004 Yılı Faaliyet Raporu [Multi-Purpose Community Centres 2004 Annual Activity Report]'. http://www. gapcatom.org/wp-content/uploads/2014/09/2004-Y%C4%B1l%C4%B1-Faaliyet-Raporu.pdf (accessed 8 March 2023).

GAP ÇATOM. 2013. 'Çok Amaçlı Toplum Merkezleri 2013 Yılı Faaliyet Raporu [Multi-Purpose Community Centres 2013 Annual Activity Report]'. http://www. gapcatom.org/en/documents/annual-reports/.

GAP ÇATOM. 2015. 'Çok Amaçlı Toplum Merkezleri 2015 Yılı Faaliyet Raporu [Multi-Purpose Community Centres 2015 Annual Activity Report]'. http://www. gapcatom.org/wp-content/uploads/2016/05/2015Yili-FaaliyetRaporu-CATOM. pdf (accessed 8 March 2023).

GAP ÇATOM. 2017. 'GAP ÇATOM | Multi-Purpose Community Centres – The Objective of the Project'. 30 November. http://www.gapcatom.org/en/about-us/ the-objective-of-the-project/ (accessed 8 March 2023).

GAP RDA. n.d. 'Multi-Purpose Community Centers (ÇATOM)'. http://www.gap.gov. tr/en/multi-purpose-community-centers-%C3%87ATOMs-page-9.html (accessed 1 November 2021).

Gardner, Katy, and David Lewis. 2015. *Anthropology and Development: Challenges for the Twenty-First Century*. London: Pluto Press.

Garland, David. 2014. 'What Is a "History of the Present"? On Foucault's Genealogies and Their Critical Preconditions'. *Punishment and Society* 16 (4): 365–84. https:// doi.org/10.1177/1462474514541711.

General Directorate on the Status of Women. 2008. 'Toplumsal Cinsiyet Eşitliği Ulusal Eylem Planı 2008–2013 [The National Action Plan Gender Equality 2008–2013]'. Ankara: The Republic of Turkey General Directorate on the Status of Women. http://www.huksam.hacettepe.edu.tr/English/Files/NAP_GE.pdf (accessed 18 May 2015).

Gezici, Ferhan, and Geoffrey J. D. Hewings. 2004. 'Regional Convergence and the Economic Performance of Peripheral Areas in Turkey'. *Review of Urban & Regional Development Studies* 16 (2): 113–32. https://doi.org/10.1111/j.1467-940 X.2004.00082.x.

Göçer, Atalay. 2018. 'Seçmeli Kürtçe Dersi Anadilinde Eğitim Talebinin Neresinde [How Selective Language Course Answers Education Native Language Demands]'.

Bianet – Bağımsız İletişim Ağı. 21 February. https://www.bianet.org/bianet/insan-haklari/183827-secmeli-kurtce-dersi-anadilinde-egitim-talebinin-neresinde (accessed 8 March 2023).

Gök, Fatma. 2007. '"The Girls" Institutes in the Early Period of the Turkish Republic'. In *Education in 'Multicultural' Societies: Turkish and Swedish Perspectives*, edited by Fatma Gök, Marie Carlson and Annika Rabo, 93–105. Stockholm: Swedish Research Institute in Istanbul.

Gökçe, Birsen. 1994. 'Suyun Öteki Yüzü GAP Bölgesi Baraj. Göl Aynasında Kalacak Yörelerde İstihdam ve Yeniden Yerleştirme Sorunları Araştırması [The Other Side of Water: A Study on Employment and Resettlement Problems in the Areas to be Dammed in the GAP Region]'. Ankara: Sosyoloji Derneği. http://yayin.gap.gov.tr/pdf-view/web/index.php?Dosya=5e4cffa363 (accessed 8 March 2023).

Göle, Nilüfer. 1996. *The Forbidden Modern: Civilization and Veiling*. Ann Arbor: University of Michigan Press.

Grabolle-Çeliker, Anna. 2013. *Kurdish Life in Contemporary Turkey: Migration, Gender and Ethnic Identity*. London: I. B. Tauris.

Günaydın, Ayça, and Zeynep Özdoğan. 2014. '"Biz Büyük Bir Aileyiz": Aile ve Sosyal Politikalar Bakanlığı Kamu Spotları ["We Are a Big Family"]'. *Kültür ve Sizasette Feminist Yaklaşımlar* 22: 53–84.

Gündüz-Hoşgör, Ayşe, and Jeroen Smits. 2007. 'The Status of Rural Women in Turkey What Is the Role of Regional Differences?' In *From Patriarchy to Empowerment: Women's Participation, Movements, and Rights in the Middle East, North Africa, and South Asia*, edited by Valentine M. Moghadam, 120–220. Syracuse: Syracuse University Press.

Güneş, Cengiz, and Welat Zeydanlıoğlu. 2013. *The Kurdish Question in Turkey: New Perspectives on Violence, Representation and Reconciliation*. 1st edn. New York: Routledge.

Güralp, Ayça K. 2015. 'Gender Equality vs. Gender Justice'. *Turkish Policy Quarterly*. 2015. http://turkishpolicy.com/debate-article/4/gender-equality-vs-gender-justice (accessed 8 March 2023).

Gürbilek, Nurdan. 2016. 'Nurdan Gürbilek Yazdı: "De"Ler Ayrı Yazılır! ["De" Is Written Separately]'. Kültür Servisi. 4 October. http://kulturservisi.com/p/nurdan-gurbilek-yazdi-deler-ayri-yazilir (accessed 9 November 2021).

Hacettepe University. 2014. 'TDHS (2013) Turkey Demographic and Health Survey'. Ankara: Population Surveys Institute, Hacettepe University. http://www.hips.hacettepe.edu.tr/eng/TDHS_2013_main.report.pdf (accessed 8 March 2015).

Halis, Müjgân. 2001. *Batman'da Kadınlar Ölüyor [Women Die in Batman]*. Istanbul: Metis Yayınları.

Harris, Leila M. 2008. 'Modernizing the Nation: Postcolonialism, Postdevelopmentalism, and Ambivalent Spaces of Difference in Southeastern Turkey'. *Geoforum* 39 (5): 1698–708. https://doi.org/10.1016/j.geofo rum.2008.03.002.

Harris, Leila M., and Nurcan Atalan. 2000. 'Developing Women's Spaces: Evaluation of the Importance of Sex-Segregated Spaces for Gender and Development Goals in Southeastern Turkey'. *Kadın/Woman* 3 (2): 17–46.

HDP. 2021. 'Seisure of Will and Realities of Trustees'. https://drive.google.com/ file/d/1hX1KkjZiShso4nVf6pUqBFdBlMH5U578/view?usp=embed_facebook (accessed 8 March 2023).

HDP Europe. 2016. 'Report on Local Governments and Appointment of Trustees to Municipalities'. Diyarbakır: Union of Southeastern Anatolia Region Municipalities. 29 November. http://en.hdpeurope.com/wp-content/ uploads/2016/12/EN_ReportonLocalDemocracy-29-11-16.pdf (accessed 6 January 2018).

Herr, Hansjörg, and Zeynep M. Sonat. 2014. 'The Fragile Growth Regime of Turkey in the Post-2001 Period'. *New Perspectives on Turkey* 51: 35–68. https://doi. org/10.1017/S0896634600006713.

hooks, bell. 1981. *Ain't I a Woman: Black Women and Feminism*. Boston: South End Press.

Hürriyet Daily News. 2015. 'One Ankara Bomber Identified: Turkish PM', 19 October. http://www.hurriyetdailynews.com/one-ankara-bomber-identified-turk ish-pm-90057 (accessed 8 March 2023).

Iğsız, Aslı. 2014. 'From Alliance of Civilizations to Branding the Nation: Turkish Studies, Image Wars and Politics of Comparison in an Age of Neoliberalism'. *Turkish Studies* 15 (4): 689–704. https://doi.org/10.1080/14683849.2014.983689.

İlkkaracan, Pınar. 2010. 'Re/Forming Laws to Secure Women's Rights in Turkey: The Campaign on the Penal Code'. In *Citizen Action and National Policy Reform: Making Change Happen*, edited by John Gaventa and Rosemary McGee, 195–216. London: Zed Books.

Independent Türkçe. 2021. 'Türkiye'de 2.8 milyon kadın okuma yazma bilmiyor, 3 milyon kadın diplomasız [2.8 Million Women Are Illiterate, and 3 Million Women Have No Diploma]'. 8 March. https://www.indyturk.com/node/326736/ haber/t%C3%BCrkiyede-28-milyon-kad%C4%B1n-okuma-yazma-bilmiyor-3-mil yon-kad%C4%B1n-diplomas%C4%B1z (accessed 8 March 2023).

İpek, Yasemin. 2006. '"Görevimiz Gönüllülük" 1990'lar, Gönüllü Kuruluşlar, Gönüllü Vatandaşlar [Volunteering Is Our Mission]'. *Amargi* 3: 17–21.

Irmak, Çağan, dir. 2010. *Baba Beni Okula Gönder!* [*Dad Send Me School!*]. https:// www.youtube.com/watch?v=9Jca31ziWk0 (accessed 12 March 2023).

Istanbul Convention Monitoring Platform. 2017. 'Shadow NGO Report on Turkey's First Report on Legislative and Other Measures Giving Effect to the Provisions of the Council of Europe Convention on Preventing and Combating Violence against Women and Domestic Violence'. https://rm.coe.int/turkey-shadow-report-2/168 07441a1 (accessed 8 March 2023).

Jahan, Rounaq. 1995. *The Elusive Agenda: Mainstreaming Women in Development.* 1st edn. Dhaka, Bangladesh: Zed Books.

Jongerden, Joost. 2007. *The Settlement Issue in Turkey and the Kurds: An Analysis of Spatial Policies, Modernity and War.* Leiden, The Netherlands: Brill.

Jongerden, Joost. 2010. 'Village Evacuation and Reconstruction in Kurdistan (1993– 2002)'. *Etudes Rurales* 186 (2): 77–100.

Kabeer, Naila. 1999. 'Resources, Agency, Achievements: Reflections on the Measurement of Women's Empowerment'. *Development and Change* 30 (3): 435– 64. https://doi.org/10.1111/1467-7660.00125.

Kabeer, Naila. 2021. 'Three Faces of Agency in Feminist Economics: Capabilities, Empowerment, and Citizenship'. In *The Routledge Handbook of Feminist Economics*, 1st edn, edited by Günseli Berik and Ebru Kongar, 99–109. Abingdon, Oxon: Routledge.

Kadın Koalisyonu [Women's Coalition] (n.d.). 'Aile ve Sosyal Politikalar Bakanığı Kadın Örgütlerini Uluslararası Siyasal Süreçlerden Dışlıyor [Ministry of Family and Social Policies Exclude Women's Organizations from International Political Processes]', http://www.kadinkoalisyonu.org/yeni/aile-ve-sosyal-politikalar-bakanl igi-kadin-orgutlerini-uluslararasi-siyasal-sureclerinden-disliyor/ (accessed 8 March 2015).

Kandiyoti, Deniz. 1987. 'Emancipated but Unliberated? Reflections on the Turkish Case'. *Feminist Studies* 13 (2): 317. https://doi.org/10.2307/3177804.

Kandiyoti, Deniz. 1988. 'Bargaining with Patriarchy'. *Gender and Society* 2 (3): 274– 90. https://doi.org/10.1177/089124388002003004.

Kandiyoti, Deniz. 1997. *Cariyeler bacılar yurttaşlar: kimlikler ve toplumsal dönüşümler.* Istanbul: Metis Yayınları.

Kandiyoti, Deniz. 1998. 'Gender, Power and Contestation: Rethinking Bargaining with Patriarchy'. In *Feminist Visions of Development: Gender Analysis and Policy*, edited by Cecile Jackson and Ruth Pearson, 108–34. London: Routledge.

Kandiyoti, Deniz. 2010. 'Gender and Women's Studies in Turkey: A Moment for Reflection?' *New Perspectives on Turkey* 43: 165–76. https://doi.org/10.1017/ S089663460000580X.

Kandiyoti, Deniz. 2011. 'A Tangled Web: The Politics of Gender in Turkey'. OpenDemocracy. 5 January. https://www.opendemocracy.net/en/5050/tang led-web-politics-of-gender-in-turkey/ (accessed 8 March 2023).

Kandiyoti, Deniz. 2016. 'Locating the Politics of Gender: Patriarchy, Neo-liberal Governance and Violence in Turkey'. *Research and Policy on Turkey* 1 (2): 103–18. https://doi.org/10.1080/23760818.2016.1201242.

Kaplan, Sam. 2003. 'Nuriye's Dilemma: Turkish Lessons of Democracy and the Gendered State'. *American Ethnologist* 30 (3): 401–17.

Kaplan, Sam. 2006. *The Pedagogical State: Education and the Politics of National Culture in Post-1980 Turkey*, 1st edn. Stanford, CA: Stanford University Press.

Karakaş, Burcu. 2019. 'Türkiye'de kürtaj hizmeti: Fiilen yasa [Abortion services in Turkey: 'De facto forbidden']'. Deutche Welle. 18 January. https://www.dw.com/tr/t%C3%BCrkiyede-k%C3%BCrtaj-hizmeti-fiilen-yasak/a-47130847.

Karayazgan, Ayşe Gül. 1998. 'Biz Kadınlar Diyememek Bir Türlü... [Inability to Say "We Women..."]'. *Pazartesi* 38: 8–10.

Kardam, Nüket. 2011. 'Turkey's Response to the Global Gender Regime'. *GEMC Journal* 4: 8–23.

Kardam, Nüket, and Selma Acuner. 2002. 'National Women's Machineries: Structures and Spaces'. In *Mainstreaming Gender, Democratizing the State: Institutional Mechanisms for the Advancement of Women*, edited by Shirin Rai, 96–114. New York: Routledge.

Karim, Lamia. 2008. 'Demystifying Micro-Credit: The Grameen Bank, NGOs, and Neoliberalism in Bangladesh'. *Cultural Dynamics* 20 (1): 5–29. https://doi.org/10.1177/0921374007088053.

Käser, Isabel. 2021. *The Kurdish Women's Freedom Movement: Gender, Body Politics and Militant Femininities*. Cambridge: Cambridge University Press. https://doi.org/10.1017/9781009022194.

Käufeler, Heinz. 2019. 'Aura und Skandal des Exotischen: Unzeitgemässe Bemerkungen zur Entzauberung der Ethnologie [Aura and Scandal of the Exotic: Untimely Remarks on the Disenchantment of Ethnology]'. ZANTHRO – Zurich Anthropology Working Papers 9, University of Zurich. https://www.isek.uzh.ch/dam/jcr:bd490a01-859a-44b5-93a3-6a965c90d8ee/ZANTHRO_09.pdf.

Keysan, Asuman Özgür. 2019. *Activism and Women's NGOs in Turkey: Civil Society, Feminism and Politics*. London: I. B. Tauris.

Kılınç, Ramazan, Jody Neathery-Castro and Selin Akyüz. 2018. 'Ethnic Conflict and Gender Inequality in Education: The Case of Turkey'. *Turkish Studies* 19 (3): 400–21. https://doi.org/10.1080/14683849.2017.1392860.

Kocamaner, Hikmet. 2017. 'Strengthening the Family through Television: Islamic Broadcasting, Secularism, and the Politics of Responsibility in Turkey'. *Anthropological Quarterly* 90 (3): 675–714. https://doi.org/10.1353/anq.2017.0040.

Kocamaner, Hikmet. 2019. 'Regulating the Family through Religion'. *American Ethnologist* 46 (4): 495–508. https://doi.org/10.1111/amet.12836.

Koğacıoğlu, Dicle. 2004. 'The Tradition Effect: Framing Honor Crimes in Turkey'. *Differences: A Journal of Feminist Cultural Studies* 15 (2): 119–51.

Konda Araştırma. 2016. ' "Türkiye'de 18 Yaş Üstü 3,4 Milyon Kişi Okuma Yazma Bilmiyor" [3.4 Million People above Age 18 Are Illiterate in Turkey]'. 8 September. https://twitter.com/kondaarastirma/status/773891493585182720.

Kuijpers, Anna Elisabeth. 2015. 'Unpleasant Relations during Fieldwork: Just Deal with It? From "Machismo" in the Field to "Machismo" in Academia'. *Tsantsa* 20: 158–63.

Kümbetoğlu, Belkıs, İnci User and Aylin Akpınar. 2010. 'Unregistered Women Workers in the Globalized Economy: A Qualitative Study in Turkey'. *Feminist Formations* 22 (3): 96–123.

Kütük-Kuriş, Merve. 2022. 'The Rise and Fall of Support for the Istanbul Convention: Understanding the Case of KADEM'. *Women's Studies International Forum* 93 (July): 102601. https://doi.org/10.1016/j.wsif.2022.102601.

Lang, Sabine. 1997. 'The NGOization of Feminism'. In *Transitions, Environments, Translations: Feminisms in International Politics*, edited by Joan Wallach Scott, Cora Kaplan and Debra Keates, 101–20. New York: Routledge.

Leupold, David. 2020. *Embattled Dreamlands: The Politics of Contesting Armenian, Kurdish and Turkish Memory*. New York: Routledge.

Li, Tania Murray. 2005. 'Beyond "the State" and Failed Schemes'. *American Anthropologist* 107 (3): 383–94. https://doi.org/10.1525/aa.2005.107.3.383.

Logar, Rosa, and Johanna Niemi. 2017. 'Emergency Barring Orders in Situations of Domestic Violence: Article 52 of the Istanbul Convention a Collection of Papers on the Council of Europe Convention on Preventing and Combating Violence against Women and Domestic Violence'. Strasbourg: Council of Europe. http://www.stabilityjournal.org/articles/10.5334/sta.gj/ (accessed 8 March 2023).

MacDougall, David. 2019. *The Looking Machine: Essays on Cinema, Anthropology and Documentary Filmmaking*, 1st edn. Manchester: Manchester University Press. https://doi.org/10.7228/manchester/9781526134097.001.0001.

Madhok, Sumi. 2013. *Rethinking Agency: Developmentalism, Gender and Rights*, 1st edn. New Delhi: Routledge India.

Mahmood, Saba. 2004. *Politics of Piety: The Islamic Revival and the Feminist Subject.* Princeton: Princeton University Press.

Maksudyan, Nazan. 2005. 'The Turkish Review of Anthropology and the Racist Face of Turkish Nationalism'. *Cultural Dynamics* 17 (3): 291–322. https://doi. org/10.1177/0921374005061992.

Malik, Khalid. 2013. 'The Rise of the South: Human Progress in a Diverse World'. New York: United Nations Development Programme. http://hdr.undp.org/sites/ default/files/reports/14/hdr2013_en_complete.pdf.

Merry, Sally Engle. 2011. 'Measuring the World: Indicators, Human Rights, and Global Governance: With CA Comment by John M. Conley'. *Current Anthropology* 52 (S3): S83–S95. https://doi.org/10.1086/657241.

Mies, Maria. 2012. *Lace Makers of Narsapur: Indian Housewives Produce for the World Market.* Spinifex Feminist Classics. Australia: Spinfex Press.

Milliyet. 2013. '2 Aylık Bebeğini Evde Bırakıp Tatile Gitti [She Left Her 2-Month-Old Baby at Home and Went on Vacation]'. 22 October. https://www.milliyet. com.tr/gundem/2-aylik-bebegini-evde-birakip-tatile-gitti-1779928 (accessed 20 September 2017).

Ministry of Foreign Affairs Department of Regional and Transboundary Waters et al. 2003. *Turkey Country Report, from The Hague 2nd World Water Forum 2000 to the Kyoto 3rd World Water Forum 2003.* Marseille: World Water Council / Conseil Mondial de l'Eau. https://www.ircwash.org/sites/default/files/Worldwaterfo rum-2003-Turkey.pdf (accessed 8 March 2023).

Mohanty, Chandra Talpade. 1988. 'Under Western Eyes: Feminist Scholarship and Colonial Discourses'. *Feminist Review* 30: 61. https://doi.org/10.2307/1395054.

Mohanty, Manoranjan. 1995. 'On the Concept of "Empowerment"'. *Economic and Political Weekly* 30 (24): 1434–36.

Mosse, David. 2011. *Adventures in Aidland: The Anthropology of Professionals in International Development,* 1st edn. New York: Berghahn Books.

Mosse, David. 2013. 'The Anthropology of International Development'. *Annual Review of Anthropology* 42 (1): 227–46. https://doi.org/10.1146/annurev-anthro-092412-155553.

Najmabadi, Afsaneh. 1998. 'Crafting an Educated Housewife in Iran'. In *Remaking Women: Feminism and Modernity in the Middle East,* edited by Lila Abu-Lughod, 91–125. Princeton: Princeton University Press.

Narayan, Kirin. 1993. 'How Native Is a "Native" Anthropologist?' *American Anthropologist* 95 (3): 671–86.

Navaro-Yashin, Yael. 2002. *Faces of the State: Secularism and Public Life in Turkey.* Princeton: Princeton University Press.

Navaro-Yaşın, Yael. 2000. 'Evde Taylorizm: Türkiye Cumhuriyeti'nin Ilk Yıllarında Evişinin Rasyonelleşmesi (1928–40) [Taylorism at Home]'. *Toplum ve Bilim* 84: 51–74.

Nivelle Cardinale, Sophie, dir. 2018. *Turquie : Erdogan Land* | ARTE Reportage. Arte G.E.I.E. and Kheops Productions. https://www.youtube.com/watch?v=EAbE i1rpg7M.

Nonini, Donald. 2016. 'Praxis'. *Dialectical Anthropology* 40 (3): 241–9. https://doi. org/10.1007/s10624-016-9429-2.

Oakley, Ann. 1974. *Housewife*. London: Allen Lane.

Öktem, Kerem. 2005. 'Faces of the City: Poetic, Mediagenic and Traumatic Images of a Multi-Cultural City in Southeast Turkey'. *Cities* 22 (3): 241–53. https://doi. org/10.1016/j.cities.2005.03.010.

Öneş, Umut, Emel Memiş and Burça Kızılırmak. 2013. 'Poverty and Intra-Household Distribution of Work Time in Turkey: Analysis and Some Policy Implications'. *Women's Studies International Forum*, Gendering Social Policy and Welfare State in Turkey, 41, Part 1 (November): 55–64. https://doi.org/10.1016/j. wsif.2013.01.004.

Öniş, Ziya. 2004. 'Turgut Özal and His Economic Legacy: Turkish Neo-liberalism in Critical Perspective'. *Middle Eastern Studies* 40 (4): 113–34. https://doi. org/10.1080/00263200410001700338.

'Oya Projesi'. 2015. Payda Platformu. http://paydaplatformu.org/projects/9.

Özbay, Ferhunde. 2019. *Kadın Emeği: Seçme Yazılar*. Istanbul: İletişim Yayınları.

Özgen, H. Neşe. 2005. 'Dünya Bankası ve Birleşmiş Milletler'in Kalkınma Politikaları ve Bölgesel Kalkınmada Yeni Kavramlar [World Bank and United Nations' Development Policies and New Concepts in Regional Development]'. *Tarım Ekonomisi Dergisi* 11 (1): 51–9.

Özgüler, Cevahir, and Betül Yarar. 2017. 'Neoliberal Body Politics: Feminist Resistance and the Abortion Law in Turkey'. In *Bodies in Resistance*, edited by Wendy Harcourt, 133–61. London: Palgrave Macmillan. https://doi. org/10.1057/978-1-137-47780-4_7.

Özkonuk, Rezan. 1947. 'Üsküdar Kız Sanat Enstitüsü [Üsküdar Girls' Institute]'. *Ev*İş* 12-13.

Özok-Gündoğan, Nilay. 2005. ' "Social Development" as a Governmental Strategy in the Southeastern Anatolia Project'. *New Perspectives on Turkey* 32 (March): 93–111. https://doi.org/10.1017/S089663460000412X.

Özyeğin, Gül. 2001. *Untidy Gender Domestic Service in Turkey*. Philadelphia: Temple University Press.

Özyeğin, Gül. 2015. *New Desires, New Selves: Sex, Love, and Piety among Turkish Youth*. New York: New York University Press.

Özyürek, Esra. 2006. *Nostalgia for the Modern: State Secularism and Everyday Politics in Turkey*. Durham: Duke University Press Books.

Pamuk, Orhan. 2005. *Snow*. New York: Vintage.

Parpart, Jane L., Patricia Connelly and Eudine Barriteau. 2000. *Theoretical Perspectives on Gender and Development*. Ottawa: International Development Research Centre.

Pearson, Ruth. 2007. 'Reassessing Paid Work and Women's Empowerment: Lessons from the Global Economy'. In *Feminisms in Development: Contradictions, Contestations and Challenges*, edited by Andrea Cornwall, Elizabeth Harrison and Ann Whitehead, 201–13. London: Zed Press.

Pedersen, D. 2008. 'Brief Event: The Value of Getting to Value in the Era of Globalization'. *Anthropological Theory* 8 (1): 57–77. https://doi.org/10.1177/14634 99607087495.

Peroni, Lourdes. 2016. 'Violence against Migrant Women: The Istanbul Convention through a Postcolonial Feminist Lens'. *Feminist Legal Studies* 24 (1): 49–67. https://doi.org/10.1007/s10691-016-9316-x.

Pervizat, Leyla. 2007. Lobbying for Women's Rights at the UN – Interview of Dr. Leyla Pervizat of Turkey Interview by Vahdati Soheila. http://wunrn. com/2007/04/lobbying-for-womens-rights-at-the-un-interview-of-dr-leyla-pervi zat-of-turkey/.

Pieterse, Jan Nederveen. 1995. *White on Black: Images of Africa and Blacks in Western Popular Culture*. New Haven: Yale University Press.

Purcell, Bridget. 2017. 'The House Unbound: Refiguring Gender and Domestic Boundaries in Urbanizing Southeast Turkey'. *City & Society* 29 (1): 14–34. https://doi.org/10.1111/ciso.12110.

Rai, Shirin. 2003. *Mainstreaming Gender, Democratizing the State?: Institutional Mechanisms for the Advancement of Women*. Manchester: Manchester University Press.

Rathgeber, Eva M. 1990. 'WID, WAD, GAD: Trends in Research and Practice'. *The Journal of Developing Areas* 24 (4): 489–502.

Rawłuszko, Marta. 2019. 'Gender Mainstreaming Revisited: Lessons from Poland'. *European Journal of Women's Studies* 26 (1): 70–84. https://doi.org/10.1177/13505 06817752012.

Razavi, Shahrashoub and Carol Miller. 1995. *From WID to GAD: Conceptual Shifts in the Women and Development Discourse*. Geneva: United Nations Research Institute for Social Development (UNRISD).

Resmi Gazete [Official Gazette] – 22937. 1997. 'Milletlerarası Andlaşma [International Treaty]'. General Directorate of Legislation Development and Publication [Başbakanlık Mevzuatı Geliştirme ve Yayın Genel Müdürlüğü]. http://www.resmigazete.gov.tr/arsiv/22937.pdf (accessed 8 March 2023).

Resmi Gazete [Official Gazette] – 26218. 2006. 'Çocuk ve Kadınlara Yönelik Şiddet Hareketleriyle Töre ve Namus Cinayetlerinin Önlenmesi İçin Alınacak Tedbirler [Measures to Be Taken to Prevent Acts of Violence against Children and Women and Honor Killings]'. https://www.resmigazete.gov.tr/eskiler/2006/07/20060 704-12.htm (accessed 8 March 2023).

Resmi Gazete [Official Gazette] – 29882. 2016. 'Analık İzni Veya Ücretsiz İzin Sonrası Yapılacak Kısmi Süreli Çalışmalar Hakkında Yönetmelik [Regulation on Part-Time Work to Be Performed After Maternity Leave or Unpaid Leave]'. https://www.resmigazete.gov.tr/eskiler/2016/11/20161108-11.htm (accessed 8 March 2023).

Rivetti, Paola. 2013. 'Empowerment without Emancipation: Performativity and Political Activism among Iranian Refugees in Italy and Turkey'. *Alternatives* 38 (4): 305–20. https://doi.org/10.1177/0304375413519191.

Rowlands, Jo. 1997. *Questioning Empowerment: Working with Women in Honduras*. Dublin: Oxfam.

Saktanber, Ayşe. 2001. 'Kemalist Kadın Hakları Söylemi [Kemalist Women's Rights Discourse]'. In *Modern Türkiye'de Siyasi Düşünce Cilt 2 / Kemalizm (Ciltli)*, edited by Murat Gültekingil and Tanil Bora, 323–33. Istanbul: İletişim Yayıncılık.

Saktanber, Ayşe. 2002. *Living Islam: Women, Religion and the Politicization of Culture in Turkey*. London: I. B. Tauris.

Saktanber, Ayşe. 2006. 'Women and the Iconography of Fear: Islamization in Post-Islamist Turkey'. *Signs: Journal of Women in Culture and Society* 32 (1): 21–31. https://doi.org/10.1086/505890.

Saktanber, Ayşe, and Gül Çorbacioğlu. 2008. 'Veiling and Headscarf-Skepticism in Turkey'. *Social Politics: International Studies in Gender, State and Society* 15 (4): 514–38. https://doi.org/10.1093/sp/jxn018.

Saltık, Ahmet. 1994. 'GAP Bölgesi'nde Kadının Statüsü ve Kalkınma Sürecine Entegre Edilmesi Araştırması [Status of Women in the GAP Region and Their Integration in the Process of Development]'. Ankara: GAP Bölge Kalkınma İdaresi Başkanlığı.

Sardenberg, Cecília. 2016. 'Liberal vs. Liberating Empowerment: A Latin American Feminist Perspective on Conceptualising Women's Empowerment'. *IDS Bulletin* 47 (1A): 18–27. https://doi.org/10.19088/1968-2016.115.

Sarıaslan, Kübra Zeynep. 2019. '(Un)Politicising Awareness: Gender Projects and the State in Southeast Turkey'. *Zanthro – Zurich Anthropology Working Papers*

6. https://www.isek.uzh.ch/dam/jcr:8baa2c63-2c67-4332-9165-4c4cf217cbcb/
ZANTHRO_06.pdf.

Sarıaslan, Kübra Zeynep. 2020. 'Capitalism's Housewife: A Biographical Analysis of
Women's Empowerment in Turkey'. *Urban Anthropology and Studies of World
Systems and World Economic Development* 49 (1–2): 85–118.

Sarıaslan, Kübra Zeynep. 2021. 'Pamuk'un Kars'ı ve Kar'ın Ötekileri [Pamuk's Kars
and Its Others]'. In *Dünya Üzerinde Kar: Kar Üzerine Yazılar*, edited by Sibel Erol,
462–77. Istanbul: Yapı Kredi Yayınları.

Savran, Gülnur. 1998. 'Yolun Neresindeyiz? [Where Are We on the Road?]'. *Pazartesi*
34: 3–4.

Schäfers, Marlene. 2018. ' "It Used to Be Forbidden": Kurdish Women and the Limits
of Gaining Voice'. *Journal of Middle East Women's Studies* 14 (1): 3–24. https://
doi.org/10.1215/15525864-4296988.

Schwartzman, H. B. 1989. *The Meeting: Gatherings in Organizations and
Communities.* New York: Springer.

Sehlikoğlu, Sertaç. 2021. *Working Out Desire: Women, Sport, and Self-Making in
Istanbul*, 1st edn. Gender, Culture, and Politics in the Middle East. Syracuse,
NY: Syracuse University Press.

Sen, Gita, and Caren Grown. 1987. *Development, Crises and Alternative Visions:
Third World Women's Perspectives*, 1st printing edn. New York: Monthly
Review Press.

Sencer, Muzaffer. 1993. 'GAP Bölgesi Toplumsal Değişme Eğilimleri Araştırması'
[GAP Region Social Change Trends Survey]'. Ankara: GAP Bölge Kalkınma
İdaresi Başkanlığı.

Shakry, Omnia. 1998. 'Schooled Mothers and Structured Play: Child Rearing in
Turn-of-the-Century Egypt'. In *Remaking Women: Feminism and Modernity
in the Middle East*, edited by Lila Abu-Lughod, 126–70. Princeton: Princeton
University Press.

Sharma, Aradhana. 2008. *Logics of Empowerment: Development, Gender, and
Governance in Neoliberal India.* Minneapolis: University of Minnesota Press.

Shostak, Marjorie. 2000. *Nisa: The Life and Words of a!Kung Woman*, 4th edn.
Cambridge, MA: Harvard University Press.

Silverstein, Brian. 2010. 'Reform in Turkey: Liberalization as Government and
Critique (Respond to This Article at Http://Www.Therai.Org.Uk/at/Debate)'.
Anthropology Today 26 (4): 22–5. https://doi.org/10.1111/j.1467-8322.201
0.00749.x.

Sözer, Hande. 2004. 'ÇATOM Project: Field Supervisors In-between "the State" and
"the Social" '. Unpublished Master Thesis, Istanbul: Boğaziçi University.

Sunier, Thijl, and Nico Landman. 2015. *Transnational Turkish Islam*.
London: Palgrave Macmillan UK. https://doi.org/10.1057/9781137394224.

Tahaoğlu, Çiçek. 2013. 'Kadınlar Diyarbakır'da Buluştu: Barışmak İçin Kardeş
Olmamız Gerekmiyor [Women Met in Diyarbakir: We Don't Have to Be Sisters
and Brothers to Make a Peace]'. Bianet – Bağımsız İletişim Ağı. 28 May. http://
www.bianet.org/bianet/toplum/146969-barismak-icin-kardes-olmamiz-gerekmi
yor (accessed 8 March 2023).

Tajali, Mona. 2015. 'The Promise of Gender Parity: Turkey's People's Democratic
Party (HDP)'. OpenDemocracy. 29 October. https://www.opendemocracy.net/
en/5050/promise-of-gender-parity-turkey-s-people-s-democratic-party-hdp/
(accessed 8 March 2023).

Tambar, Kabir. 2016. 'Brotherhood in Dispossession: State Violence and the Ethics
of Expectation in Turkey'. *Cultural Anthropology* 31 (1): 30–55. https://doi.
org/10.14506/ca31.1.03.

Tek Turan, Hande. 2016. 'Reconstruction of Regional Development Policies in Turkey
through Development Agencies'. In *New Public Management in Turkey: Local
Government Reform*, 1st edn, edited by Yüksel Demirkaya. New York: Routledge.

Tekay, Cihan, and Zeyno Üstün. 2013. 'A Short History of Feminism in Turkey and
Feminist Resistance in <Gezi'. Jadaliyya. 4 October. http://photography.jadaliyya.
com/pages/index/15037/rethinking-gezi-through-feminist-and-lgbt-perspect
(accessed 8 March 2023).

Tekeli, Şirin. 2004. 'On Maddede Türkiyede Kadın Hareketi [Women's Movement in
Turkey in Ten Bulletpoints]'. Bianet – Bağımsız İletişim Ağı. 17 June. http://www.
bianet.org/bianet/kadin/43145-on-maddede-turkiyede-kadin-hareketi (accessed 8
March 2023).

Tekeli, Şirin. 2010. 'The Turkish Women's Movement: A Brief History of Success'.
Quaderns de La Mediterrània 14: 119–23.

Tekeli, Şirin. 2017. *Feminizmi Düşünmek* [Thinking of Feminism]. Istanbul: Istanbul
Bilgi Üniversitesi Yayınları.

Tekerek, Tuğba. 2015. 'Yasal Kürtajda Kaçak Devri; Şanlıurfa'da Kürtajlar Gizli
Yapılıyor [Illegal Times in Legal Abortion; Abortion in Şanlıurfa Is Hidden]'. 25
November. http://t24.com.tr/haber/yasal-kurtajda-kacak-devri-sanliurfada-kurtaj
lar-gizli-yapiliyor,317964 (accessed 8 March 2023).

Thorp, Rosemary, Frances Stewart and Amrik Heyer. 2005. 'When and How Far
Is Group Formation a Route out of Chronic Poverty?' *World Development* 33
(6): 907–20. https://doi.org/10.1016/j.worlddev.2004.09.016.

Ticktin, Miriam. 2017. 'A World without Innocence'. *American Ethnologist* 44
(4): 577–90. https://doi.org/10.1111/amet.12558.

Titrek, Osman, Mustafa Bayrakçı and Demet Zafer Güneş. 2014. 'Barriers to Women's Leadership in Turkey'. *The Anthropologist* 18 (1): 135–44. https://doi.org/10.1080/09720073.2014.11891529.

Toksöz, Gülay. 2016. 'Transition from "Woman" to "Family": An Analysis of AKP Era Employment Policies from a Gender Perspective'. *Journal Für Entwicklungspolitik* 32 (1/2): 64–83.

Toktaş, Şule, and Dilek Cindoğlu. 2006. 'Modernization and Gender: A History of Girls' Technical Education in Turkey Since 1927'. *Women's History Review* 15 (5): 737–49. https://doi.org/10.1080/09612020600938707.

Tosun, Cevat, Dallen J. Timothy and Yüksel Öztürk. 2003. 'Tourism Growth, National Development and Regional Inequality in Turkey'. *Journal of Sustainable Tourism* 11 (2–3): 133–61. https://doi.org/10.1080/09669580308667200.

Tuğal, Cihan. 2016. *The Fall of the Turkish Model: How the Arab Uprisings Brought Down Islamic Liberalism*. London: Verso.

Tuncer, Selda. 2018. *Women and Public Space in Turkey: Gender, Modernity and the Urban Experience*, 1st edn. London: I. B. Tauris.

Türker, Duygu, and Senem Yılmaz. 2017. 'Strengthening Women Stakeholders with Social Responsibility Does It Really Work?' In *Women and Sustainability in Business: A Global Perspective*, edited by Kıymet Tunca Çalıyurt. Women and Sustainable Business. London: Routledge, Taylor & Francis Group.

Türkiye Kalkınma Vakfı. 1994. 'GAP Bölgesi'nde Kadının Statüsü ve Kalkınma Sürecine Entegre Edilmesi Araştırması (Proje Yürütücüsü: Doç. Dr. Ahmet Saltık)'. Ankara: GAP Bölge Kalkınma İdaresi Başkanlığı. http://yayin.gap.gov.tr/pdf-view/web/index.php?Dosya=da99ad75c2 (accessed 8 March 2023).

Türkyilmaz, Zeynep. 2016. 'Maternal Colonialism and Turkish Woman's Burden in Dersim: Educating the "Mountain Flowers" of Dersim'. *Journal of Women's History* 28 (3): 162–86. https://doi.org/10.1353/jowh.2016.0029.

UN. 1997a. 'Turkey – Country Profile. Implementation of Agenda 21: Review of Progress Made Since the United Nations Conference on Environment and Development, 1992'. http://www.un.org/esa/earthsummit/turky-cp.htm (accessed 8 March 2023).

UN. 1997b. 'The UN Conference on Environment and Development (1992)'. Earth Summit. 23 May. http://www.un.org/geninfo/bp/enviro.html (accessed 8 March 2023).

UN Women. 2000. 'Convention on the Elimination of All Forms of Discrimination against Women'. http://www.un.org/womenwatch/daw/cedaw/cedaw.htm (accessed 8 March 2023).

UN Women. (n.d.). 'Commission on the Status of Women'. http://www.unwomen. org/en/csw (accessed 8 March 2023).

UNDP. 2012. 'Signed Project Document: Innovations for Women's Empowerment: A Workable Model for Women in Southeast Anatolia'. https://erc.undp.org/evaluat ion/documents/download/9665 (accessed 8 March 2023).

UNDP. 2020. 'UNDP Turkey Gender Equality Strategy 2017–2020'. https://www. undp.org/turkiye/publications/undp-turkey-gender-equality-strategy-2017-2020 (accessed 11 March 2023).

UNDP Turkey. n.d. 'Support to Adaptation of Syrian Women Living in Southeast Anatolia to Social and Economic Life'. UNDP in Turkey. http://www.tr.undp.org/ content/turkey/en/home/operations/projects/syria-crisis-and-resilience-prog ram/support-to-adaptation-of-syrian-women-living-in-southeast-anatol.html (accessed 7 December 2017).

Ünal, Didem. 2019. 'The Abortion Debate and Profeminist Coalition Politics in Contemporary Turkey'. *Politics & Gender* 15 (4): 801–25. https://doi.org/10.1017/ S1743923X18000703.

Ünlü, Barış. 2016. 'The Kurdish Struggle and the Crisis of the Turkishness Contract'. *Philosophy & Social Criticism* 42 (4–5): 397–405. https://doi.org/10.1177/01914 53715625715.

Ünver, İH Olcay. 2001. 'Southeastern Turkey: Sustainable Development and Foreign Investment'. In *Conference on FDI in China's Regional Development*, 1–9. Xi'an: OECD. http://www.oecd.org/dataoecd/39/8/2350280.pdf (accessed 3 February 2023).

Ünver, İH Olcay, and Rajiv K. Gupta. 2003. 'A New Perspective on Water Development and Poverty Reduction in Southeastern Anatolia, Turkey'. In *Water Development and Poverty Reduction*, edited by İH Olcay Ünver, Rajıv K. Gupta and Aysegul Kibaroglu, 231–59. New York: Springer US.

U.S. Department of State. 2006. 'U.S. Department of State: Country Reports on Human Rights Practices for 2005 – Turkey'. 8 March. http://www.state.gov/j/drl/ rls/hrrpt/2005/61680.htm (accessed 8 March 2023).

Visweswaran, Kamala. 1997. 'Histories of Feminist Ethnography'. *Annual Review of Anthropology*, 26: 591–621.

Walby, Sylvia. 2004. 'The European Union and Gender Equality: Emergent Varieties of Gender Regime'. *Social Politics: International Studies in Gender, State and Society* 11 (1): 4–29. https://doi.org/10.1093/sp/jxh024.

Ward, Kristy, and Vichhra Mouyly. 2013. 'The Importance of Being Connected: Urban Poor Women's Experience of Self-Help Discourse in Cambodia'. *Gender and Development* 21 (2): 313–26. https://doi.org/10.1080/13552074.2013.802482.

White, Jenny B. 2003. 'State Feminism, Modernization, and the Turkish Republican Woman'. *NWSA Journal* 15 (3): 145–59.

Win, Everjoice. 2004. 'Gender Equality: Mainstreamed into Oblivion?' *Spotlight: Gender Mainstreaming: Can It Work for Women's Rights?*, no. 3 (November): 6–11.

Wohlwend, Wolfgang. 2015. '"Our Heads Did Not Accept It" – Development and Nostalgia in Southeastern Anatolia'. *Zeitschrift Fuer Ethnologie* 140 (2): 207–23.

Yabancı, Bilge. 2019. 'Turkey's Tamed Civil Society: Containment and Appropriation under a Competitive Authoritarian Regime'. *Journal of Civil Society* 15 (4): 285–306. https://doi.org/10.1080/17448689.2019.1668627.

Yazıcı, Berna. 2012. 'The Return to the Family: Welfare, State, and Politics of the Family in Turkey'. *Anthropological Quarterly* 85 (1): 103–40.

Yeğen, Mesut. 2006. 'Cumhuriyet ve Kürtler [Republic and Kurds]'. Bianet – Bağımsız İletişim Ağı. 14 March. http://www.bianet.org/bianet/siyaset/75849-cumhuri yet-ve-kurtler (accessed 8 March 2023).

Yeğen, Mesut. 2009. '"Prospective-Turks" or "Pseudo-Citizens": Kurds in Turkey'. *The Middle East Journal* 63 (4): 597–615. https://doi.org/10.3751/63.4.14.

Yeşil, Sevim. 2003. 'Unfolding Republican Patriarchy: The Case of Young Kurdish Women at the Girls' Vocational Boarding School in Elaziğ'. Ankara: Middle East Technical University. http://etd.lib.metu.edu.tr/upload/688036/index.pdf.

Yıldırım, Barış, trans. 2013. 'Kürt Meselesinin Çözümüne İlişkin Algılar, Aktörler ve Süreç [Perceptions, Actors, and the Process of Solutions for Kurdish Question]'. Istanbul: Heinrich Böll Stiftung and Diyarbakır Siyasal ve Sosyal Araştırmalar Enstitüsü. https://tr.boell.org/sites/default/files/kurt_meselesinin_cozumune_ilis kin_algilar-aktorler_ve_surec.pdf (accessed 8 March 2023).

Yıldırım, Umut. 2019. 'Space, Loss and Resistance: A Haunted Pool-Map in South-Eastern Turkey'. *Anthropological Theory* 19 (4): 440–69. https://doi. org/10.1177/1463499618783130.

Yılmaz, Aybige. 2004. 'Victims, Villains and Guardian Angels – Batman Suicide Stories'. *Westminster Papers in Communication and Culture* 1 (1): 66. https://doi. org/10.16997/wpcc.204.

Yilmaz, Zafer. 2015. '"Strengthening the Family" Policies in Turkey: Managing the Social Question and Armoring Conservative–Neoliberal Populism'. *Turkish Studies* 16 (3): 371–90. https://doi.org/10.1080/14683849.2015.1067863.

Yörük, Erdem. 2012. 'Welfare Provision as Political Containment: The Politics of Social Assistance and the Kurdish Conflict in Turkey'. *Politics & Society* 40 (4): 517–47. https://doi.org/10.1177/0032329212461130.

Yuval-Davis, Nira. 1997. *Gender and Nation*, 1st edn. London: Sage Publications.

Index

legislation 150
legislative 18, 112
Penal Code 19, 67
legitimate 111, 114, 120, 123, 127
letigimate 11–12, 16
Leupold, David XIV
Lewis, David 1
Li, Tania 7
liberal 3, 7, 11, 18, 158
liberating 7, 9
lifestyles 40, 145
literacy 35, 43, 45, 48, 61
lkkaracan, Pınar 68, 104
lknur 30, 32, 76–80, 84–5
Logar, Rosa 166
logic 11, 44, 98
long-distance 70, 139
love 10, 26, 47, 51, 65, 69, 96
lucky 101
Lüküslü, Demet 63

MacDougall, David 23
Madhok, Sumi 6
Mahmood, Saba 15
mainstream 3, 164
  mainstreaming 3, 8, 30, 32, 109–11,
    113–15, 117, 119–21, 123, 125–9,
    135, 166
Maksudyan, Nazan 10
Malik, Khalid 18
manager 54–6
Mardin 42, 99, 117, 162
marginalization 21, 133
market 11, 37, 48, 60, 72–3, 75–6, 78, 81–2,
    115, 120–1, 134
marketing 30, 49, 119
marketplace 87, 117–18
marriage 10, 14, 61, 66–8, 72, 75–7, 91,
    96–8, 110, 123, 142–4, 149, 151,
    153, 159, 164
  dowry 47, 76, 145
  marital 149, 151, 153
  married 24, 66, 69–70, 76, 80–2, 90–1,
    93, 101, 123, 143, 145, 147, 149–50
  marry 38, 65–6, 69, 132, 142–4, 148–9
  wedding 77, 149
masculinist 16, 158–9
massacre 69, 162
maternal 39, 126, 139, 150

maternity 150–1
mayor 35, 88, 114, 163, 166
measurement 5
media 10, 103, 144, 157, 164, 166
  journalistic XIII, 156
  press XV, 57, 96, 112
medical 87, 103
meeting XVII, 31, 33, 80–1, 83, 99, 105–6,
    109, 111, 116, 118, 121, 123–6, 137,
    159, 165
Melek 32, 80–2
Memiş, Emel 73
Mernissi, Fatima 88
Merry, Sally Engle 6
Mersin 52
Mesopotamia XIV, 26, 29, 82, 84
method 3, 110, 155
micro-credit 6
Mies, Maria 84
migration 27, 40, 45, 61, 68, 84, 101, 135
  migrant 4, 84, 144
military XIII, 11–12, 22, 28, 43, 57, 136,
    155–6, 162, 166
Miller, Carol 3
Milliyet 164
ministry 29, 32, 42, 44, 47–8, 58, 62, 73,
    95–6, 98–9, 103, 113–14, 138,
    162–3, 165, 167
  minister XVII, 53, 57, 89, 95, 116, 126,
    139, 164–5
minority XIV, 10, 21, 69, 163
mobility 9, 15, 38, 48, 76, 78, 83, 85, 94,
    158
moderator 120, 131–2, 136, 142, 145
modern 9, 12, 15–16, 27, 37–8, 40, 44,
    134, 148
  modernism 12, 15
  modernist 2, 12, 14, 16, 61, 157
  modernity 5, 9, 17, 37, 83, 94
  modernization XIII, XV, 1–2, 9–11, 13,
    24, 37, 44, 60, 94
modest 53, 69, 120
Mohanty, Chandra 3
money 17, 32, 36, 47–8, 64–5, 68, 71–2,
    74–7, 79–81, 84, 116, 123, 150
moral 11, 15, 121, 143
  morality 12, 144
mosques 116, 167
Mosse, Michael 2